POLICE ENGLISH

POLICE ENGLISH

A Manual of
Grammar, Punctuation, and Spelling
For Police Officers

By

PATRICK D. SMITH, Ed.D.
Chairman, English Department
School of the Ozarks
Point Lookout, Missouri

and

ROBERT C. JONES, Ph.D.
Associate Professor of English
Central Missouri State College
Warrensburg, Missouri

CHARLES C THOMAS • PUBLISHER
Springfield • Illinois • U.S.A.

Published and Distributed Throughout the World by
CHARLES C THOMAS • PUBLISHER
BANNERSTONE HOUSE
301-327 East Lawrence Avenue, Springfield, Illinois, U.S.A.
NATCHEZ PLANTATION HOUSE
735 North Atlantic Boulevard, Fort Lauderdale, Florida, U.S.A.

© 1969, by CHARLES C THOMAS • PUBLISHER
Library of Congress Catalog Card Number: 69-14794

With THOMAS BOOKS *careful attention is given to all details of
manufacturing and design. It is the Publisher's desire to present books
that are satisfactory as to their physical qualities and artistic possibilities
and appropriate for their particular use.* THOMAS BOOKS *will be true
to those laws of quality that assure a good name and good will.*

INTRODUCTION

Good English is a prerequisite for success in almost any kind of work that involves your ability to communicate with your fellow workers, with your superiors, and with the other people you come in contact with daily. Most people, however, when they think of "good English," visualize a type of written and spoken language that is extremely formal and artificial—that is, a language which few of us have any occasion to employ. This formal and artificial English is like a hothouse plant; it survives only in the environment which protects its artificiality and formality. And few people work in such an environment. Rather, most of us work under conditions which encourage the development and use of a flexible, direct, informal type of written and spoken language.

Also, most people, when they think of "good English," automatically associate the term with the concept of "good grammar." This concept of grammar, however, is frequently misunderstood. Good grammar, to many of us, really means good, or acceptable, language manners. It is analogous to knowing which fork or spoon to use first at a multiple-course dinner, or which joke or story can be told in a mixed gathering. But another meaning of "good grammar" is the knowledge of how to construct concise, unambiguous, complete sentence structures. And still another meaning of "good grammar" is the knowledge of how to spell, punctuate, abbreviate, capitalize, and so forth.

This manual deals with "good English" and "good grammar" in ways which differ greatly from those of traditional handbooks of English. First of all, this book is based on the belief that the most important structure in written English is the sentence and that the sentence is best understood when it is studied as a generated structure. Traditional handbooks employ the methodology of sentence analysis. They reproduce sample sentences and require the student to evaluate these sentences. This process of analysis stresses the ability of the student writer to identify incorrect structures that have already been produced, but it does not seem to focus upon the real problem of the student— the problem of producing, himself, correct structures. The focus of this book, therefore, is upon the process of generation: the process by which a writer can, by knowledge of the basic structures of the English language, produce correct—or grammatical—sentences that will convey his meaning clearly, concisely, and effectively to his reader.

Secondly, the viewpoint of this manual is an eminently pragmatic one. We believe that the most important thing about knowing good English and good grammar is that you be able to communicate effectively with your intended reader—that is, that you be able to tell your reader whatever it is you want to tell him in such a way that he trusts you as a source of information, understands what you have to say, and accepts or respects what it is you have said.

Finally, the three sections of this handbook are designed to clarify and simplify the student writer's concept of what is meant by "good English" and "good grammar." "Good English," as we mean the term in this manual, is the clear, concise, and effective use of the English language; it is not the prescriptive, artificial, formal language that people so often mistake for "good English"; rather, it is language which communicates. "Good grammar," as we mean the term in this handbook, consists of two parts: grammar as a clear, consistent, and natural system of relationships between units of the language; and grammar as a system of rules which govern various conventions of the English language, such as spelling, punctuation, and so forth. We have made no attempt to discuss the logical organization of report writing since this area is thoroughly covered in *A Manual of Police Report Writing* by Patrick D. Smith and Frank M. Patterson, published by Charles C Thomas. We urge those students who need help in report writing to refer to this book. In order to help the student to improve and to gain experience in his ability to write, we have provided copious exercises which we recommend that he complete; it is only by writing that one learns to write. This book was written with two goals in mind: first, that it can be used as a textbook in police schools, and, secondly, that it can be used individually.

Therefore, this book is based on the belief that the most important structure in all writing is the sentence, and that the sentence is best understood when analyzed according to sentence patterns. The majority of English sentences are based upon, or are variations of a few basic sentence patterns. Studies of the language have shown that by the time a child is six years old he has mastered the basic "kernel" sentences. As the child becomes older and progresses in school, he begins to manipulate and vary the basic sentences for more sophistication.

To accomplish the purpose of this book, the student must realize two things: (a) that learning the conventions of English will help him to communicate better and (b) that while dictionaries and hand books of English are helpful reference books, he must often be his own authority about usage.

Furthermore, the law enforcement officer must understand that probably the strongest objection to nonstandard English is social, and this objection is one of which the officer as a public servant should be cognizant. Indeed, the use of nonstandard English is usually taken as a sign of inferior social background, and the speaker of nonstandard English is handicapped in economic and social advancement. In other words, one's language not only describes things and attitudes; it also depicts the social level of the person using the language. Thus, "I have no money" and "I ain't got no money" refer to the same financial condition. One is just as clear as the other. But one sentence portrays the speaker as a speaker of standard English and the other as one of nonstandard English. Rightly or wrongly, the public judges one by the language he uses. And since the law enforcement agent is in the public eye, it is imperative that he use the appropriate English.

CONTENTS

POLICE ENGLISH

Chapter I

GRAMMAR OF THE SENTENCE

DIAGNOSTIC TESTS

Diagnostic Test 1: Recognition of Standard Sentence Patterns

THE OBJECTIVE OF this section is to determine as nearly as possible the student's ability to recognize basic sentences—in other words to determine the student's sentence sense. Choose, out of each group, the sentence or sentences which seem most acceptable (or correct) to you.

1. a. The money in 10 and 20 denominations was.
   b. The money was in 10 and 20 dollar denominations.
   c. In 10 and 20 dollar denominations, the money was.

2. a. He was supposed to catch a plane this evening.
   b. He was this evening a plane supposed to catch.
   c. He a plane was supposed this evening to catch.

3. a. He had attempted to cash a check at the hotel desk.
   b. He had a check at the hotel desk attempted to cash.
   c. At the hotel desk, he had attempted to cash a check.

4. a. During this time, the police were checking other suspects.
   b. The police, during this time, were checking other suspects.
   c. The police were checking other suspects during this time.

5. a. While trying to escape, the suspect jumped from the window and broke his leg.
   b. The suspect from the window jumped and his leg broke while trying to escape.
   c. The suspect, while trying to escape, jumped from the window and broke his leg.

3

Diagnostic Test 2: Recognition of Illogical Structures

Choose, out of each group, the sentence which seems to you to be the more logical in content.

1. a. Pulling over to the curb at the first opportunity, the fire truck passed the squad car.
   b. Pulling over to the curb at the first opportunity, the squad car was passed by the fire truck.

2. a. Many of our laws today are based on Roman laws, but being changed to fit modern needs.
   b. Many of our laws today are based on Roman laws, but have been changed to fit modern needs.

3. a. The driver failed to observe the curve sign, lost control of his car, and went over the embankment.
   b. Failing to observe the curve sign, the car lost control, thus going over the embankment.

4. a. When one is tired, you should pull over to the side of the road and rest.
   b. When a driver is tired, he should pull over to the side of the road and rest.

5. a. I have tried and always will say that he is innocent.
   b. I have said, and always will say, that he is innocent.

6. a. Drivers are more careless in the South than in the Midwest.
   b. Drivers are more careless in the South than in the Midwest.

7. a. He is as good, if not better, than any driver on the force.
   b. He is as good as, if not better than, any driver on the force.

Diagnostic Test 3: Recognition of Poor Word Choice

Choose, out of each group, the sentence which seems to you to have the better word choice.

1. a. The riots have began again.
   b. The riots have begun again.

2. a. Most of the spectators had went home.
   b. Most of the spectators had gone home.

3. a. I asked if she had seen him recently.
   b. I asked if she has seen him recently.

4. a. There are few officers more capable than him.
   b. There are few officers more capable than he.

5. a. He was the kind of driver who everybody trusted.
   b. He was the kind of driver whom everybody trusted.

6. a. Neither the boy nor his father have seen the wreck.
   b. Neither the boy nor his father has seen the wreck.

7. a. There was two mistakes made in the examination.
   b. There were two mistakes made in the examination.

8. a. Each person must contribute his share of the expense.
   b. Each person must contribute their share of the expense.

9. a. The reason they were divorced was not supporting his family.
   b. The reason they were divorced was that he would not support his family.

10. a. He wore a pair of cheap made shoes.
    b. He wore a pair of cheaply made shoes.

DEFINITION AND USE OF GRAMMAR

Grammar, as we will be using the term in this book, is the relationship between the units of the language. In the English language, the basic relationship is that of noun phrase plus verb phrase—or noun plus verb—or subject plus predicate; they are all names for the same kind of structure. All the other structures of the English language grow out of this fundamental combination. By the time that most children enter grade school, they are able to manipulate the basic sentence patterns of the language. As they grow older and more sophisticated, they vary the basic sentence patterns to show different ideas and relationships. In the first part of the grammar, we will study how to generate (create) the eleven basic varieties of the fundamental noun phrase plus verb phrase combination. In the second part of the grammar, we will study how these basic patterns or sequences can be transformed or varied to produce more complicated patterns or sequences. We can transform basic patterns by combining them with one another, by subordinating one or more patterns and inserting them into a basic pattern, or by shifting units within a basic pattern. If you master thoroughly these two skills—generation and transformation—you should have no trouble in writing grammatically correct sentences in your reports.

BASIC SENTENCE PATTERNS

Although the basic sentence patterns are very elementary—usually so elementary that they are rarely used in their original, generated form—they must be considered first because they are the units from which the more familiar, and more complex, structures of writing are formed. The exercises after each pattern are important because they illustrate and reemphasize the process of generating the specific pattern. *Study each pattern and example until you have become quite familiar with it—then move on to the exercises. By following this procedure, you are beginning to do two things. First, you are generating (creating) your own sentences. Secondly, you are learning the grammar of the language.* There are eleven basic sentence patterns.

Pattern 1:   NP + be + (int) + adj

NP in the formula stands for noun phrase; a noun phrase may be a single word—like *Sam* or *Missouri* or *he*—or a phrase like *the boy* or *several customers* or *one of the hoodlums. Be* is the symbol for any form of *to be* (am, is, was, are, were). *Int* stands for an intensifying word like *very, too, quite*, or *extremely;* the parenthesis indicates that *int* is an optional part (you may or may not use it at your own choice) of the pattern. The pattern may be complete without an *int. Adj* is the symbol for adjective, a word like *green, red, handsome, angry, tall, short,* and *sweet.*

Examples: Pattern I

1. Guns are dangerous.
   NP + be + adj

2. The woman was very angry.
   NP + be + int + adj

3. Some of the cars were rusty.
   NP   + be + adj

4. The light was green.
   NP + be + adj

NOTE: Observe that the verb *be* in this pattern is always followed by an adjective and only an adjective. This adjective has sometimes been called the predicate adjective in that it completes the meaning of the verb and refers back, modifies or describes the NP of the subject in some manner.

Exercises: Pattern I

1. Construct sentences illustrating Pattern I and using the following noun phrase and adjectives. Remember to use a form of *be*.

a. John Smith	a. dirty
b. The boys	b. belligerent
c. Many hoodlums	c. useful
d. An ambulance	d. late
e. Some of the street lights	e. bright

2. Explain why you used singular or plural forms of *be* in each of the sentences in Exercise I. By doing this you are learning the rule that the verb must agree in number (plural or singular) with the subject.

3. Supply an optional intensifier in each of the sentences in Exercise 1.

Pattern II: NP + be + NP

As in Pattern I, the NP in the formula stands for noun phrase; *be* is the symbol for any form of *to be*.

Examples: Pattern II

1. The man was a gambler.
    NP + be + NP

2. Most of the cars were wrecks.
    NP + be + NP

3. One of the drivers was he.
    NP + be + NP

NOTE: In this sentence a personal pronoun has been sub-stituted for the NP. A personal pronoun is a word like *he, him, his, she, her* etc.

4. Several witnesses were patrolmen.
    NP + be + NP

NOTE: Observe that the verb *be* in this pattern is always followed by an NP and only an NP. This NP has sometimes been called a subject complement in that it completes the mean-ing of the verb and it means the same thing as the NP of the subject.

Exercises: Pattern II

1. Construct sentences illustrating Pattern II and using the following noun phrases.

a. The officer	a. the victim
b. One of the boys	b. an elderly man
c. John Smith	c. the storekeeper
d. He	d. a college student
e. A prowler	e. one of the suspects

2. Explain why you used singular or plural forms of *be* in each of the sentences in Exercise 1.

3. Explain how the sentences in Pattern II differ from the sentences in Pattern I.

Pattern III: NP + be + adv-p

NP in the formula stands for noun phrase; *be* stands for any form of *to be*. *Adv-p* stands for adverb of place; an adverb of place may be a single word—like *there, here, home*—or a phrase like *in the street, under the bridge,* and *behind the wall.*

Examples: Pattern III

1. The point of entry was here.
   NP   + be + adv-p

2. One of the men was behind the door.
   NP   + be +   adv-p

3. Several billfolds were in his pockets.
   NP   + be +   adv-p

4. The victim was in the next room.
   NP   + be +   adv-p

NOTE: Observe that *be* in this pattern is always followed by an adverb of place.

Exercises: Pattern III

1. Construct sentences illustrating Pattern III and using the following adverbs of place.

   a. there
   b. on the desk
   c. beside the automobile
   d. under the body
   e. out of the office

2. Explain why you used the singular or the plural forms of *be* in each of the sentences in Exercise 1.

3. Explain how the sentences in Pattern III differ from those in Patterns I and II.

Pattern IV: NP + vh + NP

NP stands for noun phrase. The *vh* in the formula means a verb of the *have* class. These verbs, like *have, cost,* and *weigh,* are always followed by a noun phrase. If the *NP* is a personal pronoun, the objective case of the pronoun is used rather than the nominative case. In other words, instead of using a form of *he, she, I, they,* one uses a form of the objective case, like *him, her, me,* and *them.*

Examples: Pattern IV

1. The thieves had problems.
   NP   + vh +   NP

2. The safe weighs 500 pounds.
    NP   + vh +   NP

3. One of the necklaces cost a thousand dollars.
    NP   + vh +   NP

4. The pawnbroker had them.
    NP   + vh + NP

NOTE: Observe that the NP that follows the *vh* is different from the NP that precedes the *vh*.

Exercises: Pattern IV

1. Construct five sentences using *have* as your verb.
2. Construct five sentences using *cost* as your verb.
3. Construct five sentences using *weigh* as your verb.
4. Find five other verbs in your reading that belong to the *vh* class.
5. Explain how *vh* verbs differ from *be* verbs.

Pattern V: NP + vs + adj

The *vs* in this formula stands for a verb of the *seem* class—verbs like *seem, feel, taste, smell, look,* and *sound.* (Note: a clue to learning them is that most of them have to do with the senses.) They are always followed by an adjective (a word like *handsome, sour, angry, tall, big, fat,* and *angry*) and the adjective may be preceded by an *int.* Remember that an intensifier is a word like *very, too, quite,* and *extremely.*

Examples: Pattern V

1. The building seemed empty.
    NP   + vs +   adj

2. One of the men sounded angry.
    NP   + vs +   adj

3. His hand felt cold.
    NP   + vs + adj

4. The drink tasted bitter.
    NP   + vs +   adj

Exercises: Pattern V

1. Using the following verbs, construct sentences illustrating Pattern V.

   a. grow
   b. appear
   c. look
   d. feel
   e. smell

2. Explain how *vs* verbs differ from *vh* and *be* verbs.

3. Try to find other verbs from your reading that belong to the *vs* class. Be able to explain why the verbs fit the *vs* class.

Pattern VI: NP + vb + (int) + adj
NP

In this formula, *vb* stands for a verb of the *become* class. In American English, only two verbs fit this class: *become* and *remain*. Notice that these two verbs may be followed either by an adjective, which may or may not be preceded by an *int*, or an NP.

Examples: Pattern VI

1. The witness became angry.
   NP   + vb +   adj

2. School dropouts become troublemakers.
   NP   + vb +   NP

3. The driver remained calm.
   NP   + vb +   adj

4. The intersection remains a danger spot.
   NP   + vb +   NP

NOTE: Observe that the structure that follows a *vb* is either an adjective (predicate adjective) that modifies, describes, and refers to the subject, or an NP that means the same things as the subject. This NP is sometimes called a subjective complement because it completes the meaning of the verb and refers to the subject.

Exercises: Pattern VI

1. Construct ten sentences which illustrate Pattern VI.
2. Explain how *vb* verbs differ from *be* verbs.

Pattern VII: NP + vi

The *vi* in the formula stands for intransitive verb, a kind of verb which differs from other classes because it need not be followed by any other unit (such as NP, adj. adv-p).

Examples: Pattern VII

1. The suspect ran.
   NP   + vi

2. Some of the people laughed.
      NP   + vi

3. I fired.
   NP + vi

4. Several ambulances came.
      NP   + vi

Exercises: Pattern VII

1. Construct ten sentences which illustrate Pattern VII.

2. Make a list of ten verbs which need not be followed by any other unit. Be prepared to construct sentences from those verbs which illustrate Pattern VII.

Pattern VIII: NP + vi + prt

The symbol *vi* + *prt* stands for a subclass of Pattern VII; this subclass is distinctive because *vi* verbs are accompanied by small units (*prt*) called particles (words like *up, out, under, away, around*.

Examples: Pattern VIII

1. Most of the hoodlums ran away.
      NP   + vi + prt

2. The victim sat up.
      NP   + vi + prt

3. The car turned around.
    NP   + vi + prt

NOTE: Observe that *vi* (intransitive verbs) are not followed by a NP, adj, or an adverb of place.

Exercises: Pattern VIII

1. Construct ten sentences which illustrate Pattern VIII.

2. Make a list of ten verbs which can be followed by a *prt*. Be prepared to construct sentences which illustrate this pattern.

Pattern IX: $NP^1 + vt + NP^2$

The symbol *vt* stands for a transitive verb; a transitive verb is always followed by a noun phrase. This noun phrase always differs from the subject of the sentence and is called at times the direct object. It is the object of the action of the verb.

Examples: Pattern IX

1. The officer fired three shots.
    NP   + vt + NP

2. A car struck him.
    NP + vt + NP

3. Some of the shouts bothered her.
    NP   + vt + NP

4. The witness made a statement.
    NP   + vt + NP

NOTE: Observe that when a pronoun is used in the place of a noun, it is always in the objective case. Instead of using *he*, one uses *him* etc. e.g. *she-her; they-them.*

Exercises: Pattern IX

1. Construct ten sentences which illustrate Pattern IX.

2. Explain how transitive verbs differ from instransitive verbs.

3. Explain how transitive verbs differ from *vh* verbs.

4. Explain the difference in meaning between the following two sentences:

a. The man weighed the car.

b. The man weighed 175 pounds.

Pattern X: NP¹ + vt + prt + NP²

The *vt* + *prt* in the formula stands for a subclass of transitive verbs; this subclass is distinctive because the *vt* verbs are accompanied by small units called particles (words like *up, out, under* etc.).

Examples: Pattern X

1. The witness filled out a report.
        NP   + vt + prt   + NP

2. We looked up his name.
    NP + vt + prt + NP

3. Most crimes fall under this heading.
        NP   + vt + prt +   NP

4. The officers put down the rebellion in short order.
        NP   + vt + prt +   NP

NOTE: This combination of the verb plus a particle has sometimes been called the verb-adverb combination or merged verbs because the adverb or particle becomes a part of the verb itself.

Exercises: Pattern X

1. Construct ten sentences which illustrate Pattern X.

2. Make a list of ten *vt* plus *prt* verbs.

3. Explain how Pattern X differs from Pattern IX.

Pattern XI: NP¹ + vt + NP³ + NP²

This pattern is a subclass of the larger class of transitive verbs; this subclass is distinctive because it is followed by a noun phrase which in traditional grammar is called the indirect object.

Examples: Pattern XI

1. John Smith called the man a liar.
        NP¹   + vt + NP³ + NP²

2. The man gave him a letter.
   $NP^1 + vt + NP^3 + NP^2$

3. I threw him the package.
   $NP^1 + vt + NP^3 + NP^2$

NOTE: Observe that NP^3 always comes between the verb and NP^2. NP^2 is the direct object and NP^3 is the indirect object which is the receiver of the action of the direct object. Sometimes this indirect object is made into a prepositional phrase and then it follows the direct object—for example, *I threw the package to him.*

Exercises: Pattern XI

1. Construct ten sentences which illustrate Pattern XI.
2. Explain how Pattern XI differs from Pattern IX and X.
3. Explain the difference in meaning between the following sentences.
   a. The ball cost five dollars.
   b. The ball cost him five dollars.
   c. I hit him.
   d. I hit him the ball.
   e. The victim gave a groan.
   f. We gave the informer a reward.

Review Exercises

To the left of each number write the sentence pattern. To the right of each sentence write the structure (predicate nom., pred. adj., adverb, direct object, indirect object, objective comp., etc.) of the italicized word or phrase.

1. Mabel is *upstairs.*
2. He is a *minister.*
3. Doran became the *publisher.*
4. The coyotes howled *at the moon.*
5. He became a *different person.*
6. Murphy remained *silent.*
7. The bride wore *red.*

8. *The boiler* exploded.
9. We mailed *the package*.
10. She gave *him* the book.
11. They appointed him *captain* of the team.
12. Bradbury lowered *the boom*.
13. The troops fought *hard*.
14. He is still *here*.
15. He is *still*.
16. He thought her *beautiful*.
17. The baby is *pretty*.
18. Henry became a *musician*.
19. The lawn needed *water*.
20. Nothing remained *behind*.
21. We urged his *election*.
22. Forty people *made* the trip. (what type?)
23. Nobody *hurried* on the cross country trip. (what type?)
24. The spirit of adventure on the road is not *here*.
25. You can do absolutely *anything* with a car nowadays.
26. *Everybody* survived.
27. The pictures tell *the story*.
28. The organizer of this historic drive from Atlantic City to Los Angeles *was* John Guy Monihan. (what type?)
29. The photographs of the journey seem especially *eloquent*.
30. Bob was elected *president*.
31. Touring *cars* were open cars with collapsible tops.
32. They shot *a moose*.
33. She became a *movie* star.
34. She *remained* my closest friend. (what type?)
35. She yawned *wearily*.
36. The car looked *new*.
37. The enemy *retreated*.
38. She *sang* well. (what type?)
39. He seemed an interesting *chap*.
40. He acted *insanely*.
41. He is *insane*.
42. The club elected Bob *president*
43. They gave him *the keys* to the city.
44. Her husband gave *her* a gift.

45. No birds *sang*.
46. She sang *me* a song.
47. She *sang*. (what type?)
48. I am *tired*.
49. The eagles were *inside*.
50. He is *my English teacher*.

TRANSFORMATIONS

Although theoretically a writer could communicate intelligibly with his reader by limiting his written structures to the eleven basic sentence patterns, his writing would soon bore or annoy the reader because of its elementary and choppy units. Discourse limited to basic patterns would soon sound like sentences written for a first-grade reader. We form more complex structures of writing by taking these basic sentence patterns and combining, subordinating, shifting, or deleting them into the sentences which most of us are more familiar with—the sentences which we actually write. The point, however, is that even though we may not write basic sentence patterns, we use them to create the structures which we *do* write. This part of the grammar will deal with the three ways we transform basic sentence patterns into the more familiar structures of our everyday writing.

There is one immediate benefit to be gained from considering the process of writing from the standpoint of basic, generative patterns: In basic patterns, the relationship between subject and verb is always clear. So long as you are aware of the subject-verb relationship in your basic sentence patterns, you should have little trouble with subject-verb agreements in the structures which you build from the basic patterns.

If you have mastered the process of generation described in the previous section, and if you learn thoroughly the following procedures, you should be able to construct complex sequences that are both grammatically correct and clearly understandable to your reader.

$$\text{Listing: } SP \longrightarrow SP\text{-}1 + \begin{Bmatrix} ; \\ , \end{Bmatrix} + SP\text{-}2 + \begin{Bmatrix} \\ , \end{Bmatrix} ; + \begin{Bmatrix} \text{and} \\ \text{or} \\ \text{but} \\ \text{yet} \end{Bmatrix} + SP\text{-}3$$

A list differs from a compound in that it consists of three or more sentence patterns (SP stands for sentence pattern) that have been combined into one unit. The choice of punctuation marks used to signal the relationship between the structures is limited to the comma or the semicolon, plus an optional conjunction before the final sentence pattern. Either a comma or a semicolon may be used throughout the list, but never a mixture. If any unit in the list has internal commas, the semicolon should be used as the joining marks between units.

Examples

1. The cars arrived, the men got out, and the fight began.
2. The house was dark; the street was empty; the neighborhood was quiet.

    Sentence Connector: SP⟶ SP-1 + ; + SC + , + SP-2

A sentence connector is a word like *however, nevertheless, therefore, moreover,* etc. When it is used to join two sentence patterns, it is always preceded by a semicolon and followed by a comma. If the writer wishes, he may shift the sentence connector to the middle or to the end of SP-2.

Examples

1. The man was drunk; however, he was courteous.
2. The man was drunk; he, however, was courteous.
3. The man was drunk; he was courteous, however.

COORDINATION

After the student has studied the basic patterns, he is ready to examine coordination as a method of sentence expansion. In sentences like the following, the student needs to observe that the structures in the series are coordinate:

1. He likes swimming and hiking.
2. He slipped, fell, and broke his leg.
3. The police board scanned the applicant's transcript, recommendations and character references.

Coordinate structures are ordinarily joined by such coordinators as *and, but, nor, or, not, for, so,* and *yet;* and by the correlatives, which work in pairs, *either-or, neither-nor, both-and, not (only)-but (also)*.

Working with basic sentences, the student can combine simple techniques of combination. For example, the three basic sentences, "The man was kind. The man was energetic. The man was serene," can be combined into one sentence. "The man was kind, energetic, and serene."

As the following sentences show, coordination can be shown in three simple stages: coordination in the predicate, in the subject, and in the compound sentence.

Direct object: The suspect remembered the place, the assailant, and the fight.

Predicate complement: The suspect remained sullen and uncooperative.

Verb: He ran and jumped over the fence.

Coordination in the Predicate

Rewrite the sentences to achieve coordination.

Examples

John was a patrolman. John was a man.
John was a patrolman and a man.

1. The inspector traveled far.
   The inspector talked vigorously.
   The inspector interviewed witnesses.
Rewrite:

2. The student attended class.
   The student listened attentively.
   The student studied his lessons.
Rewrite:

3. Mr. Brown was a politician.

Mr. Brown was a statesman.
Rewrite:

4. The new district attorney became a crusader.
   He became a champion of the downtrodden.
   The new district attorney became a defender of the people.
Rewrite:

5. He spoke frequently.
   He studied diligently.
   He worked hard.
Rewrite:

6. He disliked the machine.
   He trusted the people.
Rewrite:

Coordination in the Subject

Rewrite the sentences, using coordination in the subject. Observe that changes in the verb sometimes must take place to agree with the subject.

Examples

The witness imagined plots against him.
His wife imagined plots against him.
The witness and his wife imagined plots against them.
1. Oratory was an asset for the new district attorney.
   Politically, it was an asset.
Rewrite:

2. Political ambition motivated his program.
Idealism motivated his program.
Rewrite:

3. These strengths were part of his character.
These limitations were part of his character.
Rewrite:

4. The patrolman failed to measure up to expectations.
His buddy failed to measure up to expectations.
Rewrite:

5. The desires of the people were a concern for him.
The needs of the people were a concern.
The prejudices of the people were a concern.
Rewrite:

The Compound Sentence

Combine the sentences in each group into one compound sentence.

Examples

Social legislation was passed.

The law enforcement was greatly strengthened.

Social legislation was passed, and the law enforcement program was greatly strengthened.

1. The district attorney's work drew heavily upon his stamina.
Once he became ill from overwork.
Rewrite:

2. The patrolman pursued the fleeing car.
   He arrested the offender.
Rewrite:

3. The district attorney might talk endlessly.
   He always had a purpose.
Rewrite:

4. The district attorney took everything too seriously.
   He was too intent and too intense.
Rewrite:

5. The chief of police spoke frequently about principles.
   He cared more for ends than means.
Rewrite:

COMBINING UNITS BELOW THE LEVEL OF SENTENCE PATTERNS

Structures like noun phrases, verb phrases, prepositional phrases, adjectives, and adverbs can also be combined to the above rules. The only rule which does not apply to combining units below the level of sentence patterns is the sentence-connector rule. We have already looked at some of these examples in the section on coordination. Observe the following examples:

Basic Structure	*Combined Structure*
1. A man arrived. His wife arrived.	A man and his wife arrived.
2. A simple dress. A dignified dress.	A simple yet dignified dress.

3. He borrowed it.   He borrowed or stole it.
   He stole it.

4. She was beautiful.   She was beautiful but dumb.
   She was dumb.

5. He fell.   He either fell or was pushed.
   He was pushed.

6. They were drunk.   They were both drunk and disorderly.
   They were disorderly.

7. He begged.   He begged, borrowed, and stole.
   He borrowed.
   He stole.

RULES FOR COMBINING

The simplest kind of transformation is the process of combination. This is the process of taking two or more basic sentence patterns and joining them so that the structures form one unit. There are four ways in which basic patterns may be joined: by compounding, by correlative conjunctions, by listing, and by sentence connectors.

$$\text{Compound: SP} \longrightarrow \text{SP-1} + \left\{ \begin{array}{l} \left\{ \begin{array}{l} \varnothing \\ \text{- -} \\ , \\ ; \end{array} \right\} + \text{conj} \\ \\ \left\{ \begin{array}{l} \text{- -} \\ : \\ ; \end{array} + \varnothing \right\} \end{array} \right\} + \text{SP-2}$$

As the formula indicates, you may compound or join sentence pattern 2 and sentence pattern 1 in a variety of ways. You may use either a semicolon, or a colon, or a dash; or you may use a conjunction plus a comma, a conjunction plus a semicolon, a conjunction plus a dash, or a conjunction plus nothing (or no mark of punctuation). Conjunctions (*and, or, for, nor, but, yet, so*) are grammatical signals in that they indicate relationship. Different marks of punctuation suggest different kinds of relationships between units: the semicolon is a formal mark, usually rather forceful, usually indicative of a distinct relationship between structures. The comma is a midformal mark, neutral in emphasis, usually indicative of a close relationship between structures. The dash is an informal mark, very forceful, usually indicative of a very distant relationship between structures.

Examples

1. The light changed and the car stopped.
2. I blew my whistle but the man did not stop.
3. The light was inadequate or the sign was down.
4. The hill was not steep nor was the road slick.
5. The room was quiet for the people had gone.
6. The man was sick yet he did not complain.
7. The phone rang so I answered it.

Correlative Conjunctions

$$SP \longrightarrow corr\text{-}a + SP\text{-}1 + (,) + corr\text{-}b + SP\text{-}2$$

Correlative conjunctions are word pairs like *either/or, neither/nor, not only/but also* that function together to signal a relationship between two structures. The correlatives suggest contrastive balance or sometimes emphasize parallel structure. The optional comma in the formula may be used to add emphasis to the contrastive relationship between structures.

Examples

1. Either the man was ill or he was drunk.
2. Not only did the man rob the safe, but he also cleaned out the cash register.

Exercises: Combining

1. Construct five sentence patterns. Make them into three compound sentences using conjunctions and not punctuation.
2. Make the sentence patterns in exercise 1 (above) into compounds by means of conjunctions plus a semicolon. Be ready to explain how the relationship between the compounded sentence patterns has been altered.
3. Make the sentence patterns in exercise 1 into compounds by means of a conjunction plus a comma. Has the relationship between the sentence patterns been altered? Why?
4. Make the sentence patterns in exercise 1 into compounds by

means of a conjunction plus a dash. Explain how the relationship between the sentence patterns has been altered.

5. Construct five sentence patterns and make them into lists.
6. Take two of the sentence patterns in exercise 5 and make them into a compound. Explain why a compound is different from a list.
7. Take two of the sentence patterns in exercise 5 and combine them by means of correlative conjunctions. Explain why the correlative is different from a compound.
8. Construct 5 sentence patterns and make them into compounds by means of sentence connectors. Explain why the compounds are different from the examples in exercise 1.
9. Make the sentence patterns in exercise 8 into compounds by means of a conjunction plus semicolon. Have you altered the relationship between sentence patterns? Explain.
10. Make the sentence patterns in exercise 8 into compounds by means of a semicolon. Explain how the compounds are different from those in exercise 9.

RULES FOR SUBORDINATING

The process of subordination involves transforming a basic sentence pattern into a dependent structure (usually by means of subordinating words) and connecting or inserting this subordinated pattern into an independent sentence pattern. The pattern to be subordinated is called the *insert*. The independent sentence pattern is called the *matrix.* The combination of the two is called the *result.*

Although the basic sentence pattern, as pointed out in the beginning of this chapter, is NP + VP, there are actually four possible unit positions in a kernel sentence: NP–(adj)–VP–(adv). A subordinated pattern (one which has undergone some kind of noun, adjective, or adverb, transformation), may be inserted into its corresponding position in a *matrix*: A pattern resulting from a noun transformation may be inserted into the NP position; a pattern resulting from an adjective transformation may be inserted into the adjective position; a pattern resulting from an adverb transformation may be inserted into the adverb position.

Noun Transformations

Most noun transformations produce subordinated patterns which replace the subject NP of the *matrix*. There are, however, noun transformations for patterns that can fill the traditional direct object position of a VP and also for patterns that can fill the traditional indirect object position of a VP. In all cases, the subordination pattern is the result of some kind of subordination process that has operated on a kernel sequence to reduce the original SP to a subordinate structure. We shall discuss first of all the transformations that fill the subject NP position of a *matrix;* then we shall deal with the transformations that fill the direct and indirect object positions .

NP Subject Transformations

NP subject transformations can be divided into two classes—those sequences that are subordinated by the addition of a subordinating word (*that, which, what,* etc.), and those sequences that are subordinated by a For/to or Pos/ing substitution.

1. *NP subj (wh)*
   Insert: John Smith was late.
   Matrix: This was obvious.
   Result: That John Smith was late was obvious.

As the formula indicates, the insert sentence is subordinated by the addition of a *wh* word (that). This subordinated sequence replaces the subject NP of the *matrix.* The *result* sequence, thus, is the combination of *insert* and *matrix.*

2. *NP subj (for/to)*
   Insert: John left.
   Matrix: This was a mistake.
   Result: For John to leave was a mistake.

In the transformation, the *insert* sequence is subordinated by the addition of the preposition *for* and by the changing of the verb to the infinitive (left—to leave); this subordinated sequence replaces the subject NP of the *matrix* to produce the *result* sequence.

The *result* of the transformation may be expanded by the addition of *it,* as illustrated:

For John to leave was a mistake $\longrightarrow$ It was a mistake for John to leave.

As the illustration shows, *it* is inserted before the verb of the original *matrix* sentence and the *insert* sequence (For John to leave) is shifted to the end of the *matrix*.

3. *NP subj (Pos/ing)*
   Insert: John left.
   Matrix: This was a mistake.
   Result: John's leaving was a mistake.

In the pos/ing transformation, the *insert* sequence is subordinated by the addition of possessive to the subject NP of the sequence and by the changing of the verb to an *ing* form (left $\longrightarrow$ leaving); this subordinated sequence replaces the subject NP of the *matrix* to produce the *result* sequence.

The *result* of the pos/ing transformation may undergo a deletion process as illustrated:

John's leaving was a mistake $\longrightarrow$ Leaving was a mistake.

As the illustration shows, the possessive NP of the *insert* can be deleted.

Exercises: NP Subj

1. Perform NP subj (wh) on the following. In other words the *insert* becomes a noun subordination replacing the NP of the *matrix* sentence.
   Insert: John Smith killed her.
   Matrix: This was a mistake.

2. Perform NP subj (wh) on the following using *when* as the subordinator.
   Insert: The bus arrived.
   Matrix: This was unimportant.

3. Perform NP subj (wh) on the following using *how* as the subordinator.
   Insert: The murder was committed.
   Matrix: This was a mystery.

4. Construct two pairs of inserts and matrixes and perform NP subj (for/to) on them.

5. Construct two pairs of inserts and matrixes and perform NP

subj (pos/ing) on them.

6. Put the *result* sequence of exercise 4 through an expansion transformation by the addition of it.
7. Put the *result* sequences of exercise 5 through a deletion transformation.

NP Object Transformations

There are two kinds of NP object transformations: sequences that are subordinated by the addition of a subordinating word and sequences that are subordinated by the changing of verb tense to infinitive.

Examples: NP obj (wh)

Insert: The ambulance was coming.
Matrix: The man said this.
Result: The man said that the ambulance was coming.

As the formula indicates, the *insert* sequence is subordinated by the addition of a *wh* word (that). This subordinated sequence replaces the NP object of the *matrix*. The *result* sequence of this transformation differs from the NP subj transformation in that the *matrix* sequence contains the *wh* word to be replaced, (*that, which, who, what*, etc.), as its direct object, never as its subject.

Example: NP obj (inf)

Insert: His companion drove.
Matrix: He wanted this.
Result: He wanted his companion to drive.

As the formula indicates, the *insert* sequence is subordinated by changing the verb tense (drove) to the infinitive (to drive). This subordinated sequence replaces the *wh* word in the *matrix* to produce the traditionally labeled indirect object structure as the *result*. When the *insert* contains a *be* verb, the following process occurs:

Insert: He was a coward.
Matrix: They considered this.
Result: They considered him to be a coward.

The subject NP of the *insert* (he) is changed to objective form (him). The *insert* sequence is subordinated by the changing of the verb tense (was) to the infinitive (to be). The subordinated sequence replaces the *wh* word in the *matrix*. The *result* sequence above may also undergo a deletion sequence or process:

They considered him to be a coward ⟶ They considered him a coward.

Exercises: NP obj

1. Perform NP obj (wh) on the following.
   Insert: The light was red.
   Matrix: The driver knew this.
2. Perform NP obj (wh) on the following using *how* as a subordinator.
   Insert: The robbery was committed.
   Matrix: The victim knew this.
3. Construct two pairs of inserts and matrixes and perform the NP obj (inf) transformation on them.
4. Construct two pairs of inserts and matrixes with *be* verbs in the inserts. Perform the NP obj (inf).
5. Put the result sequences of exercise 4 through a deletion process.

Adjective Transformations

Adjective transformations operate on kernel sentences to produce subordinated patterns which can fill the *adj* position of a matrix sequence.

$$NP-(adj)-VP-(adv)$$

These subordinated patterns, or relative clauses as they are sometimes identified, are related to the preceding NP by means of a relative pronoun (*who, that, which*). It is usually possible for the subordinated pattern to undergo an optional deletion process, in which the relative pronoun and the verb are removed. When this deletion process is applied, the material which is left in the pattern (usually a single word) is shifted to the pre-NP position in the matrix. Note the following example:

Insert: The man was lame.
Matrix: The man was robbed.
Result: The man who was lame was robbed.

Deletion Process:

The man who was lame was robbed ⟶ The man lame was robbed ⟶ The lame man was robbed.

Adjective transformations are of three types—those operating on *insert* sequences where the NP subject matches the NP subject of the *matrix;* those operating on *insert* sequences where the NP that matches the *matrix* NP is a direct object; and those operating on *insert* sequences where the NP that matches the *matrix* NP is a possessive.

1. Rel Adj I

Although the following examples contain slight variations, a similar process is applied to all: The insert sequence is subordinated by the substitution of a relative pronoun (*who, that, which*) for the subject NP. This subordinated sequence is then inserted into the *matrix* sequence between the NP and the VP. In each instance, the deletion process—whenever applicable—is demonstrated also.

Example 1

Insert: The car was green.
Matrix: The car belonged to the suspect.
Result: The car that was green belonged to the suspect.

Deletion Process:

The car that was green belonged to the suspect ⟶ The car green belonged to the suspect ⟶ The green car belonged to the suspect.

Example 2

Insert: The gun was on the table.
Matrix: The gun was the murder weapon.
Result: The gun that was on the table was the murder weapon.

Deletion Process:

The gun that was on the table was the murder weapon ⟶ The gun on the table was the murder weapon.

Example 3

Insert: The man is a plumber.
Matrix: The man ran away.

Result: The man who is a plumber ran away.

Deletion Process:

The man who is a plumber ran away ⟶ The man, a plumber, ran away.

Example 4

    Insert: The watchman arrived at midnight.

    Matrix: The watchman discovered the robbery.

    Result: The watchman who arrived at midnight discovered the robbery.

Example 5

    Insert: The dog was barking loudly.

    Matrix: The dog disturbed us.

    Result: The dog that was barking loudly disturbed us.

Deletion Process:

The dog that was barking loudly disturbed us ⟶ The dog barking loudly disturbed us ⟶ The loudly barking dog disturbed us.

Example 6

    Insert: The boys were watching the girls.

    Matrix: The boys stood on the corner.

    Result: The boys who were watching the girls stood on the corner.

Deletion Process:

The boys who were watching the girls stood on the corner ⟶ The boys watching the girls stood on the corner ⟶ The girl-watching boys stood on the corner.

Exercises: Rel Adj I

1. Construct five pairs of inserts and matrixes and perform Rel adj I on them.
2. Put the result of exercise 1 through deletion process wherever applicable.

2. *Rel Adj II*

This transformation operates on insert sequences where the NP that matches the *matrix* NP follows a transitive verb. This NP (in traditional terminology, the direct object) must be replaced by a relative pronoun in the objective case (*whom* or *that*). The relative pronoun is then shifted to the pre-NP position (subordinating the *insert* sequence) and the subordinated sequence is inserted into the *matrix* in the regular adj position (between the NP and the VP). Study the following examples.

Example 1
 Insert: We questioned the man.
 Matrix: The man was innocent.
 Result: The man whom we questioned was innocent.

Example 2
 Insert: The car hit the pole.
 Matrix: The pole was bent double.
 Result: The pole that the car hit was bent double.

Exercises: *Rel Adj II*

1. Construct three pairs of inserts and matrixes and perform Rel adj II on them.
2. Perform Rel adj II on the following:
 a. Insert: The man robbed the service station.
   Matrix: The service station had no burglar alarm.
 b. Insert: The students picketed the administration building.
   Matrix: The administration building had a fire.
 c. Insert: Officers arrested the students.
   Matrix: The students violated the curfew.

3. *Rel Adj III*

This final adjective transformation operates on insert sequences where the NP that matches the subject NP of the *matrix* is a possessive. The possessive NP is replaced by a possessive relative pronoun (*whose*). The possessive and the NP which it modifies are then shifted to pre-NP position. This subordinated sequence is inserted into the *matrix* in the regular adj position. Study the following examples to understand this procedure:

Example 1
 Insert: We examined the man's papers.
 Matrix: The man tried to escape.
 Result: The man whose papers we examined tried to escape.

Example 2

Insert: The officers found the man's car.

Matrix: The man had disappeared.

Result: The man whose car the officers found had disappeared.

Exercises: *Rel Adj III*

1. Perform Rel adj III on the following:
    a. Insert: We examined his ID card.
       Matrix: The student was released.
    b. Insert: Vandals had wrecked their home.
       Matrix: The couple called the police.
2. Construct three pairs of inserts and matrixes and perform Rel adj III on them.

Exercises: *Adjective Transformations*

1. Use whatever adjective transformation rules necessary to insert each of the following sentences into *matrix* A (below).
    a. Matrix: The people were traveling to Colorado.
       1. The people were poor.
       2. The people love comfort.
       3. The people lost their farms.
       4. I saw the people.
2. Where possible, perform deletion transformations on the *result* sequence of exercise 1.
3. Use whatever adjective transformation rules necessary to insert each of the following sequences into *matrix* B (below).
    b. Matrix: The robbers were frightened by the watchman.
       1. The robbers were careless.
       2. The robbers were young.
       3. The watchman had a shotgun.
       4. The watchman was alert.

Adverb Transformations

Adverb transformations operate on kernel sequences to produce subordinated patterns which can fill the adv position of a matrix sequence:

$$NP + (adj) + VP + (adv)$$

These subordinated patterns, or adverb clauses, are related

to the matrix sequence by means of an adverb (*because, when, if, although, since,* etc.), a word which relates NP + VP to space, time, frequency, probability, cause, and so forth. For example, *when* signals a relationship in time in *The cradle will rock when the wind blows.* Just as in adjective clauses, it is usually possible for an adverb clause to undergo an optional deletion process in which the subordinating word (adverb) and the verb are removed. When this deletion is applied, the material which is left in the pattern is shifted to the middle or to the beginning of the matrix sequence. However, it is also possible for an adverb clause to be shifted to the middle or the beginning of the matrix even when it has not undergone a deletion process. When this is the case, the adverb clause is unitized (or separated from the units in the matrix sequence by means of commas. Study the following examples closely to understand this process:

Insert: The boy was being noisy.

Matrix: The boy was scolded.

Result: The boy was scolded because the boy was being noisy.

Deletion Process:

The boy was scolded because the boy was being noisy $\longrightarrow$ The boy was scolded being noisy $\longrightarrow$ The boy, being noisy, was scolded.

Insert: The wind blows.

Matrix: The cradle rocks.

Result: The cradle will rock when the wind blows.

The cradle will rock when the wind blows $\longrightarrow$ When the wind blows, the cradle will rock.

There are two kinds of adverb transformations—one operates on *insert* sequences to produce subordinate adverb clauses and the other operates on *cause* and *while* adverb clauses (produced by the first type of transformation) to produce relative adverb clauses (clauses introduced by relative pronouns but which still retain their adverbial significance).

Sub Adv Clauses

The process of subordinating an *insert* to a *matrix* sequence by means of an adverb is similar to other transformations processes we have described. The adverb is placed in front of the

NP of the *insert*, subordinating the sequence. This subordinated sequence (or adverb clause as we may call it) is then placed in the adv position (at the end) of the *matrix*. If the NP of the *insert* matches the NP of the *matrix*, a personal pronoun usually replaces the NP of its second appearance in the *result* sequence. Adverb clauses, as mentioned above, may be shifted, or deleted and shifted. Note the following examples:

Example 1
> Insert: The man was driving too fast.
> Matrix: The man had a wreck.
> Result: The man had a wreck because he was driving too
> fast.

Shifting Process:
> The man had a wreck because the man was driving too
> fast ⟶ Because the man was driving too fast, he had a
> wreck.

Deletion and Shift:
> Because the man was driving too fast ⟶ driving too fast.
> Result: Driving too fast, the man had a wreck, or The
> man, driving too fast, had a wreck.

Example 2
> Insert: He was watching.
> Matrix: The bridge collapsed.
> Result: The bridge collapsed while he was watching.

Shifting Process:
> The bridge collapsed while he was watching ⟶ While
> he was watching, the bridge collapsed.

CAUTION: The process of deletion and shift cannot be applied to result sequences such as the one in example 2, because the NP of the *insert* does not match the NP of the matrix. Performing such a deletion and shift would be the kind of error traditionally identified as the dangling construction: *Watching, the bridge collapsed.* Who was watching?

Example 3
> Insert: The thief held the woman in front of himself.
> Matrix: The thief backed out the front door.

Result: The thief backed out the front door while he held
the woman in front of himself.

Expansion, Deletion Process:

While he held the woman in front of himself ⟶ While
he was holding the woman in front of himself ⟶ Holding the woman in front of himself, the thief backed out
the front door.

Shifting Process:

The thief backed out the front door holding the woman in
front of himself ⟶ Holding the woman in front of
himself, the thief backed out the front door.

The sentence in Example 3 illustrates how an *insert* sequence
with VI or VT may first be expanded (by the addition of *be*
+ *ing*) and then deleted; the deletion still retains the
adverbial relationship of time.

Example 4

Insert: The man hit the woman.

Matrix: The man stole the woman's purse.

Result: The man stole the woman's purse after he hit her.

Expansion, Deletion Process:

After the man hit the woman ⟶ After the man was
having hit the woman ⟶ Having hit the woman.

Shifting Process:

The man stole the woman's purse having hit the woman
⟶ Having hit the woman, the man stole her purse.

Example 4 illustrates how an *insert* sequence may be expanded by both *be* + *ing* and *have* + *part;* the deletion process
and the shifting of the result to pre-NP position enables the
writer to retain the time relationship expressed by *after.*

Example 5

Insert: The alarm had sounded.

Matrix: The guards were alert.

Result: The guards were alert because the alarm had
sounded.

Expansion, Deletion Process:

Because the alarm had sounded ⟶ Because the alarm
was having sounded ⟶ The alarm having sounded.

Shifting Process:

The guards were alert the alarm having sounded $\longrightarrow$ The alarm having sounded, the guards were alert.

Example 5 illustrates how an expansion and deletion process can be applied when the NP of the *insert* does not match the NP of the matrix. As the example shows, the VP is expanded by the addition of *be + ing;* then the sub conj is removed but the NP remains. The result is the traditionally labeled nominative absolute.

Exercises: Sub Adv Clause

1. Perform the sub adv clause transformation process on the following:
   a. Insert: The man ran a stop sign.
      Matrix: The accident occurred.
   b. Insert: He was cleaning the rifle.
      Matrix: The rifle went off.
2. Perform an expansion, deletion process on the following:
   a. Because the man hit the woman
   b. When the shooting stopped
   c. After I signed the ticket
   d. While the boy stole the hubcaps
3. Construct five pairs of *inserts* and *matrixes* and demonstrate the sub adv clause transformation process.

Relative Adv Clause

Relative adverb clauses originate from *because* or *while* clauses. They differ from relative adjective clauses in two ways: they are never introduced by the relative pronoun *that;* they have a *cause* or *while* relationship to the *matrix.* Relative adverb clauses are always unitized by commas. Study the following examples:

Example 1
   Insert: Because the car had a flat tire
   Matrix: The car was abandoned.
   Result: The car, which had a flat tire, was abandoned.

Example 2
   Insert: While he was talking

Matrix: The man lost control of the car.

Result: The man, who was talking, lost control of the car.

If the *cause* or *while* relationship is important to the meaning of the sentence, the writer may wish to use a stronger indicator of adverbial relationship than the relative adverb clause.

Exercises: Rel Adv Clause

1. Construct three pairs of *insert* and *matrix* sequences and perform the rel adv clause transformation process on them. Be ready to demonstrate how the *result* sequence differs from the *result* sequence of the adjective transformation processes.

WRITING AND SUBORDINATION

Subordination as a structural method is quite important in writing, for it is a way of indicating relationships whch express cause to effect, time, condition and concession. The student must be aware though that the same ideas can be expressed by the use of coordination. By being aware of subordination, the student can learn to vary his sentence structure to express subtle relationships. For example, the same sentence might be expressed either by coordination or subordination. "The old man was dying, but each day he saw a procession of visitors," or "Although the old man was dying, he saw a procession of visitors."

Working with basic patterns, the student can observe how two or more sentences can be transformed into one larger sentence which expresses a more exact relationship of ideas than could have been accomplished with two or more sentences. This simple transformation can be illustrated as follows:

John was the chief of detectives.

John became the chief of police.

John, the chief of detectives, became the chief of police.

John, who was the chief of detectives, became the chief of police.

Although John was the chief of detectives, he became the chief of police.

Notice that three different structures are possible in the transformations: the appositive; the relative clause, which needs a relative pronoun; and the adverbial clause which needs a subordination conjunction. Some subordination conjunctions are *although, after, when, if,* and *because.*

Subordination in the Predicate: Words and Phrases

Combine the following groups of sentences into one sentence, retaining the underlined sentence as the basic pattern and subordinating everything else in the predicate by using words and phrases. Observe the example: The newspapers praised Officer Coleman. The praise was generous. The newspapers generously praised Officer Coleman.

1. The children liked Bob's show. His show had appeal.
Rewrite:

2. The informer was reluctant. He left the place of rendevous.
Rewrite:

3. The man's refusal was public. He refused to move from his apartment.
Rewrite:

Subordination in the Predicate: Clauses

Combine each of the following sentences into one main sentence. Subordinate the idea of lesser importance.
Example: The force was easily stirred up. Their duty did not measure up to their expectations. When their duty did not measure up to their expectations, the force was easily stirred up.
1. Bill sat down. Cheers rang out from both sides of the gymnasium.

Rewrite:

2. The car was exceeding the speed limit. The officer arrested the driver.
Rewrite:

3. It was ten o'clock. The workers took their coffee break.
Rewrite:

Subordination in the Subject: Clauses

Combine the following sentences into one, subordinating one of them into a relative clause.
Example: Bob grew up in the West. He understood the rural population. Bob who grew up in the West understood the rural population.
1. Bob was very healthy. He passed the physical examination.
Rewrite:

2. Bob wanted to be a patrolman. He volunteered for the force.
Rewrite:

3. Bob was a good marksman. He passed his gunnery practice.
Rewrite:

Coordination: In the Predicate

Coordinate the following:
1. Bob attended the sessions.
2. Bob listened attentively.

3. Bob studied the problems.
Rewrite:

Create a compound sentence from the following:
1. Bob acted characteristically.
2. Bob refused to quit the force.
Rewrite:

Transform the following sentences into the passive construction.
1. The policeman stopped the car.
Rewrite:

2. The Speaker of the House opened the Legislature.
Rewrite:

3. The last survivor had left an account of the accident.
Rewrite:

4. The force hired Bob.
Rewrite:

STRUCTURES COMMON IN WRITING, BUT RARE IN SPOKEN ENGLISH

Purpose: to provide variety in sentence structure, emphasis of position, transition from sentence to sentence and paragraph to paragraph.

1. Pre-subject adjective or participle
Examples

Frightened, the deer plunged into the woods.

Freshly scrubbed, his face shone in the morning light.

Exercise: Write a sentence placing an adjective, participle or participle phrase at the beginning of the sentence.

2. Infinitive at the beginning of the sentence.

Example: To deliver guns were my orders.

Exercise: Write one sentence placing an infinitive at the beginning of the sentence.

3. Absolute construction—a noun and its modifiers placed at the beginning which are not part of the independent clause.

Example: The work having been completed, we returned home.

Exercise: Write one sentence with a noun and its modifiers placed at the beginning of the sentence.

4. Noun clauses used as the subject of a sentence.

Examples: That he was right is an error.

What he did at the dance shocked me greatly.

Exercise: Write one sentence with a noun clause used as the subject of a sentence.

5. Inversion for emphasis and to provide transition. (The periodic sentence.)

Examples

In the beginning, God created the heavens and the earth.

Slamming the door, she walked out of his life.

In my opinion, she was wrong.

Exercise: Write one sentence using inversion.

6. Parallelism: Any structure, phrase, adjective, noun, clause etc., can be parallel.

Examples

He likes hunting, fishing, and dancing.

They ran through the trees, around the pond, and into the woods.

Exercise: Write one sentence using parallelism.

7. Appositives derived from relative clauses.

Examples

Sally was a great reader. She enjoyed the book.

Sally, who was a great reader, enjoyed the book.

Sally, a great reader, enjoyed the book.

Exercise: Write two related sentences. Combine them into one with a relative clause. Reduce the relative clause to an appositive.

8. Participle phrases used as modifiers derived from relative clauses.

Examples

The children were teasing the cat. The children should be punished.

The children who were teasing the cat should be punished.

The children teasing the cat should be punished.

Exercise: Write two related sentences. Reduce them to one sentence with a relative clause. Reduce the relative clause to a participle phrase modifier.

9. Different ways of writing a sentence

    a. Compound sentence joined by a coordinating conjunction—Samuel was sixteen, and he got the job.

    b. Compound sentence joined by a longer conjunction—Samuel was sixteen; consequently, he got the job.

    c. Adverbial clause—When Samuel was sixteen, he got the job.

Exercise: Write two sentences which are related. Join them into a compound sentence by using one of the coordinating conjunctions, *for, and, but, or* and *nor*; then, make it into a compound sentence by using longer conjunctions such as *consequently, therefore, nevertheless,* and *hence*; finally, make the two sentences into a complex sentence by beginning the sentence with an adverbial clause.

10. Invert the following sentences for emphasis.

    a. The day of reckoning suddenly came.

    b. The bell rang loud and clear.

    c. John's old enemy was prominent among his disclaimers.

    d. His children and grandchildren stood around my uncle's death bed.

RULES FOR SHIFTING THE ORDER OF
UNITS IN A SEQUENCE

The following rules describe transformations that operate on one kernel sequence only (rather than two or more kernel sentences, as in the rules for combining or subordinating sequences). Native speakers of English perform these transformations in their writing and their speech daily. The rules are included here to show that they can be stated in forms which are as precise as the rules for combining or subordinating.

Yes/No Transformation

1. He may drive $\longrightarrow$ May he drive?
2. He has driven $\longrightarrow$ Has he driven?
3. He is driving $\longrightarrow$ Is he driving?
4. He drives $\longrightarrow$ Does he drive?

As the examples show, any time we wish to make a question that can be answered *yes* or *no,* we shift the tense and the first element of the verb to the pre-NP position. If the verb consists of one element only, then we add *do* to carry the tense.

Exercise: *Yes/No*

Turn the following sentences into yes/no questions:
1. The man has come for the flowers.
2. The girl shot the intruder.
3. The verb consists of one element only.
4. He may stay.

Neg Transformation

1. He may drive $\longrightarrow$ He may not drive.
2. He has driven $\longrightarrow$ He has not driven.
3. He is driving $\longrightarrow$ He is not driving.
4. He drives $\longrightarrow$ He does not drive.

In this transformation, a declarative sentence is made negative by the insertion of a negative word between the tense and the first verbal element. Notice that, as in yes/no rules, *do* is added to carry the tense when the verb consists of one element only.

Exercise: **Neg**

Turn the following sentences into negative structures.
1. The man is a thief.
2. The woman was crying.
3. The fire was dangerous.
4. He worried about the accident.

Wh Question Transformations

1. May he drive to town ⟶ Where may he drive?
2. Has he driven the bus ⟶ What has he driven?
3. Is he driving today ⟶ When is he driving?
4. Is he driving today ⟶ Who is driving today?
5. Has he driven the car ⟶ Which car has he driven?

This transformation operates on results of yes/no transformations. It provides for the substitution of a *wh* word (*who, what, when, where, which*) in the proper place (NP ⟶ *who, what;* adv-p ⟶ *where;* adv-t ⟶ *when;* def/nondef ⟶ *which*) and the shifting of the *wh* word to the beginning of the sequence.

Exercise: **Wh Question Transformation**

Turn the following sentences into *wh* structures:
1. Does the man take dope?
2. Is the accident serious?
3. Was the fire in the basement?
4. Has he been questioned?

Passive Transformation

The man had stolen the jewelry ⟶ The jewelry had been stolen by the man.

The example above illustrates the process of transforming a sentence into the passive voice. The passive voice always consists of some form of *be* plus the past participle of a transitive verb. In the example, the verb *stolen* is already a past participle; it remains the same. *Be* is added; because of the auxiliary verb *had, be* becomes *been* (the past participle) producing the resultant passive sequence.

Exercise: Passive Transformation

Turn the following sentences into the passive construction:

1. The man robbed a service station.
2. John Smith saw the robbery.
3. A black-haired man drove the getaway car.
4. Several people investigated the accident.

There Transformation

A man was at the door ⟶ There was a man at the door.
Several people were in the car ⟶ There were several people in the car.

This rule provides for the construction of sequences beginning with *there*. Some writers have difficulty deciding whether the verb of such a sequence should be singular or plural. If the writer keeps track of the NP and the VP of the original sentence, however, he should have little trouble in determining whether the verb of the result sequence is singular or plural. Note that the example with *man* has the singular form of *be*. The example with *people* has the plural form.

Exercise: There Transformation

Turn the following sentences into sequences beginning with *there*.

1. A number of jewels were stolen.
2. A man was stationed by the alley.
3. Several of the bills were lost in the scuffle.
4. Many crimes were committed last night.

Chapter II

THE MECHANICS AND PUNCTUATION
OF A REPORT

T HIS BOOK IS based on the belief that the most important structure in all writing is the sentence, and that the sentence is best understood when analyzed according to sentence patterns. Furthermore, the majority of English sentences are based upon, or are variations of a few basic sentence patterns. Yet unless the sentence is correctly punctuated, the reader will have trouble understanding it. Therefore, this section will deal primarily with the mechanics and punctuation of the sentence.

To accomplish the purpose of this chapter, the student must realize two things: he must realize that learning the conventions and rules of English will help him to communicate better; and he must realize that, while dictionaries and handbooks of English are helpful reference books, he must often be his own authority about usage.

Furthermore, the law enforcement officer must understand that probably the strongest objection to nonstandard English is social, and this attitude is one of which the officer as a public servant should be cognizant. Indeed, the use of nonstandard English is usually taken as a sign of inferior social background, and the speaker of nonstandard English is handicapped in economic and social advancement. In other words, one's language not only describes things and attitudes; it also depicts the social level of the person using language. Thus, "I have no money" and "I ain't got no money" refer to the same financial condition. One is just as clear as the other. But one sentence portrays the speaker as a speaker of standard English and the other as one of nonstandard English. Rightly or wrongly, the public judges one by the language that he uses. And since the law enforcement agent is in the public eye, it is imperative that he use appropriate English.

There are other reasons for learning the conventions of punctuation, but one might ask himself, "Who is going to read this report?" "Are my superiors?" Will they be pleased?" "What will they think of it?" "Will it be presented in court?" "If so, will it present what I really want to say?"

Also the purpose of punctuation is to help make clear the meaning of a report. By putting certain words together and by separating them from other words, one can see that punctuation is vital to effective communication. Observe how punctuation changes the meaning of these two sentences:

> Turn the heat on, Willie.
> Turn the heat on Willie.

We can think of the various markers or signals as roadsides on a highway. They guide the reader very much as roadsigns guide the driver of a car. Roadsigns are a signal to the driver when to slow down, to speed up, or to be aware of curves and so forth. As an unmarked highway can cause a driver to become confused, so can an unmarked sentence. A major cause of confused sentence structure is inadequate punctuation. The primary reason for correct punctuation is to prevent a confused, ambiguous, or awkward reading of the sentence. Observe how the confused sentence is made clear by the correct use of the comma. *Sergeant Walker our patrolman on the beat has been hurt.* Is this a statement about Sergeant Walker or is it a statement to Sergeant Walker? Only correct punctuation will make it clear as to exact meaning. *Sergeant Walker, our patrolman on the beat has been hurt* or *Sergeant Walker, our patrolman on the beat, has been hurt.* As a result of these illustrations, one can readily see how important punctuation might be in writing out a report.

Exercises

1. Give three reasons why a law enforcement officer should use appropriate punctuation.
2. Find in your reading of reports, magazines, newspapers, letters, or other sources, sentences which you think are incorrectly punctuated.

USES OF THE COMMA

Commas have only one real function—to make the meaning clear or more quickly understandable.

1. Use a comma or commas to set off a term in direct address.
   Sergeant Jones, will you be here this evening?
   Will you be here this evening, Sergeant Jones?

2. Use a comma to set off *yes, no,* and other introductory words and phrases.
   No, I will not be here this evening.
   Yes, the witness will be investigated.
   In my opinion, he was in error.

3. Use a comma to separate the parts of a date. Within a sentence, place a comma after the last part if it does not end the sentence.
   Columbus landed in America in October, 1492.
   The riots took place on July 4, 1967, in New York City.
   The suspect was arrested on October 1, 1967, in Dayton, Ohio.
   Captain Smith retired from the force in June, 1965.

4. Use a comma between the parts of an address. Within a sentence, use a comma after the last part of an address if it does not end the sentence.
   Police Chief Atterberry lives at 875 Washington, Nevada, Missouri.
   He formerly lived at 1900 Gersey Avenue, Nevada, Missouri, but he moved from there several months ago
   The suspect was arrested at 1109 Jefferson Street, Polk City, Missouri.

5. Use a comma to separate place names.
   The National Guard was rushed to Detroit, Michigan.
   The F.B.I. arrested the most wanted man in Kansas City, Missouri.
   Mr. George Adams, Postmaster at Hot Springs, Kansas, reported the accident.
   The driver presented a driver's license issued to a Sylvester Smith of Kansas City, Kansas.

6. Use a comma to separate words in a series.

He was arrested for speeding, careless driving, and crossing
a red line.

The inspector traveled far, talked vigorously, and interviewed witnesses.

The man was kind, serene, and energetic.

The police board skanned the applicant's transcript, recommendations, and character references.

The new district attorney became a crusader, a champion
of the downtrodden, and a defender of the people.

7. Use a comma or commas to set off an appositive. An appositive is a noun and its modifiers which modify another
noun.

Mr. C. A. Jones, our police chief, is absent today.

Mr. John B. Brown, an outstanding attorney, will defend
the suspect.

C. H. Hern, Chief of Police of Blue Springs, was at the scene.

Photographs were taken of the accident by Bill E. Bailley,
the chief photographer.

8. Use a comma to set off a direct quotation.

The passerby said, "I saw the wreck."

The witness said, "I saw him run a red light."

The witness was asked, "Did you actually see the shooting?"

9. Use a comma or commas to set off parenthetical expressions:
that is, words not necessary to the meaning of the sentence.
Usually these simply give additional information.

Yes, I saw him, wait a minute, I'm not sure that I did.

The witness, you say, is gone.

Mr. McCready stated that the railroad right-of-way shed,
located behind the housing development in Unity Village,
had been broken into sometime during the night.

10. Use a comma or commas to set off nonrestrictive modifiers.
Like parenthetical expressions, these modifiers simply give
additional information and are not necessary to the meaning
of the sentence.

Patrolmen, who are selected by physical fitness tests, should
show a lower sickness rate than that of other law enforcement officers.

Mr. McCready stated that a subject identified as John H.

Doe, who is a local resident, had seen two young men in the area.

Mr. Miller stated that he was sure that the rifle and clock had been stolen by his brother Gary E. Miller, who had been staying at his house part of the time.

11. Use a comma to separate the clauses of a compound sentence that is joined or connected by coordinating conjunctions such as *and, but, for, or, nor, so,* and *yet.*

The patrolman stopped the speeding car, and he gave the driver a ticket.

I was going to go his bail, but he skipped town.

The male subject identified himself as Charles E. Newton, but he refused to give a statement or any information about his activities.

He admitted his guilt, yet he pleaded for mercy.

You will be diligent in your duties, or you will be suspended from the force.

He was belligerent and resisted arrest, so I had to handcuff him.

12. Use a comma to set off introductory adverbial clauses, participle phrases, long prepositional phrases, infinitive phrases, or gerund phrases. (We might add that this rule is one that is broken quite often.)

In making up the checks, she and Stanford used the check protector from the Bentwood Appliance Company.

If you have a drunken man coming at you with a knife, what will you do?

If the tornado turns westward, it will miss the entire city.

According to Mr. and Mrs. Shute, the only thing removed from the trailer was a metal lock box.

Pulling over to the curb at the first opportunity, he waited for the highway patrol to pass.

In addition to his long speech, he was quite boring.

To become a good officer, one must be well educated.

Upon arriving at the hospital and checking the records, the officers learned that the boy had been brought to the hospital by his mother.

13. Use a comma to emphasize an inverted element within the sentence.

   Except for report writing, my courses aren't difficult.

   Frightened, the suspect ran from the scene.

   Long and black, the car moved slowly in the procession.

   In the beginning, the committee was for law and order.

14. Use a comma to set off contrasted elements.

   He is ill, not drunk.

   We are disgusted, not angry.

Misuse of the Comma

Do not use a comma instead of a period or semicolon between independent clauses. Ordinarily, this is known as a comma splice.

There was nothing more to be said, when they took that attitude, the officer had to arrest them.

The patrolman pursued the fleeing car, he stopped the car and arrested the driver.

The district attorney took everything too seriously, he was too intent and too intense.

Exercise

Rewrite and hand in to your instructor the following sentences, inserting as you write any punctuation which is clearly required for the improvement of the sentence.

1. It was discovered that a large crowd had assembled but no one had tried to extinguish the fire.
2. The garage was about one-half mile away and he said it would take him fifteen minutes to walk to it.
3. Baldy asked "where did you steal it, off a truck?"
4. She asked him if someone was hurt and he answered "It's me."
5. Mr. Harold a neighbor heard the blast.
6. Mr. Harold was interviewed but he could add nothing to the report.
7. On the evening of November 5 1959 Mr. Nichelson manager of the Central Hotel reported a breakin.
8. During this time the police were checking other suspects.

9. Some of the checks were written on the bank of Franklin Missouri and were signed by Charles Bobbitt.
10. While he was interviewing Charles Pruitt the reporting officer learned that Charles had also seen the accident.
11. Mr. Jones who discovered the burglary informed the highway patrol that all of the doors had been locked.
12. This door was locked however it was evident that entrance had been gained from the outside.
13. Apparently after gaining entrance the burglars had forced the glass doors back together.
14. The investigating officer observed that a large metal fire box safe which is normally located in the southwest corner of the building had been moved.
15. The money was taken from a drawer in the prescription cabinet and the narcotics were taken from shelves.
16. The combination dial and handle had been knocked, and cut off with a torch.
17. Some fingerprint lifts were made, however, there were fabric marks indicating that gloves might have been worn.
18. Photographs were made of the rear room the safe and the front area.
19. The test revealed that he was intoxicated not sober.
20. Mr. Alderman the policeman is on the beat.
21. While trying to escape the suspect jumped from the window, and broke his leg.
22. The witness resides at 1800 North Washington Joplin Missouri.

USE OF THE SEMI-COLON

1. Use a semicolon between the clauses of a compound sentence if the coordinating conjunction is omitted.
   I like my work as a policeman; my beat is also appropriate.
   The district attorney's work drew heavily upon his stamina; once he became ill from overwork.

NOTE: By observing the use of the semicolon and the comma, the writer can show different distinctions in shades of meaning; for example, in the sentence, "I liked the book; the movie was also very good," there is a relation between the two independent clauses, and the writer uses a semicolon to show this relationship.

2. Use a semicolon before conjunctive adverbs like: *however, moreover, therefore, nevertheless, consequently, hence,* or *thus* when they connect the clauses of a compound sentence.

   The car has high mileage; therefore, it would be a risk to buy it.

   It is raining outside; consequently, I will have to wear my raincoat.

   There was nothing more to be said; however, when they took that attitude, the officer had to arrest them.

Misuse of the Semicolon

1. Do not use the semicolon as the equivalent of a colon.

   My report shows that the following people have not passed their drivers test; (:) Mr. L. B. Jones, Miss Betty Smith, Mr. John Brown, and Mr. John Doe.

2. Do not use a semicolon as the equivalent of a comma.

   We stayed up until two o'clock in the morning; (,) talking about the election.

   We could come to only one conclusion; (,) that he had decided not to run for reelection.

THE USE OF PUNCTUATION IN COORDINATION AND SUBORDINATION

The expanding of basic sentences, which has been discussed in detail in Part I, by adding various structures of coordination and subordination (a) familiarizes students with these structures, (b) gives them practice in using these structures, and (c) reveals the necessary punctuation for a clear and unambiguous meaning. After the student has studied the basic patterns, he is ready to examine coordination as a method of sentence expansion. In sentences like the following, the student needs to observe that the structures in the series are coordinate and require a particular kind of punctuation.

He slipped, fell, and broke his leg.

The police board scanned the applicant's transcript, recommendations, and character references.

Coordinate structures are ordinarily, as pointed out in the use of the comma, joined by such coordinators as *and, but, nor, or, not, for, so,* and *yet;* and by the correlatives, which work in pairs, *either-or, neither-nor, both-and, not (only)-but (also).*

Working with basic sentences, the student can combine simple techniques of combination. For example, the three basic sentences, "The man was kind. The man was energetic. The man was serene," can be combined into one sentence. (Also observe the punctuation.) "The man was kind, energetic, and serene."

The sentences in each of the following groups can be joined by a coordinating conjunction to form a compound sentence, a compound complement, or a compound predicate.

In the first group the two sentences can be combined into a compound sentence by using a coordinating conjunction and using appropriate punctuation.

1. Combine the sentences in each group into one compound sentence.

Example: Social legislation was passed. The law enforcement program was greatly strengthened.
   Social legislation was passed, and the law enforcement program was greatly strengthened.

a. The district attorney's work drew heavily upon his stamina. Once he became ill from overwork.
Rewrite:

b. The patrolman pursued the fleeing car. He arrested the offender.
Rewrite:

c. The district attorney might talk endlessly. He always had a purpose.

Rewrite:

d. The chief of police spoke frequently about principles. He cared more for ends than means.
Rewrite:

e. The district attorney took everything too seriously. He was too intent and too intense.
Rewrite:

2. Combine the sentences in each group into compound predicates using the appropriate punctuation.
Example: The inspector traveled far. He talked vigorously. And he interviewed witnesses.
   The inspector traveled far, talked vigorously, and inter-viewed witnesses.
a. The student attended class.
   The student listened attentively.
   The student studied his lessons.
Rewrite:

b. The new district attorney became a crusader.
   He became a champion of the downtrodden.
   The new district attorney became a defender of the people
Rewrite:

c. He spoke frequently.
   He studied diligently.

He worked hard.

Rewrite:

Subordination and Punctuation

Subordination as a structural method is quite important in writing, for it is a way of indicating relationships which express cause to effect, time, condition and concession. (This concept has been discussed in detail in Part I on transformation. It is discussed here only as it relates to punctuation and writing.) By being aware of subordination, the beginning writer can learn to vary his sentence structure to express more exact relationships. For example, the same sentence might be expressed either by coordination or subordination. "The old man was dying, but each day he saw a procession of visitors," or "Although the old man was dying, he saw a procession of visitors." Working with the different sentence patterns, the student can observe how two or more sentences can be transformed into one larger sentence which expresses a more exact relationship of ideas than could have been accomplished with two or more sentences. This simple transformation can be illustrated as follows:

1. John was the chief of detectives.
2. John became the chief of police.
3. John, the chief of detectives, became the chief of police.
4. John, who was the chief of detectives, became the chief of police.
5. Although John was the chief of detectives, he became the chief of police.

Notice that three different structures are possible in these transformations: the appositive; the relative clause, which needs a relative pronoun; and the adverbial clause which needs a subordination conjunction similar to *although, after, when, if,* and *because.*

Exercise

Combine each of the following sentences into one main

sentence, subordinating the idea of lesser importance. Also observe the punctuation of such sentences.

Example: The newspapers praised Officer Coleman. Their praise was generous. When the newspapers praised Officer Coleman, their praise was generous.

1. The informer was reluctant. He left the place of rendevous.
Rewrite:

2. The man's refusal was public. He refused to move from his apartment.
Rewrite:

3. The force was easily stirred up. Their duty did not measure up to their expectations.
Rewrite:

4. The car was over the speed mark. The officer arrested the driver.
Rewrite:

Exercise

Combine the following sentences into one, subordinating one of them into a nonrestrictive relative clause.

Example: Bob grew up in the West. He understood the rural population. Bob, who grew up in the West, understood the rural population.

1. Bob was very healthy. He passed the physical examination.
Rewrite:

2. Bob wanted to be a patrolman. He volunteered for the force.
Rewrite:

3. Bob was a good marksman. He passed his gunnery practice.
Rewrite:

Exercise

Observe the different ways of writing and punctuating a sentence.

1. Compound sentence joined by a coordinating conjunction.
Samuel was sixteen, and he finally got the job.
2. Compound sentence joined by a longer conjunction.
Samuel was sixteen; consequently, he got the job.
3. A sentence with an introductory adverbial clause.
When Samuel was sixteen, he got the job.

Write two sentences which are related; join them into a compound sentence by using one of the coordinating conjunctions, *for, and, but, or* and *nor;* then, make it into a compound sentence by using longer conjunctions such as *consequently, therefore, nevertheless,* and *hence;* finally, make the two sentences into a sentence with an introductory adverbial clause.

THE PERIOD

The period has but two uses—to make the end of a declarative or imperative sentence and to mark an abbreviation.

1. A declarative sentence is one that makes a statement.
Today is Tuesday.
All patrolmen must be on duty on time.
It is raining quite hard.
My father is a captain in the highway patrol.
The man was arraigned at 2:00 P.M.

2. An imperative sentence makes or gives a command.
Don't do that.

Stop where you are.
John, you may wash the dishes.

3. Use a period to show an abbreviation.
Mr., Mrs., Dr., St. Louis, Ph.D., Jr., Sr., Feb., Ala., C.O.D., A.M., etc.
In general, abbreviations are avoided in writing, except in footnotes, bibliographies, formal lists, compilations of statistics, tables and addresses. For the correct form of abbreviations, however, one should consult his dictionary.

QUESTION MARK

The question mark is used to indicate that a sentence is to be understood as a question.
Who goes there?
What time is it?
You mean he's drunk?
Whose gun is this?
Did anyone see the crime?

THE EXCLAMATION POINT

The exclamation point is used to show strong emotion or feeling. One might note that the excessive use of the exclamation point is considered poor taste. One should use it only when necessary to show the correct meaning of his sentence.
Look out!
Drop that gun!
Put up your arms!
Stop that man!
Pull over to the side of the road!

THE COLON

Use a colon before a list of items when they are introduced by such words as: *the following, as follows, thus, or these,* and *or a number.*

1. To indicate that something is to follow.
Here are the facts: He appeared to be intoxicated; he was

driving fast; he was weaving in and out across the yellow line; therefore, I stopped him.

2. Use a colon between numbers showing hours and minutes.
9:00 o'clock.
10:15 P.M.
The crime took place about 2:00 A.M. in the morning.
On April 4, 1965, at 6:30 P.M., Trooper P. W. Smith was notified by Sergeant D. W. Findley of Troop F Headquarters that the victim had been taken at 1:45 A.M. to St. Luke's Hospital.

THE APOSTROPHE

The apostrophe has three general uses. The student should give close attention to the use of the apostrophe since so many beginning writers misuse it.

1. Use an apostrophe to indicate possession.
Yes, that is the boy's car. (Only one boy owns the car.)
Yes, that is the boys' car. (Several boys own the car.)
He has gone to the men's room.
The suspect had borrowed the hotel's typewritter with which he probably wrote the checks.
The subject's gun was found lying in a corner where it had fallen.

2. Use an apostrophe to show the omission of letters or figures.
I've, can't, haven't, hadn't, the class of '67.

3. Use an apostrophe to show the plural of letters or figures.
The A's looked bad last year.
You have too many L's in that word.
He threw three 8's.
There are too many *and's* in his report.

NOTE: Notice the difference between it's and its.
It's raining outside.
The bird broke its leg.

USE OF CAPITAL LETTERS
1. Capitalize the first word of each sentence.

Ask for Mr. Buck. He is in charge of traffic.

2. Capitalize the first word of a direct quotation.
   The witness answered, "I did see him run a red light."

3. Capitalize proper nouns.
   Sergeant Jones was in charge of traffic.
   He works for the National Broadcasting System.
   She works for the Red Cross.
   He dislikes English.
   The Mississippi River is one of the largest rivers in the world.

NOTE: Proper nouns identify a particular or specific person, place, or thing.

4. Capitalize nouns or pronouns referring to the deity. God, Lord, Savior, Messiah, He, Him, His, Holy Ghost.

5. Capitalize names of offices and titles only when they are used as titles.
   General Jones will be the guest speaker.
   Sergeant Troy is on duty.
   States-Attorney James will not run for reelection.

6. Capitalize north, south, east and west when they refer to specific parts of the country.
   She comes from the East.
   He lives on the West side.

7. Capitalize the names of days, months and holidays. Monday, March, Valentine's day

Observe:

He attends Central Missouri State College.
He is going to college.
The river flows south.
The Mississippi River runs up hill.
The Summer Festival of Arts begins next week.
I like summer better than winter.

NUMERALS

The following rules should be observed in writing numerals:

1. Dates, street numbers, page numbers, decimals, and per cents should be written in figures.
   Abraham Lincoln was born on *February 12, 1809.*
   She lives at *14 Elm* Street.
   Harry got *50* per cent of the vote for class secretary.

2. The sign *$* is not used for a sum less than one dollar.
   The ball cost *thirty-five cents.*

3. The general rule for writing numbers is to spell out the number if it may be done in one or two words; otherwise, it should be written in figures.
   Tom offered me a *thousand* dollars for the boat.
   Dr. Stone contributed *1437* copies of his latest book to his classes.

4. When several numbers are mentioned in a short space, use figures for all.

5. A number which represents a person's age or one denoting the hour of the day is usually spelled out.
   At *four* o'clock there is to be a meeting of the students who are between *fifteen* and *nineteen* years of age.

6. Do not begin a sentence with figures.
   Five hundred twenty-six (not *526*) people came to church Sunday.

7. It is not necessary, except in special instances to place numerals in parentheses after writing numbers; but when they are used, each should follow the number it repeats.
   I am sending you *fourteen* (*14*) blouses for school this fall.

8. In technical, mathematical, and business writing, figures are generally used.
   105 square feet, *$8.00* per pound, *2½* per cent, *10.6* meters.

Problem Exercises

Rewrite and hand in to your instructor the following sentences, inserting as you write, any punctuation and/or capitalization required by conventions. Some of the sentences may be correct.

1. Mr. Reynolds the inspector was around about 8 00 p m.
2. Men who hate walking are poor officer material
3. Did you pass your gunnery exercises
4. I dont know I havent seen the results yet.
5. What time does officer Smith report
6. When I arrested him he shouted dont shoot
7. The combination and handle had been knocked off however it did not appear that an attempt had been made to punch the spindle
8. He was supposed to catch a plane this evening for Kansas City Missouri.
9. No fingerprints were found but several glove prints were found. When they left it was by prying open a window.
10. The suspect was found in room 8 at the hotel astor.
11. At 4 oclock there is be a meeting of the candidates who are between 21 and 22.
12. The room was one hundred and four foot square.
13. The car had slid three hundred feet.
14. The pilot realizing his plight radioed for instructions.
15. The man who reported the robbery cannot be found.
16. They questioned the man who reported the robbery.
17. That they wont like it may be taken for granted.
18. He is quite inexperienced and has never worked as a detective before.
19. The officer answered I don't give advice on such questions.
20. Highway patrolman most of whom are young men lead a busy life.
21. He said I propose to transfer to the detective squad at the end of the month.
22. He said that he would transfer to the detective squad.
23. I expect he said to transfer at the end of the month.
24. Sheriff Elliott, trooper Shaw and sergeant Brown then went to Silver Missouri and made inquiries.
25. At 7 00 p m, the officers contacted Dr. Blackwell at the hospital.

Exercise

Recopy the following reports, making corrections in the punctuation and/or capitalization of the sentences.

1. On April fourth, 1965 at 6 30 p m, the reporting officer and trooper G. W. Jones were notified by sergeant D. W. Findley of Troop C headquarters that the victim of a shooting was at the St lukes hospital, St Louis Missouri. Sergeant Findley stated that he had received a telephone call from St. Louis police officer Sherman of the 7th District who notified him that Melvin Smith, age 12, had been brought to St Lukes hospital.

2. The lock box according to Mr. Smyth measures eighteen inches in height, ten inches in width, 14 inches in depth, and weighs about thirty pounds. According to Mrs. Smyth, the lock box contained between three thousand dollars and four thousand dollars in denominations up to 100 dollar bills, but mostly the money was in ten and 20 dollar denominations.

3. On the evening of November five, 1958 Mike Hearldson manager of the Central hotel of St Louis Missouri called Troop D headquarters to report what he suspected to be an operation of check forgery. Mr. Hearldson stated that he became suspicious of two people who had checked into the hotel under the names of Mr and Mrs Charles E Newsome, giving an address of 1880 east eighth Street, Detroit Michigan. Mr. Hearldson stated that the man had borrowed the hotels typewriter during the afternoon and that evening about 5:00 he had attempted to cash a check at the hotel desk. This was a company check, number 1926, of the Borderline Awning Company, 1300 North High Dayton Ohio.

4. While examining the surroundings for some indication as to what had happened officer Kennedy discovered a spot about one foot in diameter near where the horses had been standing. The substance causing the spot was dark colored and Jay said that he believed it was blood from the foot of a horse that had gotten cut in the wire fence the day before. A quart jar was also found near where the barn had burned. Although the odor from it indicated it had recently contained gasoline Jay seemed to think that it had been there several days.

Chapter III

SPELLING

ONE REQUIREMENT OF A good report is that the words be spelled correctly as recorded in dictionaries. It is for this reason that all law enforcement agencies insist that all report writing—even the most informal—show a decent regard for accepted spelling. Furthermore, conspicuously poor spelling is generally considered by the public to be a clear sign of illiteracy. Socially and professionally, a law enforcement agent who cannot spell is at a disadvantage. It is easier to judge a man's spelling than to judge other things about him; and whether it is right or not, people do jump to conclusions about a person's intelligence and ability on the basis of his spelling. A law enforcement agent who refuses to make an effort to improve his spelling penalizes himself. If an officer writes a report with several spelling errors, his supervisor will in all probability notice this weakness more quickly than any other fault. It is therefore imperative that the law enforcement agent master this mechanical ability as thoroughly as possible so as to avoid making a negative impression.

Most people who spell poorly rationalize their inability on the assumption that spelling is not important, that one can do nothing to improve his spelling, and that the only way to improve it is to memorize long lists of spelling words. None of these assumptions are true. A little conscious effort and a desire to improve can help one to overcome poor spelling habits.

The first step in improving one's spelling is to take an inventory of his errors. No one misspells all the words, but only a few; and most of them are the same ones over and over again. Also one doesn't generally misspell an entire word but syllables within the word. For example, most people who misspell *tragedy* place an extra *d* before the *g*. Another reason for mis-

66

spelling many words is that they are mispronounced. For instance, *probably* is sometimes pronounced *probly;* and, therefore, it is misspelled. The following lists are made up of words frequently used in police reports. The first part consists of words that are often mistaken for each other; these have been set apart so that they may be studied separately. It is very important that you know the meanings of each of these words since they are usually interchanged because the writer does not know their definitions. The first step to take before studying the list is to take a pretest on all of the words. The reason for this is that since you already know a lot of the words, it is only essential that you study the ones that you don't know. In fact, identifying your specific errors permits you to concentrate on that part of the word in which the error occurs. For example, if you spell *seperate* instead of *separate,* you have only to concentrate on the second syllable.

In a final analysis, spelling problems are personal, and the only way to solve them is to give them personal attention. The systematic study of the following list and the keeping of a record of misspelled words help a great deal. The spelling list does contain many of the words that are commonly misspelled on police reports. Furthermore, the spelling rules may help in that they introduce some system into the seemingly hopeless snarl of English spelling. And if one has to, he could carry a pocket dictionary in the glove compartment of his car.

Similar Forms

A study of the following list of words which are similar in sound but different in meaning may help you.

accept	except
ascent	assent
affect	effect
all ready	already
altar	alter
breath	breathe
choose	chose
coarse	course

cite .... site .... sight
bole .... boll .... bowl
detract .... distract
formally .... formerly
incredible .... incredulous
informant .... informer
principal .... principle
straight .... strait

SPELLING RULES

1. A word ending in silent *e* generally drops the *e* before an ending beginning with a vowel letter.

admire .... admiration
arrange .... arranging
believe .... believing
imagine .... imaginary
move .... movable
dine .... dining
desire .... desirous
deplore .... deplorable

But it retains the *e* before an ending beginning with a consonant letter.

arrange .... arrangement
care .... careful
force .... forceful
hate .... hateful
like .... likeness
move .... movement

But after *c* or *g*, if the ending begins with an *a* or an *o*, the *e* is retained to indicate the soft sound or pronunciation of *c* or *g*.

advantage .... advantageous
change .... changeable
courage .... courageous
service .... serviceable
peace .... peaceful
outrage .... outrageous

2. In words with *ie* or *ei* when the sound is long *ee*, use *i* before
   e except after *c*. When the sound is like *a* as in neighbor and
weight, use *e* before *i*.

i before *e*

achieve	pier
belief	shriek
believe	siege
chief	niece
besiege	cashier
reprieve	pierce
brief	priest
thief	relieve
friend	shield
fierce	shriek
grief	

except after *c*

ceiling	receive
conceive	deceive
deceit	receipt
perceive	conceit

Exceptions to the rule: science, seize, neither, weird, leisure.

3. Words in which *y* is changed to *i*. A word ending in *y*
   preceded by a consonant forms the plural by adding *ies*,
after dropping the *y*.

fly	flies
marry	marries
sky	skies
copy	copies

Ending in *y* preceded by a vowel

attorney	attorneys
destroy	destroys
enjoy	enjoys
delay	delays

When the suffix begins with *i* the
y is not changed.

carry .... carrying
marry .... marrying
spy .... spying
dry .... drying

4. Some rules for forming the plurals of nouns are the following:
   a. For most nouns add an *s*: boys, girls, cars.
   b. For nouns ending with a sound of *s*, add *es*: boxes, churches, classes.
   c. For nouns ending in *f*, *fe*, *ff*, use *s* or *ves*: chief, chiefs; staff, staffs; wife, wives; sheriff, sheriffs.
   d. For nouns ending in *o*, add *s* or *es*: solo, solos; echo, echoes; motto, mottos; potato, potatoes; tomato, tomatoes.
   e. Some nouns have irregular plurals: foot, feet; woman, women; man, men.

5. Doubling the final consonant. In words of one syllable and words which are accented on the last syllable, ending in a single consonant letter preceded by a single vowel letter, double the final consonant letter before an ending beginning with a vowel letter.

Ending begins with a vowel
One syllable word

drag .... dragging
drop .... dropped
flag .... flagged
get .... getting
plan .... planning
stop .... stopped
quit .... quitting
rob .... robbed
stab .... stabbed
step .... stepping
trim .... trimmed
snap .... snapped
sin .... sinning

Two syllable words with accent on last syllable

admit .... admitted
begin .... beginning
commit .... committed
occur .... occurrence
submit .... submitted

NOTE: Words which are not accented on last syllable, do not double the last letter.

prefer .... preference
happen .... happened
refer .... reference
benefit .... benefited

NOTE: If the ending begins with a consonant, do not double the last letter.

glad .... gladness
fat .... fatness
man .... manhood
sin .... sinful
equip .... equipment
profit .... profitless

The so-called "seed" words. Words ending with the sound *seed* are usually spelled *cede*.

Examples: accede, concede, intercede, precede, recede, secede

Exceptions: There are only four exceptions. Three of them end in *ceed;* the fourth is the only word that ends in *sede*.

1. Only one word ends in *sede: supersede.*
2. Three words end in *ceed:* exceed, proceed, succeed.

WORDS COMMONLY MISSPELLED IN POLICE REPORTS
Words Easily Interchanged

accept	effect	assistance
except	all ready	assistants
advice	already	bail
advise	all together	bale
affect	altogether	brake

break

choose

chose

coarse

course

complement

compliment

conscience

conscious

council

counsel

corps

corpse

device

devise

formally

formerly

guessed

guest

implement

impliment

its

it's

liable

libel

loose

lose

medal

metal

passed

past

patience

patients

peace

piece

personal

personnel

presence

presents

principal

principle

quiet

quite

scene

seen

sense

since

shone

shown

striped

stripped

their

there

they're

thorough

through

to

too

waist

waste

wear

where

weather

whether

your

you're

Other Frequently Misspelled Words

accessories

accident

accompanied

account

accumulate

accurate

accustomed

achievement

acknowledgement

acquaintance

acquitted

across

additional

adjust

admission

adultery

advantageous

advertisement

affidavit

affirmative

aggravated

again

airplane

alcohol

alimony

allotment

all right

alternate

although

always

amateur

ammunition

among

amount

amputation

amusement

analyze

analysis

announce

annual

answer

anxiety

anxious

apologize

apparent

appearance

application

appreciation

appropriate

arson

arrangement

arrest
artery
artificial
asked
associate
assortment
athletics
attendance
attribute
authoritative
automatic
backward
bail
bandage
beginning
behavior
believe
benefited
bicycle
bigamy
blackmail
boundary
breadth
brief
bruise
built
bulletin
burglary
business
calendar
campaign
canceled
candidate
captain
careful
carrying
cashier
casualty
catastrophe
ceiling
cemetery

certificate
character
chauffeur
chief
circle
circumference
circumstance
citizen
coincide
collar
collision
colonel
colored
column
comfortable
coming
commercial
commission
committed
committee
community
complainant
complexion
consent
conspiracy
construction
continue
convenience
conviction
cooperate
corporal
corporation
corrective
correspondence
cough
counterfeit
country
coupon
courteous
creditor
criminal

criticism
customary
cylinder
damage
deceased
deceptive
decision
defensive
definition
delinquent
demonstration
dependent
description
desperate
diagonal
diesel
different
dilapidated
dining
disappear
disappoint
discipline
discrepancy
dispatched
disperse
disposition
disease
dislocation
distinction
divide
doesn't
drunkenness
during
early
eight
electricity
eligible
eliminate
embarrass
embezzlement
emergency

employee
employment
enemy
environment
equipment
equivalent
especially
every
evidence
exaggerate
exceeding
excellent
exception
excite
exercise
excused
exhaust
existence
experience
explanation
explosion
expression
extension
extortion
factual
familiar
fascinating
February
felony
feminine
fictitious
finally
financial
forcibly
foreign
forty
fourteen
fourth
fracture
fraudulent
friend

fugitive
fulfill
furniture
gambling
garbage
gassed
gauge
generally
genuine
government
grease
grievance
guarantee
guard
guidance
half
handkerchief
hazard
headache
height
holiday
homicide
hoping
horizontal
humane
humiliate
hurried
hurrying
ideal
ignorance
illiterate
imaginary
imagination
immediately
impatient
imperfect
impossible
impression
inadequate
incidentally
incorrigible

incredible
indecent
indefinite
independent
indicate
indict
indifferent
individual
inevitable
informant
ingenious
ingredient
initial
imitation
inquiry
inquisitive
insensible
instead
instinct
insurance
intelligent
intercept
interest
interpret
intersect
interrogate
interview
intoxication
invasion
investigation
irresistible
isolate
jealous
judgment
juvenile
kidnapped
khaki
knowledge
label
laboratory
larceny

later

latter

legal

leisure

lenient

length

liabilities

license

lieutenant

lightning

likely

liquor

losing

luggage

maintain

maintenance

magazine

majority

malicious

management

maneuver

manual

margin

marriage

masculine

maturity

meant

medical

memorize

merely

microphone

mileage

minute

miscellaneous

mischievous

misspelled

motorcycle

mountainous

murmur

muscle

museum

narcotics

narrow

natural

necessary

negative

neglect

neighbor

nephew

nervous

neutral

niece

ninety

noisy

noticeable

noticing

notified

numerous

obligation

obscure

obstacle

occasion

occupant

occurrence

occurred

odor

offense

offensive

official

often

operator

opinion

opponent

opportunity

opposite

painful

parallel

partial

participate

particular

pastime

pedestrian

perform

perhaps

permanent

permissible

persecute

perseverance

persistent

perspiration

persuade

perversion

physical

physician

planning

pleasant

pneumatic

possession

posture

practically

practice

preceding

precise

predicament

prejudice

preliminary

premises

preparation

prescription

privilege

probably

procedure

progress

pronounce

pronunciation

proposition

prosecute

prostitution

psychology

publicity

pulse

pursuit

quality

quantity	schedule	tattoo
questioning	scheme	technical
quota	scarcely	telephone
racial	secretary	temperamental
raid	seize	temperature
raise	sentence	tendency
ratio	separation	testimony
readily	sergeant	theater
realize	several	thought
really	severely	throat
receipt	sexual	thieves
receive	sheriff	together
reckless	shining	tongue
recognize	signature	tonight
recollect	similar	tractor
recommend	sincerely	traffic
recreation	specimen	tragic
reduce	sprain	tranquil
reference	statement	transferred
refuse	statistics	treacherous
registration	statute	trespassing
religious	strictly	tries
remedial	stomach	trouble
remembrance	strategy	truancy
renewal	subject	truly
repeat	subpoena	Tuesday
repetition	succeed	typewriter
representation	successful	typical
reputation	suffocation	umbrella
resistance	superintendent	undoubtedly
resolution	supersede	union
revoked	supervisor	unnecessary
revolver	summons	until
ridiculous	surely	unusually
robbery	supplies	urgent
sacred	suspect	using
sacrifice	surprise	utility
salary	surrender	vacancy
satisfactory	suspicion	vacuum
Saturday	sympathy	vagrancy
scatter	symptom	validity

DATE DUE

FEB 2 9

THE PRESENT AGE

Also by Robert Nisbet

Twilight of Authority

Sociology as an Art Form

The Social Philosophers

Prejudices: A Philosophical Dictionary

The Sociological Tradition

History of the Idea of Progress

THE PRESENT AGE

Progress and Anarchy in Modern America

ROBERT NISBET

1817

HARPER & ROW, PUBLISHERS, New York

Cambridge, Philadelphia, San Francisco, Washington
London, Mexico City, São Paulo, Singapore, Sydney

FIRST EDITION

Designer: Sidney Feinberg

Copy editor: Jean Touroff

Indexer: Terry Seng

Library of Congress Cataloging-in-Publication Data

Nisbet, Robert A.

  The present age.

  Includes index.

  1. Armaments—Economic aspects—United States—History—20th century. 2. United States—Foreign relations—20th century. 3. Bureaucracy—United States—History—20th century. 4. Federal government—United States—History—20th century. 5. State, The. 6. United States—Social conditions. I. Title.

HC110.D4N57 1988   306′.0973   87-46158

ISBN 0-06-015902-2

---

88 89 90 91 92 HC 10 9 8 7 6 5 4 3 2 1

To Caroline, once more

CONTENTS

FOREWORD

It is tempting in this year of the bicentennial of the Constitution to speculate on the probable reactions of the Framers to the product of their labors and aspirations as it stands today in the world two full centuries after its inception. Such speculation need not be altogether fanciful. Some constitutional lawyers speak of recovering the "original intent" of the Framers, a not impossible feat given the clarity of the document itself and the abundance of ancillary sources of the Framers' views on government. If original intent can be reasonably retrieved after two hundred years, why not probable reaction to the present age in America?

What would the Framers be most struck by in America today? I mean after they had recovered from the shock of seeing clean, strong, white teeth instead of decayed yellow stumps in the mouths of their descendants; after they had assimilated the fact of the astounding number of Americans who were neither crippled, disease-wasted, nor pockmarked from smallpox; and, of course, after they had taken rapt eyes off the high-speed vehicles on the streets? After these astonishments, what reactions might there be to the political and cultural scene?

Three aspects of the present age in America would surely draw their immediate, concerned, and perhaps incredulous attention.

First, the prominence of war in American life since 1914, amounting to a virtual Seventy-Five Years War, and with this the staggering size of the American military establishment since World War II. The Framers had relied on two broad oceans for the license to draft the most nonmilitary constitution imaginable.

Second, the Leviathan-like presence of the national government in the affairs of states, towns, and cities, and in the lives, cradle to grave, of individuals. The Framers had worked most diligently to prevent any future hypertrophy of the federal government. They had particularly

disliked the sprawling bureaucracies of Europe in their day.

Third, the number of Americans who seem only loosely attached to groups and values such as kinship, community, and property, and whose lives are so plainly governed by the cash nexus.

In the pages following, I have enlarged upon these three aspects of the present scene in America.

Since this book contains in adapted form my 1988 Jefferson Lecture in Washington, D.C., I wish to express my deep appreciation to the National Council of Humanities for inviting me to deliver the lecture and my thanks to Dr. Lynne V. Cheney, Chairman of the National Endowment of the Humanities, for her kind interest and aid in the presentation of the lecture. I thank also Hugh Van Dusen, Senior Editor at Harper & Row, for his special help and encouragement.

THE PRESENT AGE

I

THE PREVALENCE
OF WAR

OF ALL FACES of the present age in America, the military face would
almost certainly prove the most astounding to any Framers of the
Constitution, any Founders of the Republic who came back to inspect
their creation on the occasion of the bicentennial. It is indeed an
imposing face, the military. Well over three hundred billion dollars a
year go into its maintenance; it is deployed in several dozen countries
around the world. The returned Framers would not be surprised to learn
that so vast a military has inexorable effects upon the economy, the
structure of government, and even the culture of Americans; they had
witnessed such effects in Europe from afar, and had not liked what they
saw. What would doubtless astonish the Framers most, though, is that
their precious republic has become an imperial power in the world,
much like the Great Britain they had hated in the eighteenth century.
Finally, the Framers would almost certainly swoon when they learned
that America has been participant in the Seventy-Five Years War that
has gone on, rarely punctuated, since 1914. And all of this, the Framers
would sorrowfully find, done under the selfsame structure of government they had themselves built.

Clearly, the American Constitution was designed for a people more
interested in governing itself than in helping to govern the rest of the
world. The new nation had the priceless advantage of two great oceans
dividing it from the turbulences of Europe and Asia. Permanent or even
frequent war was the last thing any thoughtful American of the time
would think of as a serious threat. Power to declare war could be safely
left to the Congress, and leadership of the military to a civilian commander in chief, the president. Let the president have nominal steward-
ship of foreign policy but let the Senate have the power to advise and
consent, and the entire Congress the power of purse over foreign policy
and war.

(1)

It was ingenious, absolutely ideal for a nation clearly destined to peace and to the cultivation of the arts and sciences. Agriculture, commerce, and manufacture were the proper and highly probable direction of the American future. The states, to which an abundance of powers and rights were left by the Constitution, would be the true motors of American prosperity.

We did a very good job, on the whole, of avoiding the traps and entanglements of the world for the first hundred and twenty-five years, and even made bold to warn the Old World that its presence in the Western Hemisphere, however brief, would be regarded with suspicion. Then things changed.

The present age in American history begins with the Great War. When the guns of August opened fire in 1914, no one in America could have reasonably foreseen that within three years that foreign war not only would have drawn America into it but also would have, by the sheer magnitude of the changes it brought about on the American scene, set the nation on another course from which it has not deviated significantly since. The Great War was the setting of America's entry into modernity—economic, political, social, and cultural. By 1920 the country had passed, within a mere three years, from the premodern to the distinctly and ineffaceably modern. Gone forever now the age of American innocence.

When the war broke out in Europe in 1914 America was still, remarkably, strikingly, pretty much the same country in moral, social, and cultural respects that it had been for a century. We were still, in 1914, a people rooted largely in the mentality of the village and small town, still suspicious of large cities and the styles of living that went with these cities. The states were immensely important, just as the Founding Fathers and the Framers had intended them to be. It was hard to find a truly national culture, a national consciousness, in 1914. The Civil War had, of course, removed forever philosophical, as well as actively political, doubts of the reality of the Union as a sovereign state. But in terms of habits of mind, customs, traditions, folk literature, indeed written literature, speech accent, dress, and so forth, America could still be looked at as a miscellany of cultures held together, but not otherwise much influenced, by the federal government in Washington. For the vast majority of Americans, from east to west, north to south, the principal, if not sole, link with

the national government was the postal system—and perhaps also the federal income tax, which was approved at long last by constitutional amendment in 1913.

The Great War changed all of this. By November 1918 after four years of war in Europe and nearly two years of it for America, the whole world was changed, Europe itself ceased in substantial degree to be a contained civilization, and the United States, after close to two years of what can only be called wrenching military nationalism under the charismatic Woodrow Wilson, was brought at last into the modern world of nations. State loyalties and appeals to states' rights would not vanish overnight; they aren't gone yet in constitutional law, and aren't likely to be. But whereas prior to 1914 one still saw the gravamen of American development in the four dozen states, "provinces" in European terms, by 1920, it had shifted to the national culture, with the states becoming increasingly archaic.

The Great War, unwanted by any nation, even Germany, unexpected, really, until it burst devastatingly and irreversibly upon Europe, was at its height by far the largest, bloodiest, cruelest, indeed most savage in history. Churchill wrote:

> All the horrors of all the ages were brought together, and not only armies but whole populations were thrust into the midst of them. . . . Neither peoples nor rulers drew the line at any deed which they thought would help them to win. Germany, having let Hell loose, kept well in the van of terror; but she was followed step by step by the desperate and ultimately avenging nations she had assailed. Every outrage against humanity or international law was repaid by reprisals—often of a greater scale and of longer duration. No truce or parley mitigated the strife of the armies. The wounded died between the lines: the dead mouldered in the soil. Merchant ships and neutral ships and hospital ships were sunk on the seas and all on board left to their fate or killed as they swam. Every effort was made to starve whole nations into submission without regard to age or sex. Cities and monuments were smashed by artillery. Bombs from the air were cast down indiscriminately. Poison gas in many forms stifled or seared their bodies. Liquid fire was projected upon their bodies. Men fell from the air in flames, or were smothered, often slowly, in the dark recesses of the sea. The fighting strength of armies was limited only by the manhood of their countries. Europe and large parts of Asia and Africa became one vast battlefield on which after years of struggle not armies but nations broke and ran. When all was over, Torture and Cannibalism were the only two expedients that the civilized,

scientific, Christian States had been able to deny themselves: and they were of doubtful utility.*

The greatest single yield of the First World War was, however, none of the above; it was the Second World War, which came a bare quarter of a century after the First, germinated and let loose by the appalling consequences of 1918, chief among them the spawning of the totalitarian state, first in Russia, then in Italy and, crucially in the end, in Germany under Hitler. World War II was fought, of course, on a much wider front, or set of fronts, than its predecessor. There was no part of the globe that was not touched in one way or other. From the Second World War, officially ended in late 1945, has come a rash of wars during the last forty years, chief among them the Cold War between the Soviet Union and the United States. But we should not overlook the dozens of other wars fought during this period, in Asia, Africa, the Middle East, the Far East, Oceania, and so on. Between the last shot fired in 1945 and the present moment, war, somewhere at some time, has been the rule, peace the exception.

There is every reason for referring to the "Seventy-Five Years War" of the twentieth century, for that is about the length of the period of wars that began in 1914 and, with only brief punctuations of peace, continues through this year, certainly the next, and to what final ending? In so referring to twentieth-century war, we are only following the precedent of what we read routinely in our textbooks of European history about the Hundred Years War at the end of the Middle Ages. That war also had its punctuations of peace, or at least absence of overt hostilities.

War is indeed hell in just about every one of its manifestations through history. But for human beings during the past several thousand years it has plainly had its attractions, and also its boons for humanity. The general who said it is "good that war is so hideous; otherwise we should become too fond of it" spoke knowingly of the mental "wealth" that inheres in most wars along with the mental and physical "illth." So practical and pragmatic a mind as William James believed that we needed a "moral equivalent of war" as the means of attaining the good qualities of war without entailing the evil ones.

Without wars through the ages, and the contacts and intermixtures

---

*Cited in Martin Gilbert, *Winston S. Churchill.* Vol. 4, pp. 913–14. Boston: Houghton Mifflin Co., 1966

of peoples they—and for countless aeons they alone—instigated, humanity would quite possibly be mired in the torpor and sloth, the fruits of cultural and mental isolation, with which its history begins. Before trade and commerce broke down cultural barriers and yielded cross-breeding of ideas as well as genetic systems, wars were the sole agencies of such crossbreeding. Individualism, so vital to creativity, was born of mingling of peoples, with their contrasting cultural codes—the very diversity aiding in the release of individuals from prior localism and parochialism, always the price of cultural insularity.

War and change—political and economic foremost, but social and cultural not far behind—have been linked in America from the beginning. War was the necessary factor in the birth of the new American republic, as it has been in the birth of every political state known to us in history. War, chiefly the Civil War, in U.S. history has been a vital force in the rise of industrial capitalism, in the change of America from a dominantly agrarian and pastoral country to one chiefly manufacturing in nature. War, in focusing the mind of a country, stimulates inventions, discoveries, and fresh adaptations. Despite its manifest illth, war, by the simple fact of the intellectual and social changes it instigates, yields results which are tonic to advancement.

By all odds, the most important war in U.S. history, the war that released the greatest number and diversity of changes in American life, was the Great War, the war that began in Europe in August 1914 and engulfed the United States in April 1917. Great changes in America were immediate.

In large measure these changes reflected a release from the sense of isolation, insularity, and exceptionalism that had suffused so much of the American mind during the nineteenth century. The early Puritans had seen their new land as a "city upon a hill" with the eyes of the world on it. It was not proper for the New World to go to the Old for its edification; what was proper was for the Old World, grown feeble and hidebound, to come to America for inspiration. A great deal of that state of mind entered into what Tocqueville called the "American Religion," a religion compounded of Puritanism and ecstatic nationalism.

What we think of today as modernity—in manners and morals as well as ideas and mechanical things—came into full-blown existence in Europe in the final part of the nineteenth century, its centers such cities as London, Paris, and Vienna. In contrast America was a "closed" society, one steeped in conventionality and also in a struggle for iden-

tity. This was how many Europeans saw America and it was emphatically how certain somewhat more sophisticated and cosmopolitan Americans saw themselves. The grand tour was a veritable obligation of better-off, ambitious, and educated Americans—the tour being, of course, of Europe.

Possibly the passage of American values, ideas, and styles from "closed" to "open," from the isolated to the cosmopolitan society, would have taken place, albeit more slowly, had there been no transatlantic war of 1914–1918. We can't be sure. What we do know is that the war, and America's entrance into it, gave dynamic impact to the processes of secularization, individualization, and other kinds of social-psychological change which so drastically changed this country from the America of the turn of the century to the America of the 1920s.

War, sufficiently large, encompassing, and persisting, is one of the most powerful media of social and cultural—and also material, physical, and mechanical—change known to man. It was in circumstances of war in primordial times that the political state arose, and at the expense of the kinship order that had from the beginning been the individual's sole community. Ever since, war has had a nourishing effect upon the state; it is "the health of the state," Randolph Bourne observed darkly but accurately, when America went to war in 1917. Werner Sombart, historian of capitalism, devoted a volume to the tonic effects of war on the rise and development of capitalism. But no less true is Max Weber's pronouncement of war and the barracks life of warriors as the true cause of communism. War communism precedes, indeed gives birth to, civil communism, Weber argued. The Communism of Soviet Russia has been based from the very beginning upon war preparation, upon the Red Army and its absolute power in the Soviet state.

War tends to stimulate intellectual and cultural ferment if only because of the mixture of ideas and values that is a by-product of combat, of victory and defeat, in any war. In both world wars, millions of Americans, men and women alike, knew the broadening and enriching effects of travel abroad, of stations in exotic places for the first time, as the result of enlistment or conscription. Granted that some were killed. Far more were not.

War tends to break up the cake of custom, the net of tradition. By so doing, especially in times of crisis, it allows the individual a better chance of being seen and heard in the interstices, in the crevasses opened by the cracking up of old customs, statuses, and conventionalities. This was remarkably true once the European war touched the

millions of lives which had been for so long familiar with only the authorities and rhythms of an existence largely rural and pretty much limited to towns of the hinterland.

Lord Bryce, who loved America, was nevertheless forced to devote a chapter in his *The American Commonwealth,* published in the late nineteenth century, to what he called "the uniformity of American life." He was struck by the sameness of the buildings, houses, streets, food, drink, and dress in town after town, village after village, as he crossed and recrossed the country by rail. Not even one great capital, one flourishing city, Bryce felt obliged to report in his classic. That, however, was before the Great War and its transformation of the United States. It brought the literature of "release" in the novels of Sinclair Lewis, Sherwood Anderson, Willa Cather, Ruth Suckow, and others, a literature constructed around the drama and sometimes agony of a protagonist's escape from Main Street or Winesburg or Elmville or wherever, to the freedoms, chilling as these could be, of a Chicago or New York. In postwar New York, America at last got a true world capital. Much of the dreadful sameness began to crack under the force of the Great War. No wonder this war remains popular in American memory; even more popular than the War of Independence with Britain, which, truth to tell, was observed at the time by a majority hostile or at best lukewarm to it. Woodrow Wilson made the war his personal mission, his road to salvation for not only America but the world; and in the process, he made the war the single most vivid experience a large number of Americans had ever known. Even the casualties among American forces (not many compared to those of France, Britain, Russia, and Germany) didn't dampen enthusiasm at home; nor did the passage of legislation which put in the president's hands the most complete thought control ever exercised on Americans.

What the Great War did is what all major wars do for large numbers of people: relieve, if only briefly, the tedium, monotony, and sheer boredom which have accompanied so many millions of lives in all ages. In this respect war can compete with liquor, sex, drugs, and domestic violence as an anodyne. War, its tragedies and devastations understood here, breaks down social walls and by so doing stimulates a new individualism. Old traditions, conventions, dogmas, and taboos are opened under war conditions to a challenge, especially from the young, that is less likely in long periods of peace. The very uncertainty of life brought by war can seem a welcome liberation from the tyranny of the ever-predictable, from what a poet has called the "long littleness of life." It

Is not the certainties but the uncertainties in life which excite and stimulate—if they do not catastrophically obliterate—the energies of men.

There is a very high correlation between wars in Western history and periods of invention and discovery. If necessity is the mother of invention, then military necessity is the Great Mother. Roger Burlingame was correct when he said that if war were ever to be permanently abolished on earth, then something would have to be found to replace it as the stimulus and the context of inventions—mechanical but also social and cultural inventions. (When Leonardo da Vinci wrote to the duke of Milan listing his greatest accomplishments as possible stimulus to patronage from the duke, more than half the list consisted of his mechanical inventions. He combined painting and sculpture into one item, the better to give prominence to the mechanical achievements, nearly all of which were military.) America between 1914 and 1918 was no exception. Inventions of preceding years like the telephone and electric light were brought to a higher degree of perfection; so were the automobile, the radio, and the prototypes of what would become cherished household appliances. The federal government, justified and encouraged by war pressure, was able to do what would have been impossible in time of peace: directly encourage and even help finance new, entrepreneurial ventures such as the airplane and radio, each to revolutionize American life after the war.

Advances in medicine rank high among the benefactions of war. The sheer number of the wounded and sick, the possibility—the necessity—of new and radical techniques of surgery, and the focus of effort that war inevitably brings all combine to make times of war periods of major medical advancement, with incalculable boons for posterity. The whole field of prosthetics, for example, opened up in World War I—to be enormously advanced in the Second War—and with it came widespread relief from the obvious disfigurements of war, so abundant and ubiquitous after the Civil War.

Revolution and reform are common accompaniments of modern national wars. America underwent no political revolution as the consequence of either world war, but in each the acceleration of social and economic reforms and the germination of still other reforms to be accomplished later were striking. Not many wartime reforms long survived the wars, but their pattern was indelibly impressed on the reform mind. Without doubt the long overdue enfranchisement of women, which took place immediately after the First War, as did Prohibition,

each the subject of a constitutional amendment, was the fruit in large part of women's conspicuous service during the war in a variety of roles, military and civil, in offices and in factories. The cause of the illiterate was stimulated by the appalling results of the mass literacy tests given recruits in the war; the cause of the unorganized worker was advanced by the special allowance for union labor during the war; the real stimulus to the work toward racial and ethnic equality that has been a prominent part of the social history of the last sixty or so years came from federal agencies in the First World War. It is a matter of frequent note by historians that almost everywhere war needs inspire, in the interest of equity and of social stability, more "socialist" reforms than does the ideology of socialism.

Sometimes, indeed, more than simple reform becomes entwined with war. Revolution takes place. This was one of Lenin's insights. The German Socialists had made peace and pacifism almost as prominent as the revolutionary cause itself. Lenin broke utterly with this position, insisting that every national war should be supported in one way or other in the hope of converting war into revolution. America did not, of course, go into revolution as a result of the Great War, nor did England or France. But a good many of the countries engaged in that war, on both sides, did know very well, sometimes very painfully, the surge of revolution. What can be said of America in the war is that the people participated widely in a revolutionary upsurge of patriotism and of consecration to the improvement of the world in the very process of making "the world safe for democracy," as the moralistic President Wilson put it.

Yet another by-product of modern wars, those beginning with the French Revolution at least, is the sense of national community that can come over a people and become a landmark for the future. In the kind of war Americans—and others too—knew in 1917 and again in 1941, there is a strong tendency for divisiveness to moderate and a spirit of unity to take over. This was particularly apparent in America in the First War. It is not often remembered or cited that economic and social tensions were becoming substantial by 1914. Very probably the nearest this country has ever come to a strong socialist movement was during President Wilson's first term. A great deal was written in those years about "class struggle," "class revolt," and "class war" in America. Unemployment was severe in many industries, unions struggled for recognition, the homeless and hungry demonstrated, sometimes rioting, and strikes in all the great industries including mining, steel, and textiles

were at times small revolutions. The entrance of the United States in the war in 1917 spelled the end of much of this tumultuous and often violent behavior. Two decades later the same thing would be true for World War II. A full decade of the deepest and most agonizing economic depression America had ever known lasted, the vaunted New Deal notwithstanding, down to our joining the war in Europe and Asia.

But economic prosperity, while vital, is not the same as the sense of community. War induces, especially in fighting forces, a sense of camaraderie and mutual recognition that becomes community. As Remarque wrote in his great World War I novels, the "Western Front" was a torture but so was "the Road Back" to civilian life at the end of the war. Even the trenches could instill a feeling of moral and social community—that was Remarque's major point, as it was of a number of novelists, dramatists, and poets in the aftermath of the war. World War I, quite unlike its successor a quarter of a century later, was both a singing and a writing war, and in song and letters the theme of war's spur to comradeship and the mordant sense too of the "spiritual peace that war brings," to cite the British L. P. Jacks, are striking.

War is a tried and true specific when a people's moral values become stale and flat. It can be a productive crucible for the remaking of key moral meanings and the strengthening of the sinews of society. This is not always the case, as the American scene during the Vietnam War made painfully clear. But that war is more nearly the exception than the rule. Even our divisive, sanguinary, radical Civil War produced a reseating of values, with the nation for the first time exceeding the regions and states in political importance.

Rarely has the sense of national community been stronger than it was in America during the Great War. True, that sense had to be artificially stimulated by a relentless flow of war propaganda from Washington and a few other pricks of conscience, but by the end of the war a stronger national consciousness and sense of cohesion were apparent. But, as we know in today's retrospect, with these gains came distinct losses in constitutional birthright.

All wars of any appreciable length have a secularizing effect upon engaged societies, a diminution of the authority of old religious and moral values and a parallel elevation of new utilitarian, hedonistic, or pragmatic values. Wars, to be successfully fought, demand a reduction in the taboos regarding life, dignity, property, family, and religion; there must be nothing of merely moral nature left standing between the

fighting forces and victory, not even, or especially, taboos on sexual encounters. Wars have an individualizing effect upon their involved societies, a loosening of the accustomed social bond in favor of a tightening of the military ethic. Military, or at least war-born, relationships among individuals tend to supersede relationships of family, parish, and ordinary walks of life. Ideas of chastity, modesty, decorum, respectability change quickly in wartime.

They did in Puritan-rooted America during World War I—changed radically in many cases, and irreversibly. Mars and Venus cavorted, as they always had in time of war, and not least in America. When the brave young doughboy in the AEF was about to go overseas, perhaps to his death, couldn't his sweetheart, even the girl next door, both honor and thrill her swain? Of course she could—in life and voluminously in fiction. The relaxation not only of ancient rules and dogmas in the spheres of marriage and family, religion and morals, but also of styles of music, art, literature, and education, although concentrated in the cities, nevertheless permeated the entire nation.

So, above all, did the new spirit of materialistic hedonism, the spirit of "eat, drink, and be merry" with or without the "for tomorrow we die," capture the American mind during the war. The combination of government-mandated scarcities in some areas, as in meat, sugar, and butter, and the vast amount of expendable money from wages and profits in the hands of Americans led to a new consumer syndrome, one that has only widened ever since World War I and has had inestimable impact upon the American economy. Manufacture of consumer goods directed at the individual rather than the family greatly increased, further emphasizing the new individualism and the new hedonism of American life.

The American Way of Life proved both during and after the Great War to be exportable, to peoples all over the world. These peoples may have had an inadequate grasp at the end of the 1920s of just where America was geographically and just what it was made of mentally and morally, but they had acquired during the decade a lively sense of Coca-Cola, the Hamburger, Hollywood Movies, Jazz, Flappers, Bootleg Gin, and Gangsters. The flapper came close to being America's First Lady in the movie houses of India, China, Latin America, and other abodes of what today we call the Third World. On the evidence of tickets bought, they adored what they saw almost as much as did the American people. Despite Prohibition, drinking was in to a degree it had never achieved when legal—that is, among young people of both

sexes but generally middle-class by the end of the twenties. The gang-ster and the cowboy both achieved a fame in that decade earlier denied their prototypes.

The 1920s was par excellence the Age of Heroes. The age had begun in April 1917 when soldiers, from Black Jack Pershing at the top down to Sergeant York, were given novel worship by Americans at home. The spell lasted through the twenties to include heroes of the industrial world like Ford and Rockefeller; of the aviation world like Lindbergh and Earhart; of the sports world like Babe Ruth, Red Grange, Knute Rockne; and of the movies like Chaplin, Fairbanks, Swanson, and Pickford. To this day names such as these are more likely to come off the American tongue than are those of any living heroes.

Almost everyone and everything became larger than life for Ameri-cans during the First World War. This began with the armed forces we sent over to Europe, a million and a half strong by the end of the war. Promotions were numerous and so were medals of one degree or other for valor, each with full publicity on the scene and back home. No military breast looked dressed unless rows of ribbons and galaxies of medals adorned it. Rife as decorations were, though, in World War I, these were almost as nothing compared with World War II. And the tendency has heightened immeasurably since that war. One illustration will suffice: In the recent, embarrassingly awkward invasion of tiny Grenada, when three American services, army, navy, and marines, were brought to combat six hundred expatriate Cuban construction workers, less than half of them armed, victory, if that be the word, was celebrated by the issuance of eight thousand decorations—there and back in Washington.

As is so often the case in history, what began in the military spread quickly to nonmilitary society during the First World War. Under George Creel, President Wilson's czar of war propaganda, about whose activities I shall say something in the next chapter, the custom arose of Home Front awards, honors, and decorations. Farmer of the Week, Worker of the Month, Lawyer of the Year, Surgeon of the Decade—these and many, many other honors festooned once quiet, modest, and shy America. The custom lasted, growing spectacularly during the 1920s, slackening somewhat in the 1930s, but regaining speed during World War II and thereafter. Today American professions spend un-countable hours giving awards to themselves. The academic profession probably leads, with journalism a close second, but lawyers, bankers, and dry cleaners are not far behind either.

A possibly more important, more creative change that came with the Great War in America was in language, written as well as spoken. It became obviously bolder than it had ever been in American history— yet another boon, or casualty, of the Great War and its smashing of old icons of respectability and conventionality. In journalism the tabloid flourished, and a newspaper vernacular came close to driving out the statelier papers such as the Boston *Transcript* and the New York *Sun.* Just as newspaper reporters had at last found a prose that brought the realities of war a little closer to readers, so, in the 1920s, they found a prose for the retailing of sex, murder, scandal, and other of the seamier aspects of life that was far more vivid than anything before. One of the great accomplishments of the respected novelists, dramatists, and critics—Hemingway, Dos Passos, Fitzgerald, Anderson, O'Neill, Mencken, and others—in the twenties was a sharper, terser, more evocative language than had prospered in the Gilded Age.

All in all, the America that came out from a mere year and a half of the Great War was as transformed from its former self as any nation in history. The transformation extended to fashions and styles, to methods of teaching in the schools, to a gradual letting down of the barriers between men and women and between the races, to informalities of language as well as simple habits at home and in the workplace.

It is not often realized that among war's occasional tonic attributes is that of distinct cultural renascences, brief periods of high fertility in the arts. Here too we are dealing with results of the shaking up of ideas and values that so frequently goes with war in history. To examine such a work as A. L. Kroeber's *Configurations of Culture Growth,* a classic in comparative cultural history, is to see the unmistakable and unblinkable connections between wars and immediately subsequent years of creativity in literature, art, and kindred disciplines. The celebrated fifth century B.C. in Athens began with the Persian War and concluded with the Peloponnesian. Rome's greatest period of cultural efflorescence, the first and second centuries, are inseparable from European and Asiatic wars. The Augustan Age emerged directly from the Civil Wars. In the more recent ages of Elizabeth I and of Louis XIV, and in the Enlightenment, we are dealing with distinct periods of cultural fertility which are inseparable from the wealth, power, and ferment of wars.

We don't often think of the 1920s in America as one of the more impressive intellectual and artistic outbursts in history, but it was. In terms of literature, we are obliged to go back to the American renas-

cence just prior to the Civil War: to the single decade, perhaps, of the 1850s when works came forth from Melville, Hawthorne, Whitman, Emerson, Thoreau, among others—a constellation of creative genius that can pretty well hold its own in world competition.

The 1920s may not quite match the 1850s, but we are nevertheless in the company of novelists of the stature of Faulkner, Cozzens, Hemingway, Fitzgerald, Dreiser, Glasgow, Lewis, and others; the poets Eliot, Pound, Frost, Robinson; and intellectual czars—a new breed—who had H. L. Mencken at their head. The war figured prominently in the early works of some, though not all, of the novelists: Dos Passos, Faulkner, Hemingway in some degree, Fitzgerald in less, and the psychological atmosphere of war in these novels was unfailingly one of disenchantment and repudiation. The literature of disenchantment with war was much more abundant in England and on the Continent than it was in America; and well it might be, given the four long, bloody, shell-shocking, and mind-numbing years in the trenches that the Europeans, unlike the American soldiers, had had to endure.

Even more historic and world-influencing than our literature of the twenties, however, was our music of that decade: first and foremost jazz in all its glories, ranging from blues to early swing; very probably nothing else of a cultural nature is as distinctly and ineffaceably tied to the American matrix as is jazz, in composition and in voices and instrumental performances. But in the musical theater of Kern, Rodgers, and Hart in the twenties America took a lead in the world that would continue for close to fifty years. These names, and also of course those of Gershwin, Berlin, and Porter, were as lustrous in the cities of Europe and Asia as in the United States.

Hollywood perhaps became the American name of greatest reach in the world. Well on its way before the Great War, it was helped immeasurably by the war; when the federal government took over the movies for propaganda uses, an assured supply of funding made possible a great many technical as well as plot and character experiments which might have been slower in coming had there been no war. And of course the opportunity to cover the actual war in Europe, its details of action, death, and devastation, provided a marvelous opportunity for further experimentation. There were excellent movies made in the 1920s in America—movies fully the equal of those in Germany and France—on war, its carnage and tragedy, romance and heroism. In any event, it is unlikely that the phenomenon of Hollywood—its tales of actors and actresses, producers and directors as well as the remarkable quantity and

quality of its films—would have burst forth as it did in the 1920s had it not been for the heady experience of the war. In art as in literature and philosophy, war can bring forth forces of creative intensity.

There was of course the myth of the Lost Generation to occupy memoirists, critics, and romantics through the 1920s and after. I shall say more about this myth in the final chapter. It will suffice here to emphasize that apart only from the appalling loss of a whole generation of brilliant minds in the trenches, there really wasn't any such thing— only the literary rumor thereof.

In sum, in culture, as in politics, economics, social behavior, and the psychological recesses of America, the Great War was the occasion of the birth of modernity in the United States. It is no wonder that so many historians have adopted the stereotype of the Age of Innocence for what preceded this war in American history.

Another national legacy of the Great War is what I can think of only as the Great American Myth. This is the myth—it sprang into immediate existence with the armistice in 1918—that America, almost single-handedly, won the war. Such was American prowess in war, derived from clean living and good hearts, that it did in a matter of months what the British and French had been at unsuccessfully for more than two years: that is, lick the Hun. In such popular magazines as *American, Everybody's, The Literary Digest, The Saturday Evening Post,* and local newspapers everywhere would appear staple pieces beginning "The reason the American doughboy won the war for the Allies was . . .". There would follow reasons ranging from the Puritan ethic all the way to the "fact" that Our Boys all came from farms where they had plenty of milk and butter, learned to shoot squirrels with deadly efficacy, and could fix anything that broke with a hairpin.

But whatever the reason was, it is doubtful that any American failed to believe, in the twenties, that American soldiers had a genius for war; could, like Cincinnatus of early Rome, take their hands from the plow one day and fight valorously for country the next. In some degree the myth is a corollary of what Lord Bryce called "the fatalism of the multitude" in America: a belief, nay, a compulsion exerted by belief that America had a special destiny of its own—one that from its beginning as a "city upon a hill" in Puritan Massachusetts, through Colonial days, the Revolutionary War, the winning of the American continent in the nineteenth century, would carry America, perhaps alone among all nations, to an ever more glorious fulfillment of birthright. Such was

the exceptional fate under which America lived, that she didn't have to be concerned about all the cares and worries, the forethought, prudence, and preparation for the worst that other nations did.

The Myth would be a commonplace, no more than a charming conceit of a kind found perhaps in every people were it not for the fact that it was and is taken sufficiently seriously by many Americans as to become a utopian block to the military preparation and industrial skill that any nation must have, even if composed of supermen. The Great Myth was operating in full force when the Second World War broke out and it operates today in the form of tolerance of a Pentagon bureaucracy that chokes off initiative and perseverence.

The stark, agonizing truth is, we Americans have not been good at war, and particularly conventional war fought on land. We won our independence from Britain all right, but it's best for the patriot not to dig too deeply into the reasons, which include key help from abroad, halfheartedness on the part of Britain, and quite astounding luck, benign accident. We were a ragtag lot, and most of the time the Continental Congress acted as if it was more afraid of a bona fide American army coming out of the war than it was of a British victory.

Our first war as a new nation, the War of 1812, was rashly declared by Congress, and it proved to be a mixed bag indeed for the United States. At Bladensburg our militia was routed without serious struggle, and the diminutive President Madison, seeking to demonstrate that he was the troops' commander in chief, was very nearly captured by the British. There followed the burning of Washington, including the White House, or much of it, and the torching of dozens of settlements on Chesapeake Bay. We were no better on the Canadian border. True, we saved Baltimore and just after the war was ended, Andy Jackson was able to become a hero at New Orleans. Not much else.

In the nineteenth century we were good at beating the Mexicans, but less good at handling the American Indians in pitched battle. From the remarkable Tecumseh and his Red Stick Confederacy in 1809 to Sitting Bull at Little Bighorn in 1876, white Americans were ragged indeed. The West was won more by the momentum of westward expansion than by crucial battles with the Indians, whom we eventually "defeated" almost genocidally through malnutrition, disease, and alcohol. No Federal leader in the Indian wars equaled Tecumseh and Sitting Bull. Custer's inglorious end at Little Bighorn is not a bad symbol of the whole of the Indian wars.

The Civil War produced, after a year or two of battles, at least two

weapons. Relations between the Americans and the British were precarious indeed, requiring constant attention by both Churchill and FDR.

American courage was not in doubt; nor was potential once adequate time and opportunity for experience had been provided. Nevertheless, the embarrassing fact is, the Americans, including Marshall and Eisenhower, who had argued so strongly for a Second Front Now on the fearfully manned and armed Normandy coast, with all stops pulled out on Can Do, looked pathetic in the far easier circumstances of Tunisia. And matters weren't different in the Pacific so far as land forces were involved. An infantry division trained for a year in the hot desert was sent, in desert clothing, for its first assignment to the bitterly cold and wet Aleutians, yielding a record toll of incapacitating frostbite. Hundreds of marines were slaughtered in the beachhead of Tarawa, largely as the result of command failure to use intelligence and readings of charts of coastal waters and island detail. Marines, it was trumpeted, Can Do and already have innate Know How. Presumably the hapless marines in Lebanon, over two hundred in number, were ascribed the same innate attributes when they were sent by Reagan in 1983 without arms, without vital intelligence, and without instructions—ending up, as we know, without lives.

The entrance of America in military array into Vietnam was begun by the Kennedy administration apparently for no other reason than impulse to show the world academic Know How of the sort illustrated by McNamara, Bundy, Hillsman, and Arthur Schlesinger, Jr., among others. We lost Vietnam after an unprecedentedly long war, one hugely expensive in lives and dollars. Desert One, in Iran, was an incredible mishmash of sheer unpreparedness and incompetence of leaders. Tiny Grenada attracted three American services— bumbling, Abbott and Costello–led services, alas—to deal with not more than two hundred armed Cubans. Most recently we have had the Freedom Fighters, and an entry into the Persian Gulf, to convoy tankers, *without minesweepers!*

Before leaving the myth, it is worth noting that it operates, and perhaps nowhere else so fatefully, in every new president's conception of himself and his command of foreign affairs. Since FDR it has become almost de rigeur for each president to make it plain to all that he will be his own secretary of state, his own master of foreign policy. The next step is usually that of creating the impression that he not only doesn't need the State Department and congressional committees to help him, but also frankly finds their presence inimical to the new, suddenly

divisions hitting "selected beaches" between Le Havre and Boulogne. These would be "nourished" at the rate of one hundred thousand men a week. The whole war-ending operation must begin in late 1942 and reach climax in 1943.

What the British, starting with Churchill, really thought of this incredible nonsense we don't know. Keeping the Americans happy in their choice of Europe First, Japan Second, was of course vital, imperative diplomacy for the British. Thus while offering frequent overt reactions of the "magnificent in principle," "superbly conceived," and "boldly projected" kind, the British leaders made immediate plans, we may assume, for weaning the Americans from a 1942 channel assault to North Africa, eased by a pledge that the so-called Second Front would take place in 1943.

Today, looking back on what was required in June 1944, two years after Roosevelt's plan was unveiled before the eyes of Churchill— required in the way of troops, landing craft, mobile harbors, planes, ships, materiel of every kind, and required too in the way of sheer luck—we can only shudder at the thought of a Normandy invasion beginning in the fall of 1942, less than a year after Germany brought the United States into the European war by its declaration of war on America.

Only the Great American Myth can possibly explain the rashness, the foolhardiness, of Roosevelt's proposal and the at least ostensible endorsement of it by American generals. Powerful defenses manned by the highly efficient German army, the treacherous currents of the channel, the terrible weather problems, the enforced insufficiency of men and materiel—what are these as obstacles when the invading troops will be joined by Our Boys, fresh from the farms, hamlets, and towns of America the Beautiful, the spirit of Galahad in every soldierly breast?

The Great American Myth fell on its face, though, in North Africa when, following our first eager and confident efforts, there were serious and indeed embarrassing reverses to American troops, whose officers were disinclined even to receive, much less ask for, advice from the well-seasoned British. The Great American Myth, absorbed in basic training, at first stood between American officers and even recognition of the sad state of their strategy and tactics. The American bumblings began in Tunisia in late 1942 and were still only too apparent in the first months of 1943, nowhere more humiliatingly than at Kasserine Pass where in addition to inflicting heavy casualties on the Americans, the openly contemptuous Germans took away half of their strategic

impetuous innocence. When Churchill was taken by General Marshall and other officers to witness for himself the "readiness for combat" of trainees at a South Carolina camp, Churchill bruised some feelings, we learn, by declaring that "it takes at least two years to make a soldier." So it does. But the Great American Myth says otherwise, and it is seemingly indestructible.

A notorious and potentially devastating instance of the myth was the American shrilling for a Second Front Now in 1942—a shrilling, alas, joined in by Roosevelt and, nominally at least, Marshall and the other Joint Chiefs. They were unimpressed by the nearly fatal experience of the British at Dunkirk in 1940; and they would remain unimpressed by the utter failure in August 1942 of the largely British-Canadian Dieppe assault in France, in which thoroughly trained, seasoned attack troops five thousand strong were repulsed easily, with 70 percent casualties, by German forces well emplaced and armed.

To be sure, Stalin, threatened by Hitler's armies in the east, was noisily demanding such a second front, in the process calling Churchill and the British cowardly; but even without Stalin's demand in 1942— instantly echoed, of course, in both England and the United States by Communist parties and their multitudinous sympathizers among liberals and progressives—the Great American Myth, the myth of Can Do, of effortless military strategy and valor, that is, American Know How, would have kept the cretinous pressure going for a storming of the cross-channel French coast, awesomely guarded by the Germans, in the fall of 1942 and early 1943.

As thoroughly mythified as anyone else, President Roosevelt himself developed a plan, as he called it, for such a blind, suicidal frontal assault by the British and Americans (in the very nature of things in 1942, overwhelmingly British) on the French coast directly across the channel. He wrote Churchill that such was the importance of his "plan" that he was sending it over by General Marshall and his aide Harry Hopkins, so that they might explain its merits personally to Churchill and his military chiefs. The decision to storm the French coast must be made "at once," declared Roosevelt through his envoys. Since only five American divisions would be ready by the fall of 1942, "the chief burden" would necessarily fall on the British, the President charmingly explained. By September 15, America could supply only "half" of the divisions necessary, that is, five, and but seven hundred of the necessary five thousand combat aircraft. FDR's plan foresaw a first wave of six

first-rate generals and some superb troops. Unfortunately these were not part of the United States forces; they belonged to the Confederate States of America. This is no place to play the game of "what if," as in, what if the South had won at Gettysburg? But the very existence of the question attests to the nearness of at least temporary Confederate victory. The United States won in the end—after the unhappy Mr. Lincoln finally got rid of timid or inept generals—through the crude but effective bludgeonings by Grant's mass army and the organized terror waged in Georgia by General Sherman.

Over the Spanish-American War, a decent curtain will be lowered here.

The American Expeditionary Force of 1917 arrived in France almost three full years after the trench slaughter there and on the Eastern Front had begun. The Allies were indeed glad to welcome the American soldiers, who did well; not brilliantly, but well, all things considered. We had our requisite heroes—Sergeant York, dashing, brilliant Doug McArthur, Black Jack Pershing whom a grateful Congress elevated overnight to the rank of George Washington himself, and others—to hear about for years and years in the thousands of little towns in America. In all truth, it is quite possible that had the war lasted a couple of years beyond 1918, had more American divisions actually been blooded in battle, and had it been given, in short, the time and seasoning necessary, the AEF might have become a sterling fighting force. But we were Over There for a pitifully short time, from the military point of view.

The American public, however, and, sad to say, the professional military in America, saw it differently. Our Boys had the strength of ten, and after the imperialist-minded, materialistically motivated British and French had stumbled and bumbled for two and a half years, Our Boys cleaned up the job. The Great American Myth gave birth to other myths: Can Do, Know How, and No Fault, myths which abide to this minute in America and yield up such disasters as Korea, Vietnam, Iran, Lebanon, and Grenada.

Under the spell of the myth, Americans begin anticipating victory and peace at about the time war is declared. In World War I and World War II, spurred on by editors and broadcasters, they were chittering within months about getting The Boys home for Christmas.

Our civilian recruits in World War II had hardly been at training six weeks when an eager citizenry proudly declared them "combat-ready right now." Sadly, some of our military leaders exhibited the same

revealed, foreign policy that he—and perhaps a Colonel House or Harry Hopkins or William Casey, but no one else—intends to broadcast to the world.

Churchill, the greatest leader yielded by the war and indeed the century, reported to his War Cabinet every day on his activities; he consulted his assembled chiefs of staff regularly; he reported periodically to Parliament; and he drew constantly on the permanent secretariat, the body of specialists that stayed through all changes of government. He would not sign the Atlantic Charter aboard the battleship off Nova Scotia until its full text had been cabled to the War Cabinet and a reply received. He was still *the* leader.

Roosevelt saw fit to consult no one but Hopkins and Sumner Welles about the charter; the idea of getting the counsel even of officers of the State Department, much less of congressional committees, would have made him laugh. *He* knew what was needed and right; experts were unnecessary and actually obstructive. FDR had never met Stalin or any other high Soviet leader; he had never been to or even read particularly about the Soviet Union. But he obviously felt the full impulse of the Great American Myth when he wrote Churchill three months after entry into the war that he "could personally handle Stalin" and do so far more ably than either the British Foreign Office or the American State Department. What Churchill thought on reading this he never told the world, contenting himself with merely including the Roosevelt message in his war memoirs.

Just as each new president must show his spurs by deprecating State Department and congressional committees in foreign policy, so, it seems, must each new National Security Adviser to the president. He too, under the Great Myth, immediately knows more than Congress or the Departments of State and Defense about any given foreign or defense issue that arises. Watching Kissinger perform as National Security Adviser, to the confusion of the State Department and congressional committees, we might have foreseen a day when a National Security Adviser would appear in admiral's uniform and define his role as that of excluding not only Congress and the Departments of State and Defense from knowledge of purportedly covert NSC operations but even his very boss, the president of the United States.

Add to what has thus far been said about the Great Myth and American Know How the attribute of No Fault, and we have the myth fairly well identified. Presidents, secretaries, and generals and admirals in America seemingly subscribe to the doctrine that no fault ever

attaches to policy and operations. This No Fault conviction prevents them from taking too seriously such notorious foul-ups as Desert One, Grenada, Lebanon, and now the Persian Gulf.

The spirit of ingrained Know How is by no means limited to the American military and the national government. Corporate America and Wall Street both bring the Great American Myth to conspicuous presence regularly. Until Black Monday, October 1987, even such un prepossessing goings-on as insider trading, hostile takeovers, flaunting of junk bonds, and golden parachutes were widely regarded by brokers and economists alike as basically healthful, nicely attuned to economic growth and productivity.

We shall not soon forget the efflorescence of the Myth in Detroit for perhaps twenty years after World War II when a vast litter of unsafe, low quality, ugly, and expensive automobiles were the issue of the Know How, Can Do, and No fault psychology of the auto industry. Not even Ralph Nader would have effected salutary change in Myth beset Detroit had it not been for the ever-widening competition—and here at home where it hurt—from Japan, West Germany and other countries.

The Great Myth provides a warm and lustrous ambiance for our towering national debt of close to three trillions, our annual budget deficits, now at two hundred billion, and our even more hazardous trade deficits. Only the intoxicating presence of the Great Myth can explain how otherwise sane and responsible people, including financial editors and professional economists, find not only no danger in such a mess of debts and deficits, but actual nutriment of economic equilibrim and growth. Historically large and prolonged national budget deficits have been almost uniformly regarded by experts as potentially crippling to any society. So has lack of savings and of investments in business been generally regarded as putting an economy in jeopardy. Consumer hedonism with its vast consumption of the fragile and ephemeral has always been looked at with apprehension by statesmen. But during the years of Reagan and his all time record setting deficits and debt-increases a new school of thought has emerged; one that declares debts, deficits, trade imbalances, and absent savings forces for the good, requiring only, if anything at all, substantial tax cuts. Needless to say, the rest of the world, starting with Japan, can only look wonderingly at the U.S. The God who looks out for fools and drunks is indeed needed for the Republic.

Fascination with the amateur steadily widens in America—amateur

in the sense of unprepared or inexperienced. We scorn professionality in appointments of officials ranging from the Librarian of Congress to Secretary of State. A Martian might think experience in national and international affairs the first requirement of the Presidency. Not so, for we fairly regularly and confidently elect Coolidges, Kennedys, Carters and Reagans to the White House as if there were a positive advantage in being ignorant or inexperienced in national and international politics. Both Carter and Reagan seemed to think this was the case when they ran for office. So, obviously, did a great many Americans. It's an old passion. In the twenties there were millions who begged Henry Ford to step down from Dearborn to Washington and "get things straightened out." In 1940 there was Wendell Wilkie and then Thomas Dewey, the while a Robert Taft could only gaze from the side line. On the whole it seems the Republicans are more easily dazzled and motivated to go for amateurs than are the Democrats. But it's a bipartisan failing, for the Great American Myth is everywhere. Naturally the first thing an amateur does when elected to the White House is appoint fellow-amateurs—not only to innocuous posts such as the Librarian of Congress but to State, Treasury, the CIA, Defense, and so on, not forgetting vital ambassadorships.

From McNamara to Weinberger we have seen off and on amateurs as Secretary of Defense. And from McNamara's TFX and computerized body counts to current miseries with the Bradley, the Sergeant York, the MX and the B1 bomber there has been a steady roster of the failed and abortive. Ten years since the mesmerizing RDF small units were announced, Pentagon is still struggling to put one such military unit into being and action. Pentagon, alas, has penetrated large areas of our economy and also, much more important, our universities and their research laboratories. We have not been in a major war since 1945, excepting perhaps for Vietnam, which was selected by the Kennedy White House as a simple counterinsurgency operation—nothing, really, but small wars, calling for special military units.

Why, then, so immense a military? The immediate answer is invariably the Cold War with the Soviet Union. The answer is indeed worth respectful consideration. The record is plain that once Japan was defeated in late 1945, America commenced an immediate pell-mell, helter-skelter demobilization that might well have denuded the nation of a military in the same measure that it did after the First World War. This demobilization stopped for one reason alone: the voracious Russian appetite for land and power that could no longer be hidden once V-E

Day came in Europe. In Poland, in the Baltic states, in the Balkans, in Iran, and in the Far East, Stalin either entered or else shored up and consolidated lands and nations he had already appropriated during the final months of the war. The roots of the Cold War are, of course, in these acts of aggrandizement, which became steadily more odious to Americans after the war, and also, by implication, threatening. But the Cold War began in full fact when Truman gave protection to Greece and Turkey, at Britain's urgent request, and Stalin realized that the United States would no longer tolerate what Roosevelt had during his presidency, when his mind was stubbornly set on winning Stalin's friendship and postwar favor.

But with all respect to the Cold War and to the highly militaristic, imperialistic nation that wages it on America, it alone is not enough to explain either the size or the type of military establishment we now have on our hands. The Cold War does not by itself come close to explaining the sheer size of the budget, well over three hundred billions a year, much less some of the specifications which are involved in military budgets. Surely a six-hundred-ship navy based upon aircraft carriers and battleships is not a requisite for any conceivable war with the Soviet Union, a war that would inevitably be land-based. The very real potential menace of the Soviets doesn't require, surely, to make it believable to the American public, that we sweep into the American-Soviet maw every little brushfire war that breaks out in Africa, the Middle East, and Latin America. The confrontations of doves and hawks, both in government and among political and military intellectuals, do indeed involve the Soviets from time to time, chiefly in respect of the size and type of our nuclear force, but far more of such confrontations are pivoted upon incidents and outbreaks only dimly connected with the Soviet Union. The Soviets just won't pass muster as the cause of everything— Korea, Vietnam, the Dominican Republic, South Africa, Iran, Lebanon, Grenada, Central America, the Persian Gulf, and so on—that we have on our post–World War II record.

There are two powerful, and by now almost inescapable, forces which operate to yield America an ever-larger military. By this late part of the century, after two world wars, a string of smaller ones, and forty years of the Cold War, these two forces would surely continue to operate even if the Soviet Union were miraculously transformed into a vast religious convent. Together the two forces, the one rationalistic, the other moralistic, conjoin irresistibly in our present society.

The first was noted profoundly by President Eisenhower in 1961 in

his cogent farewell remarks. He warned Americans against what he called the "military-industrial complex" and also the "scientific-techno-logical elite." Taken in its entirety the Eisenhower farewell address is as notable as was that of George Washington. It deserves fully as much attention as the Washington address has received over the years.

Ike was struck by how, during the Cold War—a war he believed had to be waged, given the nature of the Soviet Union—the military and the whole armaments-defense private sector had become interlocked fatefully. Each grew stronger from the nutriment supplied by the other. He was also struck by the sheer internal, indigenous power of the scientific-technological elite in the United States and its attraction to war and the military as a vast, virtually free laboratory. Moreover, Ike added, our tendency since World War II has been to meet the threat of Soviet power through "emotional and transitory sacrifices of crisis" rather than through considered planning that would meet foreign dangers without ripping the fabric of American life, without incurring expenses so vast as to worry the most dedicated of patriots. There is, Eisenhower continued, "a recurring temptation to feel that some spectacular and costly action could become the miraculous solution of all current difficulties." Could President Eisenhower have been thinking about our current Strategic Defense Initiative, or Star Wars, project, hailed in the beginning as a canopy over our heads that would forever shield us from nuclear weapons, and now estimated to cost a full trillion dollars to deploy in full—assuming it can ever be deployed at all?

The cost of alleged scientific miracles is probably less, though, than the total costs of what may from one point of view be called the militarization of intellectuals and from another point of view the intellectualization of the military. I am thinking of the fusion of the military and the university during the last half-century. Eisenhower offered this warning also in his farewell remarks: "The prospect of domination of the nation's scholars by federal employment, project allocations, and the power of money is ever present—and is gravely to be regarded." He cautioned too: "Partly because of the huge costs involved, a government contract becomes virtually a substitute for intellectual curiosity."

Eisenhower was warning primarily of what may happen to the universities as a result of their compulsive willingness to adapt, readjust, and refashion in the interest of the huge sums ever ready to be granted by the military. But a moment's thought suggests the reverse conclusion: The power of the university and the university culture in this country is such that by virtue of its union with the military, the whole

nature and function of the military establishment could become altered, and not necessarily for the better. But whichever conclusion we choose to accept, the symbiotic relationship between the military and a large and increasing part of the university world is only too obvious. The university thus joins the corporation and the technological institute in becoming willy-nilly a complex, possibly deep pattern of culture. The economy has a vested interest in the prevalence of war; that is obvious. Does the university? That could have seismic effects in the academic world.

The military, or defense, intellectual is one of the flowers of the present age, and also one of the great drawbacks in our military establishment. Probably McNamara as Secretary of Defense under Kennedy has the dubious honor of being the first intellectual to demonstrate to the professional military exactly how wars should be fought. His punishment by the gods for hubris consisted of participation in the Bay of Pigs fiasco and then his appalling leadership in the American buildup of troops in Vietnam. But there were other military intellectuals under Kennedy: Bundy, Hillsman, Rostow, and the never-to-be-forgotten Daniel Ellsberg of Defense. Who will forget the saga, now firmly in our schoolbooks, of how our military intellectuals were "eyeball to eyeball" with Khrushchev and the Soviets over Soviet missiles being fixed in Cuba? It is only today, twenty-five years later, that the truth is coming forth from the aforementioned hawks, and we now learn that the truth consists not of intellectual hawks but of doves dressed like hawks eager to make conciliatory gifts to the Soviets and to adopt secret backup lines in the event Khrushchev became hard-nosed and stubborn.

It was in the Kennedy administration that the unlamented, embarrassing Project Camelot was conceived and shortly aborted. This was a covert operation based secretly at American University in Washington and manned largely by academics and free-lance intellectuals who were apparently enchanted by the image of Kennedy and his intellectuals at the top and made eager to earn a few spurs themselves as covert hawks. A couple of dozen professors from some of America's better universities collaborated with the military to work out an intellectually—sociologically, anthropologically, and psychologically—sound covert operation by which America, with or without green berets, could spark counterinsurgency operations in countries where the resident government seemed perhaps unable to cope. Chile, of all places, was tagged secretly as the proving ground for the scheme. One of the academics became conscience-stricken, however, and blew the whistle

on the absurd venture, thus arousing the ire of the Chilean government, the front-page attention of the *Washington Star*, and an investigation by a special committee of Congress. Although the very participation of a large gaggle of American academics attests once again to the Great Myth, it has to be said that under the fools' luck codicil of the myth, all participants escaped with nothing more than temporary embarrassment.

There is no evidence that I know of that McNamara's career as military intellectual—complete, it will be remembered, with computerized body counts and TFX monstrosities—has been bettered since by any of his by now multitudinous flock of followers. More and more centers, think tanks, and institutes in Washington are directed to war policy and war strategy, and to war intelligence. Hardly a night goes by without one or other military intellectual appearing on the television screen to clear up confusions about war and the military. Intellectuals come as "terror experts," "strategy analysts," "intelligence consultants," and no one ever seems interested in where these ever-voluble experts acquired their credentials.

The liaison between scientist and technologist—connected inevitably with the liaison between the military and the corporate world—is especially productive of vast military establishments in present-day America. Eisenhower could have elaborated had he chosen to do so, even back when he said his farewell. But that day is as nothing compared to our own. It is almost as though the scientific-technological has become an immense creature with life and energy of its own. A perceptive article in *Barron's* (August 17, 1987) presents a list of "current programs," "new programs recently authorized," and "programs emerging from development within 5 years." Secret programs are not listed; those that are, run into the dozens and include both nuclear and conventional military technology.

Barron's correctly features the astronomical costs of even the overt part of the weapons program, costs which when they reach a certain not easily specifiable point will be repudiated by the people and Congress, thus presenting one kind of defense crisis. Another kind of crisis we are perhaps already reaching is that between the seemingly infinite productivity of the strictly scientific-technological elites and the very finite capacity of fighting forces, right down to the individual soldier, for assimilating all the wonders of design, for adapting them to the harsh and unforeseeable realities of the battlefield. It is as though the scientific-technological community takes on a life of its own in the design

and development of weapons, a life that becomes dangerously aloof to the needs of the soldier. Given this psychology, this urge to impress fellow scientists irrespective of cost or ultimate utility, it is scarcely remarkable that the defense budget skyrockets annually, and the list of unassimilable "problem" designs—such as the unlamented TFX under McNamara, the B-1 bomber, the M-1 tank, the Sergeant York, and the General Bradley troop carrier—keeps growing. In each of these, it would appear, the largely irresponsible imagination of technological designers has outstripped military practicality and basic need on the field.

Electronic and computerized equipment becomes more and more complicated as well as expensive. Soldiers dependent on such equipment are that much more vulnerable in war. When the cruiser *Stark* was badly crippled in the Persian Gulf by an Iraqi missile launched from a plane, it was not the complex, exquisitely sensitive radar computer system that alerted the ship's commander and crew but rather a sailor in the crow's nest—the oldest form of seagoing intelligence, we may assume, in history—who alerted the ship; too late, tragically, but that wasn't the sailor's fault.

When one reflects a moment on the failure of the computerized, electronic, mechanized system to do what it was supposed to do, warn of approaching planes and their missiles, and thinks also of the fact that in the end it was the human being using only his own eyesight who put up any kind of action whatever, we can't help mulling over something like the Strategic Defense Initiative, Star Wars. When it, in its trillion-dollar splendor, is finally deployed in space, with the security of the United States officially declared dependent upon it, will it perhaps turn out that just as the computerized *Stark* in Persian waters required the sailor in the crow's nest, the operation of SDI will require the eyes and ears of many thousands of civilians standing watch? Apparently we'll never have a chance to know, for the first use of SDI in a holocaustic emergency will be final, one way or the other.

Even if there were no Soviet Union or its equivalent to justify our monstrous military establishment, there would be, in sum, the whole self-perpetuating military-industrial complex and the technological-scientific elite that Eisenhower warned against. These have attained by now a mass and an internal dynamic capable of being their own justification for continued military spending. That is how far the military—its substance and its mystique—has become fused with economic and intellectual life. Take away the Soviet Union as crucial justification, and,

under Parkinson's Law, content of some kind will expand relentlessly to fill the time and space left.

Giving help and assistance to Parkinson's Law in the predictable prosperity of the military establishment in our time is what can only be called Wilson's Law. That is, Woodrow Wilson, whose fundamental axiom "What America touches, she makes holy" was given wording by his great biographer, Lord Devlin. The single most powerful cause of the present size and the worldwide deployment of the military establishment is the moralization of foreign policy and military ventures that has been deeply ingrained, especially in the minds of presidents, for a long time. Although it was Woodrow Wilson who, by virtue of a charismatic presence and a boundless moral fervor, gave firm and lasting foundation to American moralism, it was not unknown earlier in our history. The staying power of the Puritan image of America as a "city upon a hill" was considerable throughout the eighteenth and nineteenth centuries. America the Redeemer Nation was very much a presence in the minds of a great many Americans. American "exceptionalism" began in the conviction that God had created one truly free and democratic nation on earth and that it was to the best interests of all other nations to study America and learn from her. Even the conservative and essentially noninterventionist President Taft, in 1912, sent a detachment of marines into Nicaragua with instructions to announce to the Nicaraguan government that "The United States has a moral mandate to exert its influence for the general peace in Central America which is seriously menaced. . . . America's purpose is to foster true constitutional government and free elections."

But Taft's message was as nothing in the light of the kind of foreign policy and military ventures that began under Woodrow Wilson in the Great War—or, if it didn't begin under him, it was enlarged, diffused, and effectively made permanent. Ever since Wilson, with only rarest exceptions, American foreign policy has been tuned not to national interest but to national morality. In some degree morality has crept into rationalization of war in European countries too, but some responsibility for that has to be borne first by Wilson, then by Franklin Roosevelt, each of whom tirelessly preached the American Creed to such Old World types as Lloyd George, Clemenceau, and then Churchill in the Second World War. Those three, and many others, had thought that each of the two world wars was fought for national reasons, specifically to protect against German aggressiveness and then destroy it. Not so,

chorused Wilson and Roosevelt, the first of whom composed the Four teen Points, the second the Four Freedoms and then as encore the Atlantic Charter; and much of America has been singing those notes ever since.

Woodrow Wilson is without question the key mind; Roosevelt was simply a Wilsonian without the charismatic will and absolute power of mind that Wilson had. One thinks here of Karl Marx when someone reminded him that Hegel had opined that history occasionally repeats its events and great personages. Yes, said Marx, the first time as tragedy, the second as farce. Wilson was pure tragedy, Roosevelt farce. Wilson sought to invoke all the powers of his Calvinist god and his beloved city upon a hill, the United States of America, in order to bring about a world assembly, the League of Nations, that would realize for the entire planet the sweetness and light of America. This he sought, preached, and died for. Roosevelt, with much the same dream, spent World War II in pursuit of Josef Stalin, convinced that he, FDR, could smooth out the wrinkles in Uncle Joe, spruce him up, and make a New York Democrat out of him. That was farce—one we haven't escaped even yet.

Wilson above any other figure is the patriarch of American foreign policy moralism and interventionism. Churchill wrote, in his *The World Crisis* shortly after the Great War, that to Wilson alone had to go credit for America's entry into that war; everything depended "upon the workings of this man's mind and spirit to the exclusion of almost every other factor. . . . He played a part in the fate of nations incomparably more direct and personal than any other man."

At first Wilson fought and bled for neutrality in the war, for an America "too proud to fight" in the nasty imperialist wars of the Old World. He believed, and said to his intimates, that England and France were basically as guilty as Germany of crimes to humanity. But sometime in 1916 Wilson began to brood over his neutrality policy and to wonder if it was, in the end, the best means of putting America on the world stage as the city upon a hill needing only the eyes of all peoples on it to reform the world. Reform was the iron essence of Wilson's approach to the world. Born Calvinist, with a deep sense of sin and wickedness, and of the necessity of living by God's grace, and the necessity too of preaching and ministering this grace to the multitude, Wilson gradually transferred the content, but not the fire, of his faith to the American republic. His book *The State* enables us to see how in his mind the true church for him had become not the historic church,

the institutional church, but rather the state—provided, of course, that it was permeated by virtue, goodness, and redemptiveness.

The passion and wholeness of his desire to reform and to redeem can be seen first at Princeton where as president he put Princeton "in the nation's service." When he decided to reform the eating clubs, thus dividing university and trustees into bitter camps, he likened his work to that of the Redeemer in the cause of humanity; he did much the same thing when a little later he and Graduate Dean West were opposed as to where exactly to locate the new graduate school at Princeton. Virtually everything he touched became instantly transformed into an Armageddon. As president of Princeton, as governor for two years of New Jersey, and finally as president of the United States, Wilson burned and burned as moralist, seeing crises where others saw only problems, and endowing even his dispatch of American troops into Mexico, in retaliation for Mexican bandit crossings of the border, with a mighty purpose that would benefit all mankind.

World war was thus cut out for a mind of Wilson's passionate moralism. What he and America did had to be eternally right, before mankind and God. He had been appointed by God to serve the blessed American republic and to determine what was right in the war. His final decision, which germinated all through 1916, the year of his reelection under the banner of "He kept us out of the war," and came to thundering expression in early 1917, was that neutrality must be scrapped for intervention. He had been right in his policy of neutrality but the world and the war had changed; and now he must, with equal godliness and righteousness, do the very opposite—that is, plead with heart and soul for immediate American intervention.

Objectively prophets and fanatics change from time to time in their views of man and the world. Subjectively, however, they never change. Always the motivating principle in their lives is the same from year to year, decade to decade. It is only appearance, ever-deceptive appearance, that creates the illusion of change in the great man. Those close to Wilson learned within days of his conversion to intervention, often learned the hard way, never to speak to the President of anything that implied in the slightest that he had ever been other than a dedicated interventionist.

Actually, as Lord Devlin has stressed in his biography of Wilson, the President was in fact interventionist at heart from the very beginning; but he curbed his interventionism until the war and the international scene were just right. Devlin writes:

The Allies did not [Wilson believed] genuinely care about democracy and the right to self-government. He did; and he could proclaim his faith as they had not truly and sincerely done. *In his mind it was then and not before*, that the war to rid the world of tyranny and injustice really began. *What America touched she made holy* (emphasis added).

Thus the birth of twentieth-century moralism in foreign policy and war. From Wilson's day to ours the embedded purpose—sometimes articulated in words, more often not—of American foreign policy, under Democrats and Republicans alike oftentimes, has boiled down to America-on-a-Permanent-Mission; a mission to make the rest of the world a little more like America the Beautiful. Plant a little "democracy" here and tomorrow a little "liberalism" there, not hesitating once in a while to add a pinch of American-style social democracy.

Even before Wilson's earthshaking conversion from neutralism to intervention in early 1917, his moralism in foreign policy had been displayed to the world. Certain internal political troubles in Mexico attracted his mind and that of his populist-agrarian-pacifist secretary of state William Jennings Bryan. In 1913 the President and his secretary decided to move in. Wilson had the same dislike of professionals, diplomats and lawyers, that Roosevelt, Kennedy, Johnson, and Reagan would all have, each convinced that he by himself made the best and most enlightened foreign policy. Wilson recalled, for no given reason, his own ambassador to Mexico, immediately replacing him with a friend and former midwestern governor, John Lind. Before Lind left for Mexico, he was given a letter, written by the President himself to guide the new and inexperienced ambassador. Ambassador Lind was to make it clear from the start that the United States was not as other governments were. Never!

The letter informed Lind that the whole world expected America to act as Mexico's nearest friend; America was to counsel Mexico for its own good; indeed America would feel itself discredited if it had any selfish and ulterior purpose. In conclusion Mr. Lind was to inquire whether Mexico could give the civilized world a satisfactory reason for rejecting our good offices. Not surprisingly, the Mexican government repudiated, flouted, Wilson's great act of charity. Even when the United States, again not surprisingly, backed up its moral advice with offer of a loan, it too was rudely rejected. Wilson first adopted an air of patience, but that was soon followed by his demand that the president of Mexico step down from office. The United States, Wilson said,

would "employ such means as may be necessary to secure this result." Then, in words heard around the world, Woodrow the Redeemer said: "I am going to teach the South American republics to elect good men."

There is no need to detail what happened thereafter, first at Tampico, then at Veracruz, citing American gospel all the way: pretending to deepest wounding of American dignity in a minuscule contretemps at Tampico, then sending in several thousand naval troops at Veracruz, who inevitably met some resistance and, under orders, responded with rifles and guns, causing about three hundred Mexican dead and wounded, with fewer than a hundred American casualties, then confusedly retiring from the scene and leaving a distraught President Wilson ready to collapse in the arms of any international mediating tribunal—which he did in May 1914.

He had been blooded, though, as it were, and it was probably ineluctable that after due waiting, he would advance moralistically once again in a year or two, this time on the world stage. What America touches she makes holy. This was Wilson's adaptation of Christian blessedness to American foreign policy. He had to teach South American governments to elect good men. This earned the United States lasting impotence, save when force has been used, in all of Latin America. Next it became necessary to teach, through our intervention in the Great War, England, France, and the rest of Europe what true democracy and freedom were and how they were best seeded for posterity in all countries, great and small. Thus the birth of what shortly became known as Wilsonian idealism and became in oppressive fact American moralism abroad.

It is no wonder that Wilsonian moralism took hold of substantial segments of the American population. A whole generation of burgeoning political leaders, mostly in the East, was nurtured by Wilsonianism; they were in large part products of old wealth, of private schools and Ivy League universities, able to give ample time to international matters. Roosevelt was emphatically one of this generation, the more so perhaps in that he had served as assistant secretary of the navy under Wilson, had known him, had touched him, had had apostle's propinquity.

When World War II broke out in Europe, Roosevelt followed almost compulsively, as it seemed, the Wilson model. First neutrality, but in bemused contemplation of America's relation to the world. What America touched she made holy. It was vital therefore for her to proceed carefully. Roosevelt came to an earlier decision than Wilson had in his war; and that decision was, like Wilson's, one of intervention as soon as Congress could be persuaded to declare war. But in the meantime there was much that could be done in the way of Lend-Lease and, most especially, vital speeches and conferences in which the war's true purpose was given Rooseveltian eloquence. Thus the Four Freedoms speech before Congress in January 1941; then the Atlantic Charter conference with Churchill in August. Since the charter anticipated alliance with Stalin and the Soviet Union, which had only just been brought into the war against Hitler by virtue of the German invasion, the earlier Four Freedoms had to be cut to Two Freedoms in the charter. After all, Stalin's Russia was deficient, embarrassingly so, in freedoms.

Roosevelt had one, and only one, serious reason for taking the United States into the European war, a feat made possible in the end solely by Germany's declaration of war on the United States. That reason was the Wilson-derived mission of cleaning up the world after the war was won. Now comes the element of farce in Roosevelt that was lacking in Wilson. In Roosevelt's mind Wilson had lacked a true partner, some nation altogether free of wicked imperialism that the United States could properly, morally, work with. Britain, France, and most of the rest of Western Europe were excluded. All had indulged in imperialism. There was, however, one country that by its very nature was free of imperialism. That was Stalin's Communist Russia. He, Roosevelt, would work with Stalin during the war, acquiring his trust, perhaps civilizing him and thus Russia a little bit, and then forming a great American-Soviet partnership after the war to superintend the United Nations. All imperialism would be wiped out, all peoples, large or small, endowed with representative institutions, with human rights, and peace and democracy would be insured worldwide.

Roosevelt, like Wilson, lived just long enough to see the bitter fruits of his trust. The ink was hardly dry on the Yalta treaties and manifestoes when Stalin commenced flouting every one of the pieties and moralisms he had readily agreed to at Yalta. Yalta didn't give him Eastern Europe; his armies had already done that. What it gave Stalin was a sanctimonious imprimatur on the "democracy" and "freedom" and "free elections" the Soviets were imposing upon the subjugated Balkan and Baltic Europeans, together with Poland. Tragedy? No, farce: Can anything in political history be more farcical than an American president putting his trust in a dictator whose hands were bloodied forever by the millions he had starved, tortured, shot, and frozen in Siberia? Whose sworn purpose, inherited from Lenin, was the propagation of Communist revolution throughout the world? Who was openly contemptuous of Roosevelt, actually seeming to enjoy the company of the out-and-out imperialist—and longtime Communist foe—Churchill? Who made no bones about reducing not only Eastern but Western Europe—Britain and France foremost—to Third World status? It was Wilsonian moralism, albeit somewhat debased, that drove Roosevelt to his mission respecting the Soviet Union. He believed as ardently as Wilson had that What America Touches She Makes Holy.

Today, forty years later, moralism continues to inflame American foreign policy, Ronald Reagan being the devoutest successor thus far to Wilsonianism as interpreted by Roosevelt. He too loves to divide the world into the Good and the Evil, and to define American foreign policy as relentless punishment of the Evil by the Good—led by America. He too sees every Nicaragua, every Lebanon, Iran, Persian Gulf, and Grenada as a little bit of Armageddon, with all means justified by purity of mind.

And conceivably bankrupt. If our foreign policy were one of protecting our national security and looking out for the preservation of our political nationhood and general well-being, from time to time doing what little good for others our capacities permitted, we would not require a six-hundred-ship navy, one bulging with supercarriers, battleships, and weaponry better suited to the now historic battles of Jutland in World War I and Midway in World War II than to defense of ourselves against Soviet aggression. General de Gaulle correctly referred to "America's itch to intervene."

When we intervene the act is almost compulsively cloaked, even as Wilson's acts were, in rhetoric of pious universalism. We use our variants of Kant's categorical imperative in international affairs. We must always explain that behind our intervention lies the imperative of moral goodness—nothing less. For so simple, practical, and obviously necessary a thing as our quick aid to Turkey and Greece immediately after World War II, at England's request, a Kantian rhetoric had to be devised: that our action sprang from our resolute insistence that freedom will be supported everywhere in the world.

A few years later, in 1960, President Kennedy gladdened the hearts of all political moralists in America with his vow that we would "pay any price, bear any burden, meet any hardship . . . to assure the survival and the success of liberty." And so we have. Less apocalyptically Jimmy

Carter as president in the late 1970s declared that "a nation's domestic and foreign policies should be derived from the same standards of ethics, honesty and morality which are characteristic of the individual citizens of the nation. . . . There is only one nation in the world which is capable of true leadership among the community of nations and that is the United States of America."

Such language would surely arouse the mingled concern and amusement of the Framers. It was a constitution for one nation that they designed, not one for the prosecution in all parts of the world of the native values of the thirteen colonies. There is none of the world-saving rhetoric to be found in our constitution that would be found a decade later in the successive constitutions of the French Revolution. Treatment of the armed forces is spare indeed in the American constitution, and it is oriented austerely to "the common defence." The purpose of the whole document is that of establishing "a more perfect union," not that of spreading America's sweetness and light to the needy world. Nor is there hint of worldwide soul-saving in *The Federalist.* The closest to a treatment of America and the world is Federalist No. 2 by John Jay, and it is directed solely to the necessity of protecting American riches from "Foreign Powers."

George Kennan is the most notable of living Americans to understand the purpose of a foreign policy in our time. In 1948 he argued that we should stop putting ourselves in the position of "being our brothers' keeper and refrain from offering moral and ideological advice." More recently he has said that American interventions in the world can be justified only if the practices against which they are directed are "seriously injurious to our interest, rather than to our sensibilities." Too many of our foreign interventions, Kennan declares, have served "not only the moral deficiencies of others" but "the positive morality of ourselves." It is seen as the moral duty of the United States "to detect these lapses on the part of others, to denounce them before the world," and even to assure "that they were corrected." How often, Kennan also notes acerbically, the purported moral conscience of the United States turns out to be a set of moralisms limited in fact to a single faction or special interest group. That American foreign policy should be framed within the borders of morality, Kennan does not doubt. Americans have the right to see to it that the government never acts immorally abroad or at home. But it is a far cry from eschewing the immoral and locating the bounds of morality to the kind of assertions just cited from Wilson, Roosevelt, Kennedy, and Carter.

South African apartheid is indeed a repugnant system—as is the system of one or other kind found in a large number of contemporary governments on the planet. We should and do wish apartheid early disappearance, as we do the repressive practices of the Soviets and their satellite governments. But on what basis does the United States attack apartheid? The gods must have been convulsed when, under the heavy pressure of black organizations and student bodies across America, our government was pressed into service for disinvestment and, if possible, sanctions and even a blockading of South African ports. The United States of America, Mrs. Grundy herself, overbearingly teaching another people how to be decent to blacks? America was the very last civilized country to abolish out-and-out black slavery—and this only by Lincoln's agonizing change of mind on the subject and use of war powers—and then, put the millions of freed blacks in a state of unspeakable segregation—a type of segregation more punishing in many respects than what exists in South Africa, a segregation that finally began to be broken only in the 1960s in a crusade for civil rights that barely missed being a revolution, a full century after emancipation from legal slavery.

There is another form of blindness to reality that can and often does spring from minds beset by moralism and ideology. This is likely to be present more often in the political Right than the Left. It is well illustrated by the fever of "world Communism" that came over right-wing groups in this country in the late 1940s. Everything unpleasant that happened in the world, whether in Egypt, Kerala, or China, was believed to be part of a world conspiracy hatched by the Kremlin. When, in the late 1950s, there were unmistakable signs of a growing rift between Communist China and Communist Russia, the official position of the United States, a position largely initiated by the Right, was for some time that no rift existed, that Mao's China was a Soviet pawn.

Those who knew their Chinese-Russian history were not at all inclined to doubt the existence of growing hostility between Mao and the Kremlin, for hostility between the two empires, Russian and Chinese, went back several centuries and had not infrequently broken out in fierce fighting. It was the Chinese who coined the name "Great Bear" for the Russian empire. Granted that Mao was a Communist as were Stalin and his successors. Only eyeless ideology could have prevented leading American figures in and out of government from recognizing that just as capitalist nations can engage in bitter warfare with one another, so, obviously, can and will Communist nations. We might

have been alerted by the early disaffection after World War II between Russia and Yugoslavia—so confidently but ridiculously denoted as a Russian pawn by our moralist-ideologists in the beginning—and then Albania. Historical, geopolitical, and fundamental military-strategic considerations will always triumph over purely ideological alliances, unless of course one nation has been taken over by cretins, which has assuredly not been the case with either China or Russia.

Moralists from the Right, blinded by their private picture of "world Communism," fail to see the undying persistence in the world of the nation-state, be it capitalist or communist. Nationalism has spawned more wars than religion—and Communism is a latter-day religion—ever has or ever will. All the while Stalin was bending, rending, torturing, and terrorizing, always shaping Russia into an aggressive military nation, with Marxism-Leninism its established religion, our right-wing moralistic ideologists in this country were seeing stereotypes, pictures in their heads, of the defunct Trotskyist dream of Russia not a nation but instead a vast spiritual force leading all mankind to the Perdition.

This kind of moralism is still a menace to our foreign policy. It is the mentality that converts every incident in the world into an enormously shrewd, calculated operation by the KGB. To sweep every North-South happening into an East-West framework is the preoccupation of the Right—religious and secular. So was it the preoccupation of the Right when for years, all evidence notwithstanding, it insisted that because Russia and China were both officially Communist, therefore they had to be one in faith, hope, and destiny. Richard Nixon was and is no ideologue; neither is Henry Kissinger. Result? Our celebrated entry into China and what now appears to be a very genuine thawing of Communist orthodoxy.

Vigilance is a cardinal virtue in international affairs. But when it hardens into an unblinking stare off into the horizon, a great deal in the vital foreground is overlooked. The plainest trend in the world since the death of Stalin is the gradual, halting, often spastic, movement of the Soviet Union from its iron age to something that, while not yet entirely clear, is a long way removed from the Russia that under Stalin in 1945 very seriously contemplated a European sphere of interest that included Western as well as Eastern Europe. It is entirely likely that only the atom bomb, then in the exclusive possession of the United States, posed a threat serious enough to dissuade Stalin. After that came the Marshall Plan and then NATO, and the Stalinist dream of suze-

rainty over Western Europe collapsed along with the Stalinist reality of permanent terror over the entire Russian people.

The Soviet Union remains an enigma. It remains also a dangerous adversary in the world, the one other superpower. It bears American watching and American military preparation is necessary for any of several possible threats. But to pretend that the Russia of Gorbachev is still, just under the skin, the Russia of Josef Stalin is as nonsensical as was the inflexible belief in some quarters back in the 1950s that Maoist China was a willing pawn of the Soviet Union—or the still earlier dogmatism that insisted long after the fact that Tito's Yugoslavia was but a Stalinist plaything. I take some pleasure in citing some words I wrote more than a quarter of a century ago:

> When I am told that Russia—or China—is dangerous to the United States and to the free world, I can understand this and agree. When it is suggested that the United States should suspend nuclear testing, as an example to the rest of the world, I can understand this and emphatically disagree. But when I am told that the real danger to the United States is something called "world Communism" and that our foreign policy must begin with a 'true understanding' of the moral nature of Communism, and not rest until Communism has been stamped out everywhere, I am lost. Meaning has fled into a morass of irrelevancies, half-truths, and apocalyptic symbols.*

No nation in history has ever managed permanent war and a permanent military Leviathan at its heart and been able to maintain a truly representative character. The transformation of the Roman Republic into the dictatorial empire was accomplished solely through war and the military. Is the United States somehow the divinely created exception to this ubiquitous fact of world history? Not, assuredly, if instead of a foreign policy based upon national security and finite objectives associated with this security, we indulge ourselves in a foreign policy with an "itch to intervene," and a purpose flowing out of the preposterous fantasy of a world recreated in the image and likeness of that city on a hill known as the United States of America. That way lies total confusion abroad and an ever more monolithic and absolute military bureaucracy at home.

---

*Commentary, September 1961. p. 202–203

II

THE NEW ABSOLUTISM

Any returned Framers of the Constitution would be quite as shocked by the extent and depth of the power of the national state in American lives today as they would be by war and the gargantuan military. The most cursory reading of the Constitution itself tells us that behind the labors which produced this document lay an abiding fear, distrust, hatred of the kinds of political power identified with the government of George III and with the centralized despotisms, such as France, Prussia, and Russia, on the Continent. Add to reading of the Constitution even a scanning of the Federalist Papers followed perhaps by a brief dipping into the annals of the Convention, and there can be no doubt of what the Framers most definitely did not want: a highly centralized, unitary political Leviathan.

That, however, is what their work of art has become in two centuries. And with this has come, has had to come, a political absolutism over Americans that would not be lessened or mitigated for the Framers by its manifestly, unchallengeably democratic foundations. There is not the slightest question but that ours is still what Lincoln called it, government of the people, by the people, for the people. But it is still absolutist.

The fact is, democracy can yield a higher degree of absolutism in its relation to the individual than is found in any of the so-called absolute, divine-right monarchies of the early modern era in European history. Louis XIV's *L'état, c'est moi*, notorious for its purported absolutism, was actually a confession of weakness whether the king knew it or not. In between divine-right monarchs and any possible absoluteness of rule lay a thick stratum of intermediate authorities, starting with church and aristocracy, that made farce of any claim to personal authority. The absolute state of the sixteenth century is in fact as much a sham as was the Holy Roman Empire before it. What Walter

Lippmann wrote a half-century ago in his *A Preface to Morals* remains apposite:

> A state is absolute in the sense which I have in mind when it claims the right to a monopoly of all the force within the community, to make war, to make peace, to conscript life, to tax, to establish and disestablish property, to define crime, to punish disobedience, to control education, to supervise the family, to regulate personal habits, and to censor opinions.
>
> The modern state claims all of these powers, and in the matter of theory, there is no real difference in the size of the claim between communists, fascists, and democrats. There are lingering traces in the American constitutional system of the older theory that there are inalienable rights which the government may not absorb. But these rights are not really inalienable for they can be taken away by constitutional amendment. There is no theoretical limit upon the power of ultimate majorities which create the civil government. There are only practical limits. They are restrained by inertia, by prudence, even good will. But ultimately and theoretically they claim absolute authority against all churches, associations, and persons within their jurisdictions.*

Much of the energy of political intellectuals, of what I shall call in this chapter the political clerisy, has gone since the New Deal into the demonstration that although state authority has grown constantly heavier, reaching more and more recesses of life, there has not been any real compromise of liberty, inasmuch as the authority has the sanction of the people, and the theory of democracy (the theory at any rate of Jean-Jacques Rousseau) holds that no people can by its volition tyrannize itself. I shall come back to this later.

In our politics as well as in our military, the present age begins with the Great War and with Woodrow Wilson's powerful effect upon America.

"All men of military genius," wrote Tocqueville, "are fond of centralization and all men of centralizing genius are fond of war." The history of the United States is ample illustration of the general soundness of Tocqueville's principle. If we look at the presidents, starting with Andrew Jackson, who if they have not actually relished and sought out war have nevertheless taken to it and to the use of war powers rather more easily than others have, we must include some of our greatest presidents. There was Jackson and Lincoln (who was exceeded by no

---

A Preface to Morals. New York, 1929. p. 80

one in the American presidency in alacrity in precipitating a war and in the free use of war powers during it); there was Theodore Roosevelt, Wilson, Franklin Roosevelt, Kennedy, Johnson, Nixon, and, very much in the procession, Ronald Reagan.

In each of these presidents there is a conspicuous readiness to turn to political centralization, bureaucracy, and the heaping up of powers, so far as possible, in the central government even at the expense of a strictly read Constitution. Woodrow Wilson is the master of them all, in respect to his union of strong instincts toward centralization and use of war powers. His political, economic, social, and even intellectual reorganization of America in the short period 1917–1919 is one of the most extraordinary feats in the long history of war and polity. Through artfully created board, commission, and agency he and his worshipful lieutenants, drawn from all areas—business, academia, law, even entertainment—revolutionized America to a degree never reached in such a short period of time by either the French or the Russian revolution. And Wilson, let it be remembered, in diametrical opposition to the Robespierres and Lenins, demobilized completely the militarized society he had built only a couple of years earlier.

But it was by no means the war imperative alone that spurred Wilson to his work of political power in the Great War. He was an ardent prophet of the state, the state indeed as it was known to European scholars and statesmen. He had written a book on it. He preached it, especially in its American revelation, as no one before had. From him supremely comes the politicization, the centralization, and the commitment to bureaucracy of American society during the past seventy-five years. He only began this evolution, and what he did was chiefly apparent during the two years we were at war with Germany. But the wartime powers assumed by the national government proved to be durable seeds, and by 1939, only twenty years from the time when they had been nominally jettisoned for good, Wilsonian centralization and collectivization were, under FDR, as pervasive as they had been during the Great War. Ever since there has been a unitary, unilinear pattern of development to be seen, only rarely punctuated by sign of reversal, that has centralization of government its embedded goal, with all forms of decentralization and pluralism declared by political elites to be mere eruptions of the dead hand of the past. From Wilson through FDR, Truman, Kennedy, Johnson, Nixon, and Reagan we have seen America develop from its state of innocence in 1914 down to the highly sophisticated power complex that marks American democracy today.

Wilson began it chiefly within the context provided by the Great War. Within a few months he had transformed traditional, decentralized, regional, and localist America into a war state that at its height permeated every aspect of life in America. I shall describe some of the political changes he effected, in a moment. But I think the following passage from the English historian A. J. P. Taylor is an important prefatory note. It is directed to English experience but it is highly relevant to America:

> Until August 1914 a sensible, law-abiding Englishman could pass through life and hardly notice the existence of the state beyond the post office and the policeman. . . . He could travel abroad or leave his country forever without a passport or any sort of official permission. He could exchange his money without restriction or limit. He could buy goods from any country in the world on the same terms as he bought goods at home. For that matter a foreigner could spend his life in the country without permit and without informing the police. . . .
>
> All this was changed by the impact of the Great War. . . . The state established a hold over its citizens which though relaxed in peace time, was never to be removed and which the Second World War was again to increase. The history of the English people and the English State merged for the first time."*

Much the same merging of people and state took place under Wilson after Congress declared war on Germany in April 1917. Congress not only obeyed Wilson's request for a state of war—made with the same prophet's intensity that had, until a few months before, supported his insistence upon neutrality—it also showered war powers on him beyond the dream of an early Caesar. Wilson accepted them as if he had created them himself. "It is not an army we must shape and train for war," he said, "it is a nation." His words came from the mind and heart alike.

No one knew better than Professor Wilson, student of American government, just how unfitted for the demands of the Great War raging in Europe the American constitutional system was. Founded on the sacredness of states' rights, permeated with the philosophy of a weak central government which by design left all powers possible to the states, and crowned, as it were, by the doctrine of separation of powers in the national government, the Constitution was only too obviously a charter for peace, not war. That is, unless or until the Constitution was

---

English History: 1914–45. Oxford University Press, 1965. p. 1

set aside for the duration, to be succeeded by a more practical scheme
in which, effectively, the entire government of the United States would
be delegated to the president alone—for the duration of the war, no
longer.

Not Britain, not France, not even the hated Germany had the kind
of dictatorial power vested in any one figure or office that the United
States did shortly after American participation in the war began. Gone
completely was the political character of government that had made the
United States almost a curiosity in the eyes of European scholars and
statesmen, who professed indeed to be able to find no true sovereignty
in America nor even a "theory of the State," as Lord Bryce put it in
his widely acclaimed *The American Commonwealth*. In a word, decentralization was banished; centralization ruled supreme. Charles and
Mary Beard wrote:

> In a series of the most remarkable laws ever enacted in Washington, the
> whole economic system was placed at his command. Under their provisions
> the President was authorized to requisition supplies for the army without
> stint, to fix the prices of commodities so commanded, arrange a guaranteed
> price for wheat, take possession of the mines, factories, packing houses,
> railways, steam ships, and all means of communication and operate them
> through public agencies and license the importation, manufacture, storage
> and distribution of all necessities."*

Novel boards and agencies were fashioned to assimilate the whole
American economic and social fabric in their workings. The most powerful of the economic bodies was probably the War Industries Board.
From it, and it alone, came the authorizations, licenses, and permis-
sions—and with these, absolute orders and mandates—by which the
American economy operated during the war. Railroads, mines, and
other interstate industries were nationalized, made wards of Washington, D.C. There was a War Labor Policies Board, a Shipping Board,
a Food Administration, and before the ending of the war many another
centralized, national authority created by the Congress or the executive
in which absolute power was vested in its own sphere. Nothing even in
Europe equaled the degree and intensity of American political absolutism during its brief period in the Great War. General Ludendorff
acknowledged American initiative in this respect when, in a last great
effort at German victory, he instituted "War Socialism." Lenin's War

---

*Charles and Mary Beard, *The Rise of American Civilization*. New York, 1930. p 635

Communism, with its thicket of centralized agencies of regulation or ownership, was indebted to what America did first and so successfully. Mussolini's early structure of Fascism in Italy, with its powerful national agencies controlling factory production, labor relations, the railroads, took a leaf from the American wartime book of three years earlier.

The blunt fact is that when under Wilson America was introduced to the War State in 1917, it was introduced also to what would later be known as the total, or totalitarian, state. There is this important point to add: The acts which transformed laissez-faire, entrepreneurial America into a total state for the duration were acts of Congress, not of a revolutionary minority as in Russia and Italy. And, to repeat, there was not the slightest difficulty after the armistice in putting a terminal date to the various elements of the total state, though not all of the elements—railroads, unions, other industries and associations—appeared to be happy in their return to freedom from the state. Certain figures, intellectuals and business executives included, began to think of techniques for escape from that freedom. Considerable thought was given to ideas, for example, that would under FDR go into the National Recovery Administration, the life of which was rudely ended by the Supreme Court in the early thirties.

But with full understanding of the democratic instauration of the Wilson War State and of its equally democratic termination a couple of years later, it is entirely proper, nay, obligatory, to see this state as total, as a brief forerunner to the kinds of state that would be "managerial states" in the thirties including those known as totalitarian. Just about everything in America that was susceptible of being brought under the direct rule of the federal government in Washington, was brought under.

Wilson had shrewdly realized that in mobilizing the all-important industries and services in the war effort, some of the popular mind needed also to be mobilized, to be fixed, willingly or unwillingly, on the goal of military victory. He brought George Creel, previously a newspaper reporter and writer, to head the ministry of war information, one that turned out almost immediately to be an agency of war psychology, morale, patriotism, and vigilance against any excess of free thought in the country. There is no record of Wilson ever disapproving a single act of Creel's. Creel saw his job as that of bringing, through every conceivable instrument, the patriotism of the American people up to the highest possible level. After all, at least half of the American people had been strongly opposed to American intervention, and they included

what used to be known as hyphenated Americans, those naturalized or native citizens who sprang from ethnic minorities, starting with the German-Americans. There were Americans, the hundred-percenters argued, who weren't as dedicated to war and victory as they might be. They must be watched and monitored. They must also be apprized directly of how important their patriotism was, to the country and to themselves. Several hundred thousand Americans volunteered, when called for, to be neighborhood watchers, that is, of their own neighborhoods, and to report to appropriate agencies, including the police, any suspicious scraps of conversation or any reports of such scraps. Creel also had the inspiration to create what he called the four-minute men. These numbered some seventy thousand at their height. They were empowered by the President to speak for four minutes on the war before any club, lodge, school, labor union, service club, whatever, whether invited or not, theoretically to give war information—their real purpose being, of course, that of lauding the war aim and the government.

The schools and churches were affected. Throughout America, citizens' groups, and sometimes more official agencies, went through schoolbooks in order to remove all pieces written or otherwise composed by Germans, no matter how classic they had become. (I recall vividly that as long after the war as 1926, none of the music books in the school I attended had a single composition by a German—all such had been removed in 1917.) Multifold "suggestions" were received from Washington or local patriotic win-the-war groups to bring the living reality of the war into every class, no matter what the subject. The churches, or a great many of them, yielded to the pressure of propaganda from the Creel office. There was no want, apparently, of preachers who were only too willing to present arms almost literally from the pulpit. *Preachers Present Arms* is the unappetizing but accurate title of one major study of the militarization of the American pulpit.

There were millions of Americans with German names, and a substantial number of them knew the torment and humiliation of being pilloried for their German ancestry; more than a few of them found it expedient to anglicize their names—from Weber to Wuybur, for example—the while American patriots were transforming hamburger to "liberty steak." In 1917 the Espionage Act was passed by Congress at the behest of the White House, making life even more difficult for German-Americans no matter how long they had lived in this country; and the following year the even more deadly Sedition Act was passed, making it easy to charge and often indict the most casual comment in public

as seditious to nation and war effort. Eugene Debs, Socialist and famous labor leader, spoke publicly against American participation in the war, for which he received a ten-year sentence in a federal prison. Even when the war was over, Wilson coldly refused to commute sentence or pardon Debs. President Harding pardoned Debs within days after he took office in 1921. Under the Espionage and Sedition acts just under two hundred thousand Americans were accused, or indicted, or found guilty and fined heavily or imprisoned for remarks heard or overheard in public. Turning in "German spies" or "pro-Germans" became a veritable sport for large numbers of American patrioteers in 1917 and 1918.

And yet despite the atmosphere of outright terror in the lives of a considerable minority of Americans, despite the food shortages for civilians, despite the presence throughout the country of superpatriots serving the government as neighborhood watchers for the purpose of reporting any act or word that seemed suspicious, despite the virtual militarization of the local schools and their textbooks, despite the maleficent custom of white feathers being pinned by women volunteers on the lapels of men seen rightly or wrongly as slackers—despite all this, many Americans seemed to become fond of the War State. Lost neighborhood, local, and other liberties didn't seem too high a price to pay for the economic benefits in the form of high wages, props to unionism, quick and generally favorable arbitration agreements for workers, and the novel availability of spendable money, cash in hand. And how exhilarating to see the speed with which the national government could move in matters where local governments stalled and stalled.

It was all a great lesson, slowly but surely learned by those of nationalistic disposition: that it is far easier to promote the state's power when a trade-off in the form of economic and social goods is effected. Also, crisis, whether actual war or something else, is a valuable means of acceleration of political power. Wilson, whose feeling for the state was almost religious, sensed this. So while he spurred on the Bernard Baruchs, Hugh Johnsons, Gerard Swopes, and other appointed, absolute industrial czars in their planning and managing of the economy, he also found the time to give aid and sustenance to the class of political intellectuals just coming into existence, those for whom service to the central state in the interest of the people would become a creed. Wilson had been impressed by a book by one of them in 1909: *The Promise of American Life* by Herbert Croly, a plea for the conversion of the abstract, constitutional state into a national community. Wilson was similarly impressed by a young Socialist just out of Harvard, Walter

Lippmann, whom he placed in the secret group of scholars that was at work drawing up the Fourteen Points and possible postwar realignments in Europe. I shall say more about the New Class a little later in this chapter.

The Wilson War State was from the beginning a structure of unprecedented mixture of parts—in Europe as well as in America. On the one hand it was humanitarian to the core: in high wages approved by the government, improved working conditions, moderation of ethnic tensions in the workplace, and a variety of reforms aimed at the working class and the indigent. To many workers in the Northeast and Midwest, these reforms added up to the kind of socialism they had learned about in Europe and preached after coming to the United States. But the other side of the War State was different, making it difficult of acceptance even by academic socialists and liberals. This was the repressive side, the side presided over by George Creel, the side of repression, intimidation, and quick, summary justice. It was the side of the ugly "Palmer Raids" by the attorney general, A. Mitchell Palmer, with no known dissent from President Wilson. For all the delicate socialistic touches given the war economy by the government, there was no mercy extended to even the most peaceful and law-abiding of socialists and social democrats when the fancy seized Palmer. Throughout 1919 the raids took place, rarely if ever based upon legal warrants, invading without notice the homes, businesses, even churches of suspected socialists, anarchists, and ordinary dissenters.

This was the divided legacy of the War State of 1917–1919: on the one hand a centralized, planned economy that seemed to work and work well, at least with the stimulus of the Great War; on the other hand a police-state atmosphere, with the watchers serving secretly as monitors of their neighborhoods, ever ready to report a suspicious remark or alleged remark; and the Four-Minute Men empowered by law to invade any meeting, civil or religious, in order to warn of any departures from strict and absolute support of the war—and the Palmer Raids.

On the whole it was the first legacy that survived, the second that eroded away under the heady influences of the 1920s and then the chilling effects of the Great Depression. The national state never really went back to its prewar laissez-faire identity. Return to Normalcy, which President Harding made into a kind of national slogan—at least as a chapter title thenceforth in American history books—was really not much of a return. If nothing else there were the dispositions toward the

national state acquired under the heady atmosphere of the Wilson War State.

But there was more. To begin with, the Eighteenth Amendment passed in 1919 after years of work toward it by teetotalers. However tempted Wilson might have been (he loathed it for its effect on the working class) to ban liquor as a war measure, he desisted; it would be pushing American tolerance of lost liberties too far, he may have thought. But what a monarch might draw back from, the people can confront and adopt. It is possible that all that saved America from an insurrection during the 1920s was the fact that the Volstead Act, passed to implement the Prohibition amendment, was from the start lightly and loosely enforced. The bootlegger became almost a heroic figure.

Another blow for the residual power of the democratic state was yet another constitutional amendment passed while a couple of million American men were in uniform, mostly abroad: the Nineteenth Amendment, in 1920, which forbade thenceforth any state or munici-pality from denying women the vote. For the many millions of zealots for states' rights as well as for the perhaps larger number of male chauvinists, the Nineteenth Amendment was bitter brew, calculated, it was widely believed, to subvert the family and to bring the republic down in a soggy feminist mess.

Furthermore, in 1924, the mild President Coolidge—alleged physi-ocrat in economic views and veritable anarchist in fear of the central state, so it was said—appointed J. Edgar Hoover to take direction of the Bureau of Investigation with clear instructions to improve and enlarge it and set it on a track that would in a very few years make it the first federal police force in American history.

These are highlights, of course. But in dozens of laws passed and decrees issued, the 1920s proved to be anything but a return to the America of the first decade of the century. In national projects of reclamation, in agriculture, in educational assistance to the states and cities, in social work for the indigent, and in investigations of central-planning possibilities, the federal government often came closer in the twenties to the Wilson War State than to anything that had preceded it in American history.

Throughout the 1920s a vein of thought was visible that can be nicely summed up by the title of one of the books that nourished the vein: *We Planned in War, Why Not in Peace?* Such journals as *The New Republic* and *The Nation* and writers like John Dewey, Stuart

Chase, Walter Lippmann, and literally dozens of university social scientists kept up a steady beat for the increased partnership of the state and the economy, one akin to that which had existed during the Great War but, of course, without war and without the repression of civil rights that had gone with it. Even some of the heads of great corporations spoke out in ways that would have shocked the business titans of a generation earlier. The state was very much in the air in the twenties as the possible pivot of what could be a national community.

The Great Depression hit the United States at the end of the 1920s, to be met within a couple of years by the New Deal under Franklin Roosevelt. He had served Wilson as assistant secretary of the navy in World War I, and had been one of those thrilled by Wilson personally and by certain aspects of the War State. It is interesting to speculate on what form American response to the depression of the 1930s would or might have taken had it not been for the legacy of government planning and regimentation left by the First World War. It is at least possible that some kind of response by government and business beginning in 1933 would have been a great deal less centralized and bureaucratized than what actually came into being.

In striking measure the response made by FDR and his chief aides, men like Raymond Moley and Rexford Tugwell, Henry Wallace and Harold Ickes, one and all political intellectuals rather than businessmen, was simply a revival of structures and relationships which had characterized the Wilson War State. With altered names, many of the same production, labor, banking, and agricultural boards of World War I were simply dusted off, as it were, and with new polish set once again before the American people. This time the enemy was not Germany or any other foreign power but the Depression; this did not, however, prevent Roosevelt from literally declaring war on it and likening himself and his associates to a "trained and loyal army willing to sacrifice for the good of a common discipline." In his inaugural address in 1933 the President pledged to "assume unhesitatingly the leadership of this great army of our people dedicated to a disciplined attack upon our common problems." He perceived America, he said, as a vast army needing only to be mobilized for the war against depression to begin.

The New Deal is a great watershed not only in twentieth-century American history but in our entire national history. In it the mesmerizing idea of a *national community*—an idea that had been in the air since the Progressive era, featured in books by Herbert Croly, Walter Lipp-

mann, John Dewey, and others, and had come into full but brief
existence in 1917 under the stimulus of war—was now at long last to
be initiated in peacetime, as a measure to combat the evils of capitalism
and its "economic royalists."

"At the heart of the New Deal," William Schambra has percep-
tively written, "was the resurrection of the national idea, the renewal
of the vision of national community. Roosevelt sought to pull America
together in the face of its divisions by an appeal to national duty,
discipline, and brotherhood; he aimed to restore the sense of local
community, at the national level. He once explained the New Deal's
'drastic changes in the methods and forms of the functions of government' by noting that 'we have been extending to our national life the
old principle of the local community.' "

Schambra continues:

> The New Deal public philosophy, then, may be understood as a resurrec-
> tion of the progressive vision of national community: a powerful central
> government in the service of the national idea, a president articulating that
> idea and drawing Americans together as neighbors, or as soldiers facing a
> common enemy. This vision of the national community, this public philos-
> ophy, would continue to dominate American politics for three decades, and
> to this day it strikes a responsive chord in the hearts of millions of Ameri-
> cans. As Irving Howe wrote recently, the "lasting contribution of the
> Roosevelt era" was the "socialization of concern, the vision of society as
> community."*

The New Deal did not, alas, have any discernible impact on the
economic problems of deflation, unemployment, reduced profits, and
the virtual disappearance of growth. In this respect we were somewhat
behind not only England but Hitler's Germany as late as 1938, which
was well before either power commenced rearmament on a significant
scale. Neither country suffered the deep recession of 1937, a recession
within a depression, that America did.

It was therefore a matter of supreme luck for the New Deal and the
national community dream that World War II broke out in September
1939. For the war not only brought the Depression at last to an end
in America—once war orders from Europe assumed massive enough
force to break all vicious circles in the plight of the American economy—but there was, once again, war to serve the drive toward national

---

*The Quest for a New Public Philosophy. American Enterprise Institute. Washington,
D.C., 1983

community, the while it deluged and intoxicated many millions of long-unemployed, dispirited American workers with high wages, ample jobs, and a very cascade of long-sought economic and social reforms. American soldiers seemed less inspired by war, more prone to seek draft deferment at almost any cost, but from early on, they were promised educational, home-buying, and business benefits after the war that would make it all worthwhile.

Without doubt the idea of national community burns brightly in the American consciousness at the present time. Initiated by President Roosevelt, the idea has been nourished, watered, and tended in one degree or other by each succeeding president. When Governor Mario Cuomo of New York delivered his now historic speech in San Francisco in 1984 before the Democratic Convention, he made the national community his central, spellbinding theme. Over and over he referred to "family" and "community," and once or twice to "wagon train," meaning in each use, not the actual family or local community or wagon train crossing the prairies of earlier America, but rather the national state, the centralized, collectivized, and bureaucratized national state of this late part of the century.

Perhaps only under the camouflage of the rhetoric of freedom is the actual power of the state increased more easily than under the camouflage of the rhetoric of community. The greater despots of history, which is to say twentieth-century history, like Lenin, Mussolini, Hitler, Mao, and Castro, have turned to both rhetorics—of freedom and community. Here the Rousseauian vision in Western political thought plays a major role. Rousseau designed, in his *The Social Contract* and even more perhaps in his *Discourse on Political Economy,* the most powerful state to be found anywhere in political philosophy. There must be, wrote Rousseau, a social contract among the people. "Each of us puts his person and all his power in common under the supreme direction of the general will, and, in our corporate capacity, we receive each member as an indivisible part of the whole."

Properly understood, Rousseau insists, there is "the total alienation of each associate, together with all his rights, to the whole community; for, in the first place, as each gives himself absolutely, the conditions are the same for all and, this being so, no one has any interest in making them burdensome to others." True community for Rousseau is not anything arising out of kinship, religion, ethnicity, or language. True community lies only within the purview of the state, the state conse-

crated to the virtue of its citizens, to be sure, but the state, once and for all. The general will, to which Rousseau gives absolute sovereignty, is the collective will purged of all marks of purely individual wills—with their egoisms, avarices, and selfishnesses.

But, Rousseau enjoins, the absoluteness of power of the general will and the new political community resting on the social compact, is only freedom, real freedom, in disguise:

> In order then that the social compact may not be an empty formula, it tacitly includes the undertaking, which alone can give force to the rest, that whoever refuses to obey the general will shall be compelled to do so by the whole body. This means nothing less than that he will be forced to be free; for this is the condition which, by giving each citizen to his country, secures him against all personal dependence.

From this it is really but a short step for Rousseau to the idea of a civil religion, the note on which he ends his *Social Contract.* The civil religion, Rousseau insists, is to be limited to a few common articles which are "not exactly dogmas," being more nearly in the nature, he writes, of "social sentiments." While the sovereign "can compel no one to believe them, it can banish from the State whoever does not believe them. . . . If any one, after publicly recognizing these dogmas, behaves as if he does not believe them, let him be punished by death: he has committed the worst of all crimes, that of lying before the law."

It remains for Rousseau only to point out that while the sovereign general will is created by the social compact and is the emanation of the whole people, the ascertainment of this will on any given issue does not absolutely require such devices as voting and systems of representation. In fact, especially in larger states, these are undesirable. They would tend, Rousseau explains, to corrupt the purity of the general will by making appeal to the mere "will of all" with its undesirable attribute of majority opinion. Fortunately, Rousseau continues, elections, votes, and representatives are "hardly ever necessary where the government is well-intentioned. . . . For the rulers well know that the general will is always on the side which is most favorable to the public interest, that is to say, the most equitable; so that it is needful only to act justly to be certain of following the general will."

And whoever heard of a government, from ancient imperial Egypt down to Stalin's Soviet Union, that did not believe it acted justly? We are more likely to ascribe the totalitarian mystique in modern Western

thought to Marx, with his "dictatorship of the Proletariat," or to Lenin and the "dictatorship of the Party," or to Hitler and his "dictatorship of the Volkstum," that is, the true German people, than to Rousseau, but in all truth it was he who converted the democratic ethos into the totalitarian dogma.

Rousseau is the man of the hour at this juncture in American political thought. Unlike Marx, for more than half a century the invisible guru of the clerisy in America, Rousseau is clean; that is, without the tarnish that the practical reality of the Soviet Union has put on Marx's name for the last seventy years. The only major event or emergence in modern history that Rousseau can be connected with is the French Revolution. The Jacobins virtually memorized him in order to guide the revolution to its totalitarian apogee in 1794. But who today remembers or gives thought to the French Revolution?

Rousseau's paean to the absolute power of the state is offset in any event for most intellectuals by the other, seemingly unconnected, faces he presents to readers: the face of the romantic in his novel La Nouvelle Héloïse, on the surface no more than an idyll of spontaneous affection and love; the face of the artless believer in the purity of the state of nature and in the intrinsic, ineffaceable goodness of man—"corrupted only by institutions"; and the face of the tutor in Émile, dedicated to the task of teaching by tireless attention to natural right, to educing and evoking the good from the pupil rather than imposing harsh and alien idols of the mind upon him. And, finally, implacably, there is the Rousseau, the very central Rousseau, of the general will and its absolute power over the individual, of insistence that when the individual enters into the social contract that yields the general will, all liberties and rights are automatically surrendered.

Rousseau, as I have stressed, did not—in his estimation and in the estimation of countless worshipers since—thereby snatch freedom away from the individual. On the contrary, Rousseau guaranteed for man a higher form of freedom, that of participation in the being of the collective sovereign. And when this sovereign appears to be lowering its absolute power on the citizen's head for whatever reason, this is only an act of "forcing the citizen to be free."

Is it any wonder that Marx is rapidly being consigned to the charnel house of history, save among cultists, with only his "humanist" attributes preserved—preserved for fusion with the near totality of agreeable attributes in Rousseau. Rousseau is, at least to the mind of the late-twentieth-century clerisy in this country, the saint of saints. He offers

absolute power in the form of divine grace, of the community of the elect.

This is perhaps the single most important fact there is about Rousseau the political thinker, the fact that makes him just as attractive to certain marginal conservatives like the followers of Leo Strauss as to all-out radicals. Of all the philosophes that the late Carl Becker brilliantly assigned to *The Heavenly City of the Eighteenth-Century Philosophers*, written over half a century ago, Rousseau is the most interesting and also the most important. Rousseau transferred, as it were, grace from the body of the church to the body of the state, the state based upon the social contract and the general will. His doctrine of the general will was regarded in his day as it is in ours as beyond the power of pure reason to understand, to assimilate. He could have said what Saint Augustine said in effect: To understand, one must first believe, have faith. The general will is the will of the people but it is not the will of all people. This is precisely what Rousseau tells us. The resolution of the paradox, like the resolution of the paradox of the Christian Trinity, lies in a kind of transrational or pararational imaging of the general will as the mind of the organism properly formed, no more capable of being understood by rationalistic dismemberment into tiny molecules than is the human mind itself. Rousseau is the political mystic, rivaled in this respect only by Plato, whom Rousseau declared the greatest of his teachers.

It is testimony to the religious element in Rousseau's political philosophy that he endowed his collective monolith of power in the pages of *The Social Contract* with a religion of its own—the civil religion— to which I have already referred. The general will is of course the godhead.

There was a certain unwonted historical wisdom in Rousseau's act of creating a church for his state. State and church, although archenemies over long periods of time in the annals of civilization, have more in common than either does with the economic realm—the common butt of both religious and political condemnation for its alleged crassness and egoism. And it is a fact that in the succession of power that forms the greatest single pageant in Western history, the state has succeeded the church in the detailed and minute custodianship of the individual. The state for a long time in history was obliged to wear the mantle of other, more respectable institutions. Thus the patriarchal state of yore, followed by the religious or divine-right state. But since

the eighteenth century, the state has walked on legs of its own, and in so many respects has taken over once-ecclesiastical functions.

In Western Europe, throughout the Middle Ages, the majority of Europeans lived cradle-to-grave lives in the church. There was no aspect of life that was not either actively or potentially under the ordinances of the church. Birth, marriage, death were all given legitimacy by the church, not the state. Property, inheritance, work conditions, profits, interest, wages, schooling, university admissions, degrees, licenses for professional practice, workdays, holidays, feasts, and commemorations, all were subject not to secular but to ecclesiastical governance. The Middle Ages represented the height of ecclesiastical absolutism. That particular absolutism has vanished in the West—though not of course in other parts of the world, beginning with an Iran—but no vacuum has been left. Much of modern European history is the story of the gradual transfer, as it were, of ecclesiastical absolutism to monarchical and then democratic-nationalist absolutism. Medieval man was so accustomed to the multitudinous ordinances of the church governing his life that he didn't even see them. That is more and more true today of modern man, democratic man.

There are respects, as I have suggested, in which the contemporary democratic state is like the totalitarian states of this century: in the number and scope of political laws governing the most intimate recesses of our lives, in the sheer comprehensiveness of political identity, role, law, and power in each state. But there is one large and sufficing difference between even the most bureaucratized and paternalistic of the democracies and the totalitarian states we have seen thus far, in Russia and Germany foremost. In the total state there is no pretense of free elections, free political association, and free choice of representatives in political office. Moreover, there is no instance, thus far at least, of a heavily bureaucratized, ordinance-saturated, democratic Leviathan ever evolving into the total state as I have just described it. All totalitarian states we are familiar with are the consequences of armed revolution, are based upon their armies, and exist literally by command. There is no suggestion that apart from military and party command there is any kind of law that operates, certainly none of common-law character.

But while democratic absolutism of the kind and extent we are now thoroughly familiar with poses no threat of evolution into a Soviet Union or Nazi Germany, it does not follow that it may not possibly grow almost insensibly, by infinitesimal degrees, into what is nothing less, for all practical purposes, than legal and administrative tyranny. Our con-

sciousness of freedom is something more likely to be reserved for the interstices of the laws we pass annually rather than to be found in the laws themselves. There comes a time when no matter how much "representation" we as citizens have, laws—of taxation and disposition of property, of choice of schooling, of penetration even of the bedroom, of pornography and obscenity, of race, color, and sex, and of all else involved in the business of living—become burdensome to even the thickest-skinned.

Freedom, whether in the sense of *from* or of *to,* is not a virtue in itself. It is a virtue only when there goes with it personal privacy, autonomy in some degree, and creativeness to the limit of one's faculties. To be free merely to be free is the stuff of inanition—like making hammers to make hammers to make hammers, as Chesterton has suggested. Democratic absolutism, chiefly in the manifestation of the thick, heavy bureaucracies we build today, can be as oppressive to the creative instinct, the curiosity itch, and the drive to explore as anything that exists more blatantly in the totalitarian state. It is interesting to observe in the Soviet Union right now a marked relaxing of law and ordinance taking place, especially in the economy. The reason for this is emphatically not some sudden reconsideration by the politburo of the values of liberalism; it is solely because after seventy years of Communist central planning and control, production, distribution, and consumption are in a more and more hopeless condition. Love freedom or hate it, there is a minimum without which there is no significant thought and action.

Tocqueville, first and even yet greatest theorist of democracy, was clear, as he surveyed the European democracies coming into existence in the 1830s, that democracy, more than any other genus of state in history, introduces and then refines and strengthens the power of the majority, the centralization of government, the leveling of social ranks in the name of individual equality, and the bureaucratization of society. On the last, Tocqueville went so far as to say that the progress of bureaucracy in modern Western history is the infallible augury of democracy coming up in the rear.

The Framers would be stunned by the mass and the labyrinthine complexity of the American bureaucracy today. It covers the country like a blanket and it does not by now hesitate to intrude into the most intimate details of our economic and social lives. The Framers knew from afar the kind of oppressive, suffocating bureaucracy that lay in

Prussia, France, Russia, and other European countries. They didn't like it. They would have agreed with Tocqueville's famous description in *Democracy in America:* "It covers the surface of society with a network of small, complicated rules, minute and uniform, through which the most original minds and the most energetic characters cannot penetrate, to rise above the crowd." They would have seen with Marx "an appalling parasitic body which enmeshes the body of French society like a net and chokes off its pores." The Framers would have quickly understood Parkinson's Law—the inverse ratio between significance of function and size of attending bureaucracy—for they had seen it operate under George III.

But would they be prepared, could they possibly be, for the current reality of American bureaucracy, answering as it does to both Tocqueville's and Marx's characterizations but going far beyond the reality of any national bureaucracy in the nineteenth century. Consider the vast payroll, the number of jobs, tiers of responsibility, departments, subdepartments, commands, and cross commands, assistants to assistants to assistants in the chain—if that can possibly be the right word—of command in the military bureaucracy, the Pentagon. The Joint Chiefs valiantly pretend to be in charge of the American military, but they aren't really, and they must know it. No one is in charge. No one can be. The system is too elephantine and cumbersome, too much a vast prehistoric type of monster, for any one person or any tiny group to control it. Even if the military bureaucracy were small and manageable, joint—and incessantly conflicting—responsibility of the president and the Congress would make any kind of leadership by top brass unlikely.

Being elephantine, the Pentagon can apparently think only in terms of the elephantine. Since World War II the planet has known only small wars—Korea, Vietnam (far from small by the end, to be sure), Dominica, Iran, Grenada, etc., to limit ourselves here to American wars. Small wars would appear to be the wave of the future. Apart from the exceedingly unlikely war between the Soviet Union and the United States, there really isn't the possibility of a war like either of the two world wars in this century. Small wars call for different kinds of forces from those which fought the Civil War, the Napoleonic Wars, and World Wars I and II. What is manifestly needed is the highly mobile, rapidly deployable, specially trained, and relatively small fighting force. The Joint Chiefs know it, we assume. But the enormous bureaucracy with its tentacles stretched out in every possible direction, tripping over one another, threatening to strangle the monster they are connected

with, has apparently made it impossible for the great military bureaucracy in America to develop proper forces for the late twentieth century's kinds of war. A single strike force, operating swiftly and responsibly, would have been more than enough for tiny Grenada and its primitive defensive forces. Instead there were three vast services put into place at or on the island.

If the Pentagon is the most glaring, and downright dangerous, of our mammoth bureaucracies, it is far from being the only one. There isn't an aspect of individual life, from birth to death, that doesn't come under some kind of federal scrutiny every day, and that means of course bureaucratic scrutiny. Horror stories are legion and related to every bureaucracy from the Internal Revenue Service to Commerce, Labor, Human Services, and so forth.

Even so, Americans are ambivalent about bureaucracy. They hate it, suffer from it, yet find it tolerable. In the first place, it is, with all its clumsy steps, the bearer of goodies. Once the American middle class became a full-fledged part of Social Security and Medicare, and then of an escalating abundance of still other goodies such as low-interest loans for their children's precious college degrees, animosity toward bureaucracy began to retreat. "Damned bureaucracy" may be one word in most conversations, but it is said with more and more toleration, even affection.

The second reason that bureaucracy is acceptable is that it operates as a brake on the muddleheaded, brash, and sometimes cretinous ideas of government, of war and peace, brought to Washington by each new administration. As I noted in the preceding chapter, under the enchantment of the Great American Myth, each new president, secretary of state, of defense, and other departments is convinced of his effortless wisdom of leadership. The bureaucracy checks many of the gaffes and blunders, though not all. True, the bureaucracy would doubtless be equally vigilant against good and meritorious ideas, simply on the grounds that they were new and had never been tried before. But there haven't been many of those in the modern age.

Reagan promised, vowed, swore that the size of the bureaucracy and with it the size of the national debt would be dramatically decreased. Those promises came in the fall of 1980 and in the first months of 1981. But things changed. And it is recorded in the books of Reagan's own government, now in its second term, that his administration has presided over the largest budget increases and the largest budget (and also trade) deficits in American history, and that the size of the federal

bureaucracy has shot up 13 percent, with not one significant bureau or department, not even Energy or Education, despite promises, dropped.

Nor is that the entire story. For, again beyond any predecessor in the White House, the rhetorically sworn apostle of laissez-faire President Reagan has sought, promised, and backed increases in the powers of the centralized state which would carry it into the intimacies of the bedroom and the cloister of the church: constitutional amendments, in other words, to forbid abortions on the one hand and mandate religious prayers in the schools on the other. Not even Hitler dared carry the state, the totalitarian state, that far into the home and the church. But absolutist democracy dares!

Arresting—egregious, some would say—as the Reagan spectacle is, however, it not unfairly epitomizes the attitudes of a great many Americans toward bureaucracy and state centralization. They curse it, deride it, abhor it, all the while they are beckoning it to them with one hand. Any reader can verify this easily. Whenever there is a dispute of some kind going on over a moral, social, economic, cultural, or even religious issue, the words "The government must . . ." lead all proposed solutions offered on the spot. Whether it is drug abuse, child molesting, obscenity, housing, educational quality, sickness all the way from AIDS down to the common cold or headache, the appeal to government—and necessarily bureaucracy—leads the field. Americans may hate bureaucracy, as they piously insist over and over, but any reduction whatever in the vast number of entitlements and other political subsidies, whether in money or in kind, would (indeed, does!) bring on avalanches of despair and hatred of the suspected malefactor.

There are two activities which account for well over half the annual budget and contribute most to the size of bureaucracy: the social services and the military. The middle class, the largest and overall wealthiest segment of American society, receives the most and the greatest of federal entitlements, thus being a major burden upon the taxpayer. But since the major taxpayer is the middle class, the happy theory is that it is all an ingenious and providential trade-off. Actually it isn't, because seemingly no government, Republican or Democratic, dares to pay through current revenues the massive costs of the welfare state and the military, and therefore annual budget deficits of over two hundred billion dollars a year have become commonplace. The almost equally massive military budget is, as I explained in the preceding chapter, the consequence not so much of the sheer danger posed by the Soviet Union, but of the popular passion, inflamed first by Woodrow Wilson,

then by Franklin Roosevelt, to intervene anywhere in the world that seems to be less than democratic, liberal, and humanitarian in the American image.

Together the social welfare bureaucracy and the military bureaucracy add up in the contemporary democratic United States to the largest bureaucracy in the history of the world, including even the Soviet Union. In fact, all else being equal, democratic absolutism creates larger bureaucracies—by virtue of the humanitarian factor—than does totalitarianism.

For a long time, until the aftermath of World War I, the main Western ideologies were checks on the idea of the omnicompetent state. All these ideologies—essentially socialism, liberalism, and conservatism—had developed in consequence of two great events of the eighteenth century: the French Revolution and the Industrial Revolution. The first epitomized the birth of modern nationalism, the second capitalism. But in actuality the role of the state was about as prominent in the second as in the first. As an increasing number of historians have demonstrated, the creation of nineteenth-century capitalism required a good deal more than simpleminded laissez-faire. The landscape for the new industry had been reordered by a number of activities. These included the enclosure acts of the English Parliament; other politically driven erasures of the Old Order, manifest in the lingering villages and outdated boroughs; special new laws and decisions the political state, after obliterating much of the old, made to provide reinforcement to the new, its factories and mills, its wage-earning labor force, and the "free" market required for cheapest possible production and distribution.

That is why all three ideologies, in the United States as well as Great Britain, found themselves in an often combative role toward the state. Even though socialism for the most part made the economic the dominant force in the long run, it (including Marxian but especially in its Proudhonian quasi-anarchist form) saw the state and the army and police as the very first target of the dreamt-of revolution. For Marx and Engels as well as for Proudhon and Kropotkin, the abolishment of the bourgeois state and its appalling bureaucracy was a goal of highest priority. Although neither Marx nor any other champion of socialism was ever able to set forth clearly the kind of society future socialism would actually usher in, a fundamental dogma of socialism declared that whatever the future might hold, the centralized, bureaucratized, and

unitary national state would be gone, driven out by the Revolution.

So did nineteenth-century liberalism and conservatism make assault upon the state basic in their doctrines. For liberalism the individual and his maximum possible freedom formed the basis of opposition to the state. Conservatism rested its opposition to the unitary state on its defense of the social order—family, neighborhood, guild, and property—and the necessity of autonomy from political centralization.

The nature and significance of all three traditional ideologies have been drastically changed during the decades since World War I. Marx's and Engels' antipathy toward the state found no echo in Lenin and Stalin, who made the land of the first great socialist revolution a setting for the centralized state in the single most repressive form it has ever taken in history. Totalitarianism had its origin in our century in the events of 1917 when the Bolsheviks, under Lenin's generalship, set up the first totalitarian state in history. A considerable number of Western socialists persist, of course, whose opposition to the Soviet Union is unqualified, and often bold and courageous. But what is sometimes called "the death of socialism" in our era is actually the collapse of a once vigorous and exciting crusade against the national state into yet another form of statism. Between democratic socialism and the omnipresent, current humanitarian bureaucratic state there is too little difference to be worth spelling out.

Liberalism had its notable reversal of values in the United States during the New Deal. The New Deal is second only to World War I under Wilson as a cause of the steady politicization of a doctrine founded originally on the freedom of the individual. The central value of contemporary American liberalism is not freedom but equality; equality defined as redistribution of property. Not autonomy from power but participation in power follows, as tenet, directly from the new equalitarianism.

A veritable renascence of conservative ideology was under way by the end of the fifties; it was sufficient to carry with it an interest in both Edmund Burke and Tocqueville greater perhaps than any in prior decades. Overwhelmingly the new conservatism—in resolute opposition to liberals above all other groups—followed Burke and Tocqueville in espousing decrease in centralization, pluralism over monism in government, the free market in basic economic production and distribution, intermediate social groups like family and local community and voluntary associations—all calculated to take some of the load of responsibility from big government—and, inevitably, substantial decrease in

bureaucracy. The new conservatism also emphasized some of the traditional moral values which, it was plausibly argued, had gotten battered into passivity by the forces of modernism, political modernism most of all. In a word, the *autonomy* of social order and culture was the prized objective of the new conservatism.

At the present moment, however, militant conservatism has as little to do with its historic substance as contemporary liberalism has to do with its birthright of devotion to individual liberty. What is most likely to be labeled "conservative" by the media—and with considerable basis in reality—is militarism on the one hand and Christian Far Right evangelicism on the other, which is far more interested today in extending the power of the state into the intimate recesses of life through legislation and constitutional amendment than in a free religion in a free political society. In large measure conservatism has become, within a decade or two, an ideology seeking to capture democratic absolutism rather than secure from it social and moral authority distinct from political power.

Conservatism has had severe difficulties ever since the Reagan coalition captured the government in 1980. Given the sharp differences in the ideologies forming the coalition—military hawkishness, evangelicism, libertarianism, supply siders, the power-obsessed Right, and others equally discordant—it is probably remarkable that the Reagan coalition lasted as long as it did. It does not now look as though it will be missed.

Politics is king, having deposed economics in World War I. That war proved that however insane a given economic measure might seem when examined strictly on its own merit, its success was virtually guaranteed in the marketplace if the state chose to mandate it, to make it a part of the state's official strategy, and to frost it with the rhetoric of freedom and equality. Jacques Ellul, in his *The Political Illusion*, has written powerfully on politics in the present age:

> To think of everything as political, to conceal everything by using this word (with intellectuals taking the cue from Plato and several others), to place everything in the hands of the state, to appeal to the state in all circumstances, to subordinate the problems of the individual to those of the group, to believe that political affairs are on everybody's level and that everybody is qualified to deal with them—these factors characterize the politicization of modern man, and, as such comprise a myth. The myth then reveals itself in beliefs, and as a result, easily elicits almost religious fervor . . . To act in a contrary fashion would place us in radical disagreement with the entire

trend of our society, a punishment we cannot possibly accept . . . We consider it obvious that everything must be unreservedly subjected to the power of the state.*

Vital to the contemporary bureaucratic, centralized, omnicompetent democratic state is its clerisy, by which I mean the aggregate of intellectuals and scholars dedicated to the state precisely as their medieval forebears were to the church. The medieval clerisy was formed chiefly of theologians but was not without *politiques*, theorists and practitioners of power. The clerisy of our day in America is mostly *politiques* pure and simple, but it has its full share of theologians too, as almost any academic journal of political science attests.

Predictably, the contemporary political clerisy was born of the Wilson War State in 1917 and 1918. Wilson, himself a reverent *politique*, of course, and the very idol of America's intellectual classes, sent out a call for fellow intellectuals to aid him in the winning of the war and the planning of the peace. A secret group of intellectuals with the distinguished geographer Isaiah Bowman of Johns Hopkins its chairman, and containing also the youthful Walter Lippmann, almost literally wrote the famed Fourteen Points that Wilson thrust upon the world.

But there were many others marshaled by Wilson as clerisy—historians like Guy Stanton Ford and Stuart P. Sherman, novelists including Booth Tarkington and Samuel Hopkins Adams, and many others from various sectors of society. Europe had been familiar with the political intellectual for a long time, certainly since the philosophes in France in the late eighteenth century. They were the earliest of a long procession of thinkers and doers through the European nineteenth century who saw capture of the state and its sovereign powers as the first step toward bringing about the good society. For centuries most intellectuals had been more closely attached to the church or to the aristocracy for support. Now, increasingly, emotional, and not seldom financial, attachment was to the secular state.

It is difficult to find a class of political intellectuals, a clerisy, in America in the nineteenth century. Utopian and reform energies were characteristically expended from religious or philosophical bases—as in the great wave of Protestant social reform in the century and the many and divers utopian communities. Edward Bellamy's widely read *Look-*

The Political Illusion. Tr. from the French by Konrad Kellen. New York, Alfred A. Knopf, 1967. p. 12

ing Backward, in which a powerful and militarized state is portrayed as America's salvation, was a conspicuous exception.

In the 1920s the political intelligentsia grew appreciably in size and influence. The Wilson War State had left indelibly imprinted on a great many minds, academic foremost perhaps but legal and business minds too, the spectacle of intellectuals serving the state in the interests of moral betterment and economic reform. Where the church had been for so long the most widely accepted institutional base for reform of society, a constantly increasing number of social scientists, philosophers, and critics now, in the 1920s, put full emphasis on the national state. John Dewey, America's most respected and influential philosopher in the twentieth century, put the stamp of approval upon a liberalism in which the state would be the tireless champion of the people, as against the varied factions of business, religion, and ordinary politics.

The onset of the Great Depression at the beginning of the 1930s carried with it the greatest opportunity yet for the expansion and popularization of the political class. The almost instant odium that fastened itself upon the business community made the hypertrophy of the state and its apparatchiks the easier. So did the presence of Herbert Hoover in the White House when the stock market crash and then the pall of depression settled over the land. Hoover's reputation is and doubtless always will be that of a strict apostle of laissez-faire. He was anything but that. An engineer by profession, he tasted of social engineering under Wilson in World War I. He was food administrator for the United States and important in a variety of other government connections. He was the strongest member of the Harding and Coolidge administrations, always known for his keen interest in the use of the national government to build up the country. When depression came, Hoover launched a considerable number of governmental schemes and programs for relief of the people—many of them to survive and be used by Roosevelt in his first term of office. Hoover really began modern peacetime political and social engineering; Roosevelt simply enlarged upon it.

It was Roosevelt, though, who led all predecessors in the sheer number of intellectuals he attracted to Washington. What James Burnham has called the managerial revolution took place in America under Roosevelt all the while, in different setting and with different result, the same managerial revolution was taking place in Europe. Burnham was struck in the 1930s by the ever-increasing power of management in the great corporations of America, almost always at the expense of

the stockholders who in theory owned the corporation and possessed all the usual rights of control which normally go with ownership. Many times the most powerful individuals in the corporations were managers who didn't own a share of stock in their corporation. Their power came from a managerial role that was in effect crowding out the actual owners.

Burnham saw the same type of managerial revolution taking place in Western governments. Political intellectuals and bureaucrats—one and all appointed, not elected—were taking over powers which once belonged to the people and their elected representatives. In Europe this managerial revolution yielded up the totalitarian regimes of Russia, Italy, and Germany. They could be seen as extreme, deeply ideological manifestations of the revolution. But in other parts of Europe—France and Great Britain, for example—the managerial revolution had very much the same character and substance as it did in the New Deal in America. Under the spur of the crisis of the world depression, even the democracies were succumbing to the allure of a managerial class, thus in their own way adding to the crisis of democracy.

I believe that the legal fraternity, especially in some of the more influential law schools, is rapidly becoming the most powerful wing or sector of the political clerisy in America. The idea of working directly through law and the courts in order to accomplish major changes in economy and social order, even in government itself, has its modern origin in Jeremy Bentham. Not that Bentham for a moment liked the English common law or the courts in which it was practiced. He loathed the jury system, ridiculing the idea that a pickup group of men could rationally and logically make its way to the truth in law any more than in philosophy or mathematics. Nor did Bentham like the accumulating paraphernalia of democracy in Britain. Democracy is ultimately based upon the will of the majority; this implies minorities, Bentham observed, and with majorities and minorities, the danger of chaos and anarchy becomes threatening. Working through parliaments and congresses, Bentham believed, was a time-consuming, infinitely circuitous, and ultimately self-defeating approach to the good state.

Bentham's solution was what he called the Magistrate; that is, a man or tiny group of men, acting more in the role of grand inquisitor than of any king, president, or legislative body, who by the special nature of his exalted being would always be in perfect synchronization with the will—that is, the *real*, the *true*, the general will of Rousseau, essentially—of the whole people. Congresses inevitably fragmented the

populaces; kings and presidents were hamstrung by intermediate institutions serving actually as obstacles to truth and justice. The only way of overcoming the clutter and slowdown of representative institutions and of electorates—masses of incompetent citizens voting their feebly understood will—was through a great system of law, one based upon the principle of the greatest happiness for the largest number of people. This system of law would be personified, acted for, served, and above all dominated by the Magistrate—ill-defined by Bentham but plain enough in his fevered prose.

We are not likely to hear about a sovereign magistrate or the general will from our increasingly active, change-oriented legal clerisy. They appear to be quite satisfied with the present system of federal courts rising to the Supreme Court. Why not be satisfied? The Supreme Court is the single most glittering prize to be had in America for the activism-, reform-, or revolution-seized political mentality. We have learned over the past several decades, most resplendently in the Warren Court, how great, far-reaching changes can be effected by a majority of the Supreme Court without having to go through the channels set up and favored by the Framers—that is, the legislative and the executive working together.

How long, it has to be asked, would it have taken for state legislatures, Congress, and the presidency to have brought about desegregation, the principle of one man, one vote, and the total legalization of abortion? A long time, obviously. Tocqueville, who admired America's localist and regionalist political institutions, confessed that these would never, by themselves, overcome the "terrible evil" of slavery or, for that matter, if slavery was somehow abolished as law, overcome too the still fiercely segregated position of the races. Only a great central power, a kind of superemperor, was capable, Tocqueville thought, of abolishing slavery and its segregationist aftermath. Tocqueville was very far from recommending such a central power, though he did comment on some of the great things which can be accomplished only by centralization.

To return to the present age: Law, especially the law of the entire nation, federal law, presents itself as the most potent force for social change now imaginable. Inevitably, therefore, the attention of the eager, impatient, and activist among humanitarians and reconstructionists is already being turned from the presidency and the Congress—and conspicuously the merely state-level political offices—to the federal judiciary with its grand prize of the Chief Justiceship of the United States. It will be interesting to historians of the next century or two to

see in what measure the Supreme Court—consisting today of nine unelected individuals, still of the traditional conviction, for the most part, that the proper business of the Court is the interpretation, not the making of law, least of all the making of large reconstructive law—evolves, if it does, into an entity at least suggestive of Bentham's Magistrate.

Irrespective of all that, the present fact is that federal law, the federal courts, and above all the Supreme Court offer a challenge to eager spirits of the political clerisy that was not possible a generation or two ago when virtually all law practiced was at the local and state level. Law is, as Bentham saw brilliantly, the most egalitarian of all institutions in present society, and, as Tocqueville foresaw, the quest for equality would be the most consuming of all quests in the future. Given the vital place of the Supreme Court in this respect, we may expect to see nominations of justices by the Executive Branch henceforth subjected to ever more bitter confirmation fights in the Senate. The inquisition of Judge Robert Bork in late 1987 will have frequent followups in the years ahead.

In politics the best of all known reinforcements of an ideological position is a philosophy of history. It has the effect of making your particular goal seem a part of the constitution of mankind, of the movement of the stars in their courses.

Karl Marx learned this, and what he learned has had great influence on other political and social causes, including that today of the centralized national state. In his youth Marx was a seething cauldron of desires, fantasies, utopian ecstasies—all the product of his deeply dyed hatred of the institutional setting in which he lived, all catalyzed by his apocalyptic vision of the great, cleansing revolution. But by the time Marx had spent a few years in Paris, had met Engels, and had written with him the historic *Manifesto of the Communist Party*, he had a philosophy of history in which personal craving was hugely reinforced by the vision of all history as class struggle, with each stage a moral step above the preceding one. This was for Marx "scientific" socialism. Social action, including the revolution, was not proscribed; merely adjusted to the great "law of motion" of human history.

A similar philosophy of history in stages contributes to democratic absolutism and its prosperity: first the family, then religion, then the local community and cooperative. These, like the family itself, served human beings well in their time. But, the argument goes, their time is

now gone, leaving the political state as the lineal, progressive replacement of the family, church, and traditional local community. The highest form of community is today, the argument continues, the political community; that is, the state suitably equipped with largesse in every form.

It is not enough to say that the national state is simply a *good* community; it must be presented as the *only* possible community in the late twentieth century, the single form of community that has emerged from the whole historical process and is thus, whether we recognize it or not, an inevitable stage in the evolution of human society. We must be able to sing with our hearts: The state is necessary and the inexorable outcome of Western history. All other forms of association intermediate to man and state are at best sentimental reminders of the past—the dead, soon to be the forgotten past.

Within the larger frame of asserted evolution lies the narrower but trenchant evolution of the state itself. This evolution, it is declared, has moved in unilinear fashion from the primitive kingship through the patriarchal, the religio-sacred, the oligarchic, the contractual, and the laissez-faire state, each a necessary stage in its time, down to the twentieth-century people's state, to the *nation* as family, church, and above all community.

The great advantage of a philosophy of history or theory of social development, however subjective and fanciful either is in fact, is that the holder of the philosophy or theory is then able to point out confidently those elements of the present which are "progressive," "modern," and "functional" as contrasted with other elements of the present which are "obsolete," "archaic," and "reactionary." These latter are survivals of some earlier, now outmoded, stage of human development, and no matter how attractive, how desirable, how seemingly efficient they are—like the family, church, and local community, like the free market, the private sector, and the voluntary association—they must be sternly repudiated. Repudiated in favor of the national, democratic, central people's state hereinafter known as the true "family," "community," and "wagon train," all courtesy of Governor Cuomo. Thus centralization, nationalist administration of government, and within this the presidency over Congress and the judiciary, and a generally unitary type of society are all to be preferred to pluralism, decentralization, particularism, and the private sector because these last are mere reminders of the past, "communities of memory," and the stuff of nostalgic romance.

Armed thusly, the contemporary clerisy is mighty and its consensus supreme—in sophisticated society, at any rate. The polemical advantages are obvious. No longer must one justify his predilection for the centralized national state bureaucratically thrust into our most intimate lives by naive expressions of desire and preference. With a little experience any apprentice in the clerisy can quickly snap out "Modern" and as quickly the epithets "Outdated" or "Archaic" and thus have the battle won immediately. Only an Alice in Wonderland would be struck by the weirdness of dividing the present, or any historical time period, into the Modern on the one hand and the Archaic on the other. But as the queen would doubtless inform Alice tartly, a theory of history is exactly what I want it to be, no less, no more.

The same myth of an ordered, necessary development of the state works admirably for the clerisy in foreign policy. There are many despotisms in the world. On any rational scale, the Soviet Union has by far the worst record of repressiveness, one that includes, over a few decades, genocide, terror, torture, show trials, and the Gulag. States made in the image of the Soviet Union, like Bulgaria, Cuba, and Albania, are not far behind in internal, permanent terror. But on the other hand, the world's despotisms can be arranged in terms of a different scale, that of the archaic and reactionary to the modern and progressive. In the first category fall such states as the South Korea of Syngman Rhee, the South Vietnam of Diem, South Africa, and the Philippines under the Marcoses. Without doubt these are repugnant governments—but hardly the equals in systematic repression and flouting of human rights of the Soviets and their shadow states.

But beginning with the 1930s a very considerable number of American liberals, members all of the political clerisy, have found it much easier to swallow the Soviet Union and its minions than the South Koreas and South Africas. As Jeane Kirkpatrick pointed out in a now historic essay, a great many political intellectuals in the United States confront the world's dictatorships armed with double standards: one standard (usually in fury) for the "reactionary" and "archaic" and "capitalist" nations such as South Vietnam under Diem; another standard for the Soviet Union, Castro's Cuba, and Sandinista Nicaragua. The double standard rests precisely on the dogma of a pattern of political development, or progress, that divides the present world into the reactionary and the progressive.

Roosevelt had a great deal to do with the coining and broadcasting of this dogma and the distinctions among nations that flow from it. He

made no bones, during World War II, about his preference for Stalin's Communism over Churchill's British imperialism. The Soviet leaders, FDR told Frances Perkins one day, after the Teheran summit, have "an almost mystical devotion" to their people. "They all seem really to want to do what is good for their people instead of wanting to do for themselves." Despite the totalitarian structure of the Soviet Union and its appalling record, it was not this nation that FDR foresaw as the enemy of democracy but rather British imperialism. He seems to have actually believed that the United States had more in common with the Soviet Union than with Great Britain. The Soviets were somewhat barbaric, FDR agreed, but in comparison with imperialism practiced by capitalist states, mere barbarism was venial and could easily be overcome, especially if there was someone like Roosevelt to guide Stalin after the war.

Roosevelt commissioned a special report on imperialism, particularly British, from his dutiful aide General Patrick Hurley, who required no instruction as to FDR's likes and dislikes. In a report to the President—which Roosevelt sent immediately along to Churchill, indicating that in general he approved of it—Hurley declared that at that very moment the blood of thousands of brave American boys was being spilled in their forced position of defense of British imperialism. He added that the great struggle ahead was that between democracy and imperialism—not, be it noted, between democracy and totalitarianism. Finally, in the general's judgment the Soviets, as Hurley found them in Iran, were very exemplars of modern efficiency and world citizenship.

Armageddon would be, in short, between the modern United States and the "archaic" and "reactionary" imperialism of states like democratic Great Britain, not between democracies and totalitarianisms— the latter a concept seemingly unknown to Roosevelt and Hurley. However odious in short-run situations the Soviets might be, as in Poland, the Balkans, and the Baltics, and however cruelly destructive of all parliamentary, representative states which they subjugated and occupied, the Soviets yet had to be recognized as vastly ahead in the line of progress of the imperialistic czarist regime they had vanquished and ahead, too, in any proper philosophy of world history, of the Great Britains and the Frances of Europe. These were still democratic, representative, attentive to human rights, and all that, but they were archaic, basically great fossils harking back to the outstripped past. As the Churchill-Roosevelt wartime correspondence amply attests, FDR spent at least a part of the war lecturing Churchill on the sin of imperialism— with India the great object lesson, of course—the while he seems to

have stomached everything in the Soviet Union, even finding in the Soviet leaders, as I have noted, a mystic bond of consecration to the people.

At bottom it is the same conception of history, of some believed logic or pattern of history, that leads the political clerisy in the democracies to speak so assuredly of "developed" nations on the one hand, and the "undeveloped" on the other. Empirically, logically, and scientifically, the distinction is fatuous when applied to the peoples of the earth. How can we declare any people undeveloped? It has presumably had a long history and quite possibly has undergone as many fundamental changes over time as any people we describe as developed. The United States, three centuries old, is developed. India, several millennia old in its constitutive elements of family, village, and caste is undeveloped.

The distinction is ridiculous by the criteria of ordinary logic, but it exists and is widely used as the consequence of the philosophy or theory of progress that the West has sustained for many centuries and that has been the very life's blood of modernity. Under the Western canon of progress, the West itself is deemed to be in the vanguard of the advancement of humanity. Other peoples are ranked unprogressive or undeveloped in accord with a scale. Those peoples most different in customs from the West are *ipso facto* not merely most different but most undeveloped; they are, it is said, primitive, barbaric, savage, or, commonly, reactionary if there is property coupled with strong kinship and caste ties and with a system of political representation different from ours.

Limited use of the political government in the lives of citizens; considerable reliance upon family, clan, religion, and class or caste in matters of self-government and mutual aid; a suffusion of life by the sacred and its symbols; decentralization and localism; and a jealous regard for private property and its place in the family or caste—all such traits, commendable though they may be in many contexts on earth, are deemed reactionary and undeveloped by the West's political clerisy. Political omnicompetence, with the state the spearhead of all social and cultural life; industrialization, however farcical in context; nationalization of education; rampant secularism; and growing consumer-hedonism—all this bespeaks modernity to the Western clerisy and the welcome sign of the developed, the progressive. When there is evidence of a burgeoning socialism, or at least of socialist thought styles, joy runneth over, it would seem, in the political and bureaucratic

offices of the World Bank and other sanctuaries of world homogenization, American style.

The Soviet Union, it will be noted, ranks very high on the scale of development and modernity. This puts the Soviets well above a South Africa or a South Korea unless one happens to be affronted by genocide, permanent terror, a totalitarian government, and militaristic imperialism.

The word *politicization* may not be felicitous, especially off the tongue, but it is an indispensable word to any faithful account of the present age. "The Politics of . . ." is the beginning of many a title or subtitle of book and article in this epoch. Once it was the economic factor that was emblazoned on books about the Constitution, the Civil War, Hollywood, or World War I. But economics' place has been overwhelmed by the political. Now it is the politics of the family, the school, relationships in industry, the Supreme Court, and the environmental movement. Power, not money, is the great commodity to be brokered and traded.

There is a very considerable actuality behind the triumph of the political in print. Under the spur of this actuality, Washington, D.C., is at last on its way to becoming a city, that is, a city with some identity. It should be. Before World War II there weren't a dozen trade associations headquartered in Washington; they were mostly in New York and Chicago. There are thousands now in the capital, and they include lobbies for every conceivable economic, social, and cultural interest in this country. There is almost nothing, from art to zoos, in which the politics of the interest doesn't come close to outweighing the intrinsic subject matter. It is not so much freedom from bureaucracy as it is participation in it that seems to matter the most.

Until the early 1960s, the fondest wish of most evangelicals—a term I take to include fundamentalists, Pentecostals, and charismatics of all colors—was seclusion: from the inquiry of the state, from political processes, and from publicity. The humiliations suffered by the fundamentalists alone in the famous Scopes trial in Tennessee in 1925, from the defense of Scopes by master defense attorney Clarence Darrow, with the once-revered William Jennings Bryan the chief scapegoat, were enough to make them covet the anonymity of seclusion. They were not likely, either, to forget for a long time the brilliant and widely printed lacerations by America's reigning critic and wit, H. L. Mencken.

But when religion generally became popular in the 1950s, not least on college campuses, the evangelicals began to seek the sunlight again, and within a decade they had become not only religious but political forces to deal with. For whatever reasons, Americans flocked to the ranks of born-again Christians and to the arms of the Oral Robertses, the Pat Robertsons, the Jerry Falwells, and many others. I shall say something about their economic significance in the next chapter. Here I want simply to point out the extreme politicization their religious message has undergone in very recent years. The political communiqué or handout often seems to have succeeded the New Testament as the organ of the Good News. The agenda of the group that began under the label of the Moral Majority was as political, as concerned with strictly political ends, political techniques, and political power plays, as anything witnessed back in the 1930s in the labor unions.

We have no difficulty in seeing three stages, all recent, of the evangelical affair with politics. Its first motivation was acquisition of enough political influence to protect religious exceptionalism in America. This was followed by stage two in which political power, the engine of the national state, was sought in order to advance, indeed to force upon the whole of America, certain moral objectives—such as the criminalization of all abortion and the establishment of prayers in all public schools—which were the possession of a distinct minority of Americans. Stage three is well symbolized by the entry into the presidential race of one of the most powerful of the evangelicals, Pat Robertson. What we shall see in the future no one can foretell. But it is well to remember that politics and religion have always been the pristine areas of human division and difference, of blinding hatred uncoiled in terror, arson, and wars without limits of mercy. There is much food for reflection in the history of Christianity. Beginning as a sect, or rather a multitude of sects, in the early years of the Roman Empire, with simple desire for autonomy and growth its obsession, it had become the official religion of Rome by the end of the third century. A thousand years later it was the supreme power—at once religious, moral, economic, and political—in Western Europe.

I do not question that the majority of Christians in America are basically uninterested in wielding the sword of political power. Their chief interest—as Christians, that is—is that of preserving spiritual and moral autonomy under existing political power. But there is a large, and apparently fast-growing, minority of Americans whose zeal for Christ and overwhelming confidence in their righteousness make politics an

irresistible beacon. If politics is the name of the game, and it is in our age, then let born-againness become a political as well as a spiritual rite.

Thus the nakedly political approach of the evangelicals to such matters of morals and faith as abortion, prayers in the schools and other public places, and the so-called right to life of the comatose in hospitals. There will be a great deal more of this in the decades ahead.

Labor unions in the United States offer a panorama of politicization, with the political function of unionism now superior to the economic function that led to unions in the first place. Prior to World War I, the unions were just as eager for autonomy in the state as were universities and churches. The war changed that. It was part of war strategy for the home front to make everybody, capitalist and wage earner alike, happy. Unions were accorded a special honor and privilege by the several economic czars Wilson appointed. After the war the famous labor leader Samuel Gompers chose the older course of keeping unions as free as possible of political involvement. He was totally opposed to the course of politicization he could see in Europe, a course that transformed mutual aid economic associations into political parties, even parts of the state.

But Gompers's philosophy did not win out. Increasingly, the unions saw the capture of political power as the quickest way of enlarging membership and their rights against employers. The Norris-LaGuardia Act of 1932 exempted unions from antitrust laws and outlawed use of injunctions in labor matters; the National Industrial Recovery Act of the following year, and especially the National Labor Relations Act of 1935, went a long way in the politicization of the American trade union simply through heaping ostensible privileges, special protections by the state, upon labor leaders. It was strengthening to the unions for some time, but in the long run the politicization of the unions has contributed a great deal to their waning importance as economic powers. So thick are the political restrictions now—with the federal government even directly governing at least one large union—that there is little room for autonomous mobility by the unions today. Basically the unions no longer have the once-feared strike threat. The AFL-CIO headquarters in Washington is close enough to the White House to suggest a government bureau, and that is about what organized labor has become—to consequent erosion of morale.

So do the great universities threaten, by the sheer volume of political demands upon the federal government, to become in due time as politicized as the universities in Europe and Latin America. Among

several meanings of academic freedom is that of a college's or university's freedom from the power of government ministries or departments. Until World War II the unwritten law of laws in the university world was the duty of the university to stay as clear of the national state as possible; that is, not to allow its academic freedom to be jeopardized by government bureaus sniffing and poking around. Although Wilson had drawn heavily on scholars to engage in war propaganda work, he did not involve the universities themselves.

That changed dramatically in World War II when, by early 1942, the militarization of the university was well in progress. Courses were hastily adapted to "national defense" curricula, young soldiers were marched from class to class, whole colleges were occasionally taken over for war training, and research was almost totally military in character in the sciences and remarkably so even in the humanities.

Today the university is becoming a creature of the national state, in funding primarily but thereby, almost necessarily, in impact upon university policy, and in general orientation to political strategy. The recent powerful demonstrations of students and faculty in the major universities on disinvestment in South Africa were only the latest illustration of the political power possessed by campuses at the present time. To what extent the university will remain an academic instead of a political university of the kind that has become legion in Latin America, the Far East, and other parts of the world is still unclear. Such is the extent to which the forces of militarization and politicization have already left heavy impress on the American university.

Without doubt one of the most vivid and ominous tendencies in our present age is the politicization of mind and behavior that is to be seen in the churches, the labor unions, the universities, the professions, and indeed so much of ordinary social concern. For the most part the object of the drive toward politicization is the state at its highest level. As I write, we read in the press of the televangelist Pat Robertson, currently a candidate for the U.S. presidency. A decade and a half ago, in a personal testament published and sold widely, the Reverend Mr. Robertson wrote that God had commanded him for Himself, and not, therefore, for politics. God, we can only conclude at this point, has changed his mind or else found even himself impotent before the spell of politics in America in the present age.

Accompanying the rage to political power in our age is the relentless march of royalism in the federal government. We see this in the presi-

dency perhaps foremost, and I shall restrict myself for the most part to this office. But it would be negligent to overlook the trail of royalism in other departments of government also: in the Supreme Court where, as I have just emphasized, the temptation to make law instead of merely interpreting becomes ever stronger; in the Congress, especially the Senate, where more and more recourse is had to televised performances of Senate committees sitting inquisitorially over individuals, hailed commandingly by subpoena to come in front of it and be interrogated, often sharply, before the many millions of the television audience—descendants perhaps of those who used to enjoy public hangings. Everywhere, in the federal courts, in the halls and offices of Congress, in the White House, the mantle of luxury shines—a luxury of appointments, architecture, and style that one cannot often find in Europe anymore.

This is particularly noticeable in the presidency, in the present-day, post–Kennedy White House, never as resplendent before as under the Reagans; in the luxuriousness that pervades every corner and crevice of the presidential life; in the incessant imaging of the president for public purposes; and in the palace intrigues by now rife in every White House. Capture of the White House has appealed to utopians, reformers, and plain movers and shakers since the beginning of the century. From the time Wilson assumed the absolutism of his war powers in 1917 and commenced the radical transformation of America implicit in the War State, there has been a kind of dream of the strong, active, robust, commanding president that included more than a mere touch of plebiscitary democracy in it.

Basic to the clerisy strategy of magnifying the presidency in the eyes of the people is the parallel work of denigrating Congress and the departments. It is usually a toss-up between Congress and the Department of State as to which will be made, in any given year, the chief donkey of government. It is nearly instinctual in the political clerisy— and this holds true whether the administration is Republican or Democratic—to portray the president as the elected representative of the entire people, "The People," as it is commonly put, with congressmen portrayed as like mayors and city councilmen, mere representatives of wards, sections, and districts, thus a cracked mirror of the People.

This is not, of course, the way the Framers of the Constitution saw the ideal of American government. Ben Franklin is said to have replied, when an outsider asked him which was being effected by the Constitutional Convention, a republic or a monarchy: "A republic, if you can keep it." Franklin's answer would no doubt be the same today were he

on the scene, but the words might be uttered with somewhat less confidence or optimism. During the past half-century we have seen the spirit of royalism rise considerably. Wilson is prototypical; not since have direct, personal powers been showered on a president by Congress, and with the approval of the Supreme Court, as they were on Wilson. But his presidency was one of austerity, and when the armistice came, demobilization of forces and return to constitutionality were immediate.

Present-day royalism in the federal government began with FDR. Few then present are likely to forget the excitement generated by his seeming assumption during the Hundred Days of just about all the powers of government. Congress was for the time relegated to the shades; the air was filled with alphabetical symbols of the agencies, bureaus, strategies he was pursuing on his own. He found it possible to receive credit even for entities like the Tennessee Valley Authority and the Reconstruction Finance Agency in which his role was slim at best. He did create on his own the ill fated National Recovery Administration, a fusion of government and business that suggested Italian Fascism and was rather quickly ruled unconstitutional by the Supreme Court. With undiminished effort at autocracy, FDR sought to get a bill through Congress that would have—on the pretext of enhancing the Court's efficiency—increased significantly the size of the Court, thus making it possible for him to add justices of his own predilection. He was defeated on that by Congress.

Royalism is the essence of Roosevelt's wartime stance. Churchill, true architect of the salvation of the West from both Nazism and Soviet Communism and resplendent leader in action, was obliged, as noted above, to report regularly to Parliament and almost daily to the powerful War Cabinet. In no way was his leadership diminished; he thought, indeed, that Roosevelt would have been aided by a similar regimen. Roosevelt would have had none of it under any circumstances. His consultation of Congress, once the war was entered, was infrequent and minimal. So was his consultation of the Cabinet. So was his consultation of any high official of government, including the Secretary of State, Cordell Hull. Churchill became the war's most illustrious leader without departing from constitutionalism. Roosevelt came very close to flouting constitutionalism, electing to confide in and listen to Harry Hopkins and, to somewhat less degree, General Marshall.

Under the Kennedy administration royalism was reinvigorated. From the beginning the theme, broadcast widely through a compliant

press, was the "power of the president." To this end courtiers—there is no other appropriate word—appeared named Rostow, Schlesinger, Bundy, McNamara, Rusk, Hillsman, and Goodwin. This is the group given journalistic immortality by David Halberstam in his *The Best and the Brightest.* Although they all held regular governmental positions, including high Cabinet secretaryships, the real influence of the group came from their direct, *personal* fealty to the young and histrionic president.

Under President Kennedy's authority alone the number of military advisers to Diem in South Vietnam was increased from a few hundred to more than fifteen thousand, commanded by a four-star general. Under the same authority came the tragic and fateful decision to depose President Diem, thus leading to Diem's murder and also to our eight-year nightmare of war in Asia, eight thousand miles away. Precisely the same kind of exercise of presidential authority, nourished only by courtiers, not genuinely constitutional bodies of advisers like congressional committees and full departments like State and Defense, led at the very beginning of the Kennedy administration to the Bay of Pigs fiasco.

Royalism has not disappeared since Kennedy's assassination, only subsided slightly from time to time. Lyndon Johnson's Tonkin Gulf ruse gave him individual war powers suggestive of Roosevelt's and Wilson's. So did his reshaping of domestic bureaucracy through the Great Society program. Intrigue in the palace was constant; so was public discontent over his war in Vietnam. The President was in effect deposed, saved from that actuality only by grace of the election of 1968.

Since then in the reigns of Nixon and Reagan there have been analogous, even worse, incidents of extreme hypertrophy of White House power. National security, that ancient refuge of despotic monarchs, has become the portmanteau for at least two clutchings for personal power by the president: Watergate and, most recently, Irangate. National security as shield takes on some of the odor of *raison d'état* in Renaissance Europe, the plea of "reason of state" to conceal crime, heresy, or treason, or all three, in a given kingly court. The National Security Adviser—who has his own special power undergirded by a large and growing staff and which is composed for the most part of individuals sworn in fact to the personal being of the president rather than to the seals of government—would make the Framers rub their eyes. For in it, as it has been interpreted almost continuously since the Kennedy administration, lies, by implication at least, almost everything

the Fathers of the Constitution loathed and abominated in the Old World.

National security is, like *raison d'état*, a wonderful umbrella for extensions of the presidential-royal power. Whether the president personally, consciously, participates in these extensions in domestic and foreign matters is just as hard to discover as ever it was when a Henry VIII or Louis XIV was involved. For the vast White House power is wielded today by a score of loyal, faithful personal retainers dedicated to protection of the royal presence and largely out of reach of legislative bodies. Government of laws and of offices threatens thus to be supplanted by government of personal retainers, of courtiers—hit men, jesters, confidential clerks, envoys of the most personal and secret responsibility, one and all thrilled at the work of guarding, when necessary, the government and the people from their duly elected, constitutionally vested representatives.

Perhaps the ultimate thus far in *raison d'état* in the name of the higher patriotism and morality that is above the law is the recent Poindexter-North intrigue, possibly even a small coup d'état, as it all unrolled. Here, an admiral and a marine lieutenant-colonel between them, serving as members of the National Security Council staff, took upon themselves the engineering of foreign policy to a degree that strains the vocabulary of the comic as well as the ominous. The height of the dark comedy was reached when the admiral relieved the President of the-buck-stops-here responsibility for the execution of a major, if ultimately farcical, coup in foreign policy.

Inevitably, given the temper of the times and the ubiquity of the political clerisy, the blame for White House coups and secret governments and grossly illegal operations abroad falls on Congress, sometimes the Court but never the royal presence of the president. For the clerisy that would amount to *lèse-majesté*. To shield, protect, conceal, dissemble for the president is now high among the responsibilities of the several hundred *politiques* who fill the White House and adjoining buildings as "staff." This began in the Kennedy administration; there the gravest offense any one of the protecting aides could be found guilty of was failing to absorb the possible blame to the President created by his own actions or words. The president is never wrong! If he appears to be wrong in the eyes of press and people, someone in the White House curia, or janissariat, has failed in his job by not instantly absorbing full responsibility. Repeatedly during the Iran-*contra* hearing, Admiral Poindexter and also Colonel North made evident their devotion

to the principle that the President must be protected even from his own judgment. This was the ground on which the admiral justified not only his withholding of vital information from the President but his actual destruction of documents signed by the President. Such treatment may be proper occasionally for traditional heads of state, whether kings, emperors, or presidents, who by office and tradition must be above the fray at all times. But it is hardly a fit role for the executive of the government.

Government by deception, by flat lying, grows apace in America. Prior to Franklin Roosevelt deliberate lies by chief executives, or indeed public officials of any considerable consequence, were few and, when detected, deemed reprehensible. Presidents before FDR were charged with everything from sexual immorality to blind political stupidity, but not with calculated deception of the public. When Roosevelt declared to the people that his reason for wishing to see the Supreme Court enlarged was a desire for greater judicial efficiency, he lied and everyone knew it. When, after the Germans invaded the Soviet Union in June 1941 and Roosevelt took the lead in organizing a vast program of Lend-Lease for the Soviets, such was his desire to whiten their reputation that he even called a press conference in the fall of that year in order to declare that despite all misunderstanding, the Soviet constitution did grant freedom of religion. He didn't have to go that far, but he did. When he returned from Yalta in early 1945, he would have been forgiven had he said nothing about what was done at the Crimean conference. But he chose to go before Congress and lie about concessions to the Soviets in Eastern Europe, the Far East, and the United Nations. Again, he didn't have to; but he did, by politics-governed choice.

Between Roosevelt's death in 1945 and 1960 when the Kennedy administration took office there was something of a moratorium on lying in the White House, though Eisenhower shocked the country when he lied in whole cloth about the U-2 spy plane shot down by the Soviets. Unlike the "Gay Deceiver" who had been his commander in chief in the war, Eisenhower didn't present the image of the liar.

The Kennedys did, however, and they lied with maximum confidence. There were the lies covering the buildup of American military forces in South Vietnam; about the threat of Soviet missiles coming to Cuba—lies which persisted until the last minute despite Senator Keating's public warnings, followed by the all-out "eyeball to eyeball" crisis involving Kennedy and Khrushchev; about the bugging of Martin Luther King, Jr.; about Chappaquiddick; about the gangster's moll mistress, and so on.

Johnson gave the world the biggest lie yet to come from the president of the United States: the Tonkin Gulf lie, which led to the notorious Tonkin Gulf Resolution and then to the War Powers Act, and who knows what yet to come.

With Nixon came the crescendo of lying that went with Watergate, not to forget the fateful bombing of Cambodia. It would be tedious to go further here and also needless. Before it is over the Reagan administration may well be proved to have captured the prize for systematic lying to the public. The Iran-*contra* episode alone has made the administration a formidable contender for the century's prize. But it is well to recall that an imposing background exists for the Reagan accomplishments in public deception, a background going all the way back to President Wilson's assurance to the country in 1916 that no secret understandings existed with Great Britain and, despite the poisonous "rumor," no secret plans for an American military draft.

Journalists have estimated that not more than about 20 percent of the American people will by this late date believe the White House or the president personally when a major announcement is made. More than a decade ago I wrote the following lines; I see no reason to qualify them:

Of all passions, A. E. Housman wrote, passion for the truth is the feeblest in man. Of course. Who will not lie to save himself? Neither the common law nor the American Constitution demands that any individual tell the truth when such act would tend to incriminate him. Lying in behalf of self, of friends, of family, of military allies: all this is as old surely as mankind. Casuistical nuances in matters of truth and falsehood are a part of the fabric of traditional morality and law.

It is different, however, with the great mass societies we call modern democracies when habitual, institutionalized lying comes to be considered a part of the governmental process. A fateful circular pattern develops: the more that credibility in the government's capacity to do all that it arrogates to itself drops, the greater is the amount of lying necessary by bureaucracies and officials; and the greater the amount of lying, the faster the decline in government credibility.

* * *

A final example, and glittering emblem, of the royalization of the American presidency is what has recently come to be known as the president's living memorial; that is, a monument built in his lifetime, during his presidency perhaps, to the stipulated greatness of his reign. Money for construction is raised among private citizens, but thereafter the memorial becomes a responsibility of the federal government—like the Washington Mall or the Jefferson Memorial. In the beginning, with FDR's Hyde Park home made an official archive of personal papers, the justification was simply that: an archive to facilitate scholars' study of a presidential administration. There was little if any pretense of a "memorial," for in American history memorials were posthumous, like the memorials to Washington, Jefferson, Lincoln, and others in Washington, D.C. A long time passed before the greatness of those three was recognized by monuments.

Not so today. The moment a new president takes office work begins, or is jolly well expected by the White House to begin, on the living memorial. As for archives, yes, some space will indeed be allotted, but the Carter and now the Reagan plans for personal monuments include a great deal more than collections of papers. If each is to be a living memorial, it must be the setting for more than scholars. It must be a pulsating matrix of possessions of presidents, reminders, photographic and other, incunabula, period pieces, and general memorabilia attesting to the expanse of the empire this president ruled over. There must be large parking lots, special throughways built, day-care centers, restaurant facilities, conference rooms galore, movies, tableaus, etc.—all in memory of a president, probably still living well and healthily, of whose real importance in political history no one has the remotest idea. For Reagan, whose living memorial bids fair to become the grandest of them all, even a substantial piece of the Stanford University campus was not too egregious a demand; and when the trustees finally summoned up the courage to deny the campus to the Reagan memorial, the bitter howl of ideology and politics was raised immediately.

Pyramids like those of the ancient pharaohs would be cheaper in the long run; even less royal in thrust.

III

THE LOOSE INDIVIDUAL

REPEATEDLY in history the combination of war and political centralization leads to a fraying effect upon the social fabric. Threads are loosened by the tightening of power at the center. Dr. Johnson once told Boswell of a man in London he knew who "hung loose upon society." Loose in the sense of the loose cannon, the ship that slips its hawser, the dog its leash, the individual his accustomed moral restraints.

Without doubt there are a great many loose individuals in American society at the present time: loose from marriage and the family, from the school, the church, the nation, job, and moral responsibility. What sociologists are prone to call social disintegration is really nothing more than the spectacle of a rising number of individuals playing fast and loose with other individuals in relationships of trust and responsibility. From the right level, it could all look like what physicists call a Brownian movement, one in which molecules fly about in no discernible patterns. It is not entropy, as Henry and Brooks Adams thought, but Brownian. The cause may not lie within the group but in some distant magnet, such as the centralized state or capitalism become seductive, which loosens the individual's relationships with family and other ascribed institutions.

Tocqueville put his finger on political centralization, upon "despotism," in his word, as the principal cause of the waves of egoism, selfishness, and self-seeking which from time to time roll over societies—as has been the case in the West at least since post–Peloponnesian Athens, the age that dismayed Plato and led to *The Republic*. Tocqueville's own France of the early nineteenth century—the France, too, of Balzac and his brilliant landscapes and portraits of the French social and economic scene in *The Human Comedy*—was in many respects like our own at the present time in America.

The chief aspect of the society around him was, for Tocqueville, the

eroding away of traditional associations like family, social class, and "craft fraternities" of economic life. With the disappearance of such associations the individual is left freer and freer of the restraints which normally establish checks upon behavior. The government, Tocqueville argues, far from trying to impede this erosion of limits, encourages it in the interest of its own power.

Money becomes the common denominator of human life. It acquires an "extreme mobility" and "everybody is feverishly intent on making money. . . . Love of gain, a fondness for business careers, the desire to get rich at all costs . . . quickly become ruling passions under a despotic government."* Government is the primary force in it all; such government weakens where it strengthens: weakens normal social authority as it strengthens itself through laws, prohibitions, and taxes. As the blood rushes to the head of society, it leaves anemic the local and regional extremities.

Others, however, including Burke, Carlyle, and Marx, have made the economic factor central in the process of loosening ties and multiplying loose individuals. It was the vast debt of France, Burke insisted, that formed the background against which "a great monied interest had insensibly grown up, and with it, a great power. . . . The monied power was long looked on with rather an evil eye by the people. They saw it connected with their distresses, and aggravating them. . . . The monied interest is in its nature more ready for any adventure, and its possessors more disposed to new enterprises. Being of recent acquisition, it falls in more naturally with any novelties. It is therefore the kind of wealth which will be resorted to by all who wish for change."**

Burke gives the label "new dealers" to the members of this monied class. Later Carlyle, responding to what seemed to him a "spiritual emptiness" of his age, called in the "cash nexus" as the main force. Cash payment, he wrote, is "the sole nexus between man and man." Relationships of kin and neighborhood which had been fundamental in human society for countless ages were of a sudden, as it seemed, transposing themselves into relationships of money alone. Not long after, Marx and Engels in the *Manifesto* wrote of the bourgeoisie that "wherever it has got the upper hand, [it] has put an end to all feudal, patriarchal, idyllic relations. It has pitilessly torn asunder the motley

*Alexis de Tocqueville, *The Old Regime and the French Revolution* (1856). Doubleday Anchor Books, 1955. Foreword, xiii
**Reflections on the Revolution in France* (1790). New York: Holt, Rinehart and Winston, 1959. p.133f

feudal ties that bound man to his 'natural superiors,' and has left remaining no other nexus between man and man than naked self-interest, than callous 'cash payment.' "

Two ideal types come to mind which give emphasis as well as perspective to the kind of society that Carlyle and Marx sought to limn. In the first, possibly the kind that Marx called primitive communism, all relationships in a community are formed solely of the trust, allegiance, fealty, and responsibility which emanate from the kinship roles of the members of the community. No monetary or other denominator exists to dilute the directness of the social bond.

In the second ideal type, there are no such personal, role-determined relationships at all in society. Every act of service, responsibility, protection, and aid to others is an act presupposing or calling for monetary exchange, for cash payment. What individuals do for their spouses, for their children and kinsmen, for neighbors and all other common partners in the business of maintaining family, job, citizenship, and even personal identity itself, rests upon the cash nexus and nothing else.

Most Americans, if asked which of the two ideal types just described most resembles American society at the present time, would doubtless choose the second, and who is to say they are wrong? It is evident that while ancient personal values of trust, loyalty, and selfless service to others have by no means disappeared, they do not count as much in the marketplace as they once did. And "marketplace" as a setting has come to include more and more relationships once declared utterly alien to it. When Balzac said that "the power of a five-franc note has become sovereign," he was referring to the France of the post–Napoleonic age. The power of the five-dollar bill, sufficiently exerted, is enough to open all doors in America today.

The loose individual is a familiar figure in our age. Whether in the role of the deviant, delinquent, alienated, anomic, bored, narcissistic, as the case may be, he displaces a good deal of social atmosphere. Beginning with the economy, I want to suggest in this chapter some of the haunts of our ubiquitous nonhero.

The economy is rich in such figures. I take "economy" in its proper, large sense to include in our day evangelists of the television ministries, who alone form an economic system of profit and loss running into the billions; the baseball, football, and basketball stars; the university, once as noneconomic in function as a monastery, but no longer; and the now thick crowd of ex-generals, ex-admirals, ex-ambassadors, and ex-presi-

dents who, whether in lecture fee, corporate directorship, book author-
ship, or consulting business, demonstrate how often and quickly the
revolving door turns.

I shall come back to these individuals; but let us first look at the
economy proper, site of property and profit in the old sense. Almost half
a century ago, the distinguished Harvard economist Joseph Schumpeter, in his *Capitalism, Socialism and Democracy,* laid out clearly the
essential processes leading to the business and financial scene of the
present. Schumpeter referred to an "evaporation" of property; more
particularly, an "Evaporation of Industrial Property" and an "Evaporation of Consumer Property," both reflecting a historical trend of tidal
proportions that had been going on in the West and especially in
America over the past century. The effect of Schumpeter's evaporation
of industrial property—looking at the matter solely from the property-
holder's viewpoint—was the substitution of the "soft" property of
shares of stock and bonds for the "hard" property of land, buildings,
and machines that the property-holder had once managed as well as
owned in the passive sense and had been very much a part of in its
operation. Independently of volition such a property-holder had a distinct stake in society, a role of social responsibility based upon day-to-
day mingling with managers, workers, and consumers.

Very different is the "evaporated" property owner, typically possess-
ing shares of stock existing in their own seemingly detached, stock
market world, independent of their owner's will beyond the buying and
selling of the shares. There is far less stake in society in this kind of
property. After all, a single safe-deposit box can hold many millions of
dollars of property, the whole requiring little of the attention and
responsibility that are mandatory when property exists in the forms of
land, buildings, and machinery. An atmosphere of not only impersonal-
ity but irresponsibility is created by evaporated property. The fabled
miser hoarding his gold must be changed as metaphor to something like
the man-about-town enjoying his debentures, if we are to do justice to
the present age. Less and less seems to depend upon the traditional
virtues of prudence and social responsibility in the husbanding of one's
wealth, and more and more depends upon Fortuna. Thus the atmosphere of the gambling casino begins to permeate not only one's economic but also one's familial and community life.

The evaporation of hard property makes for a liquefied atmosphere
that alternates in individual lives from trickle to cloudburst. We learn
to travel lightly on the principle that he who does so can eat up vaster

distances in a lifetime. Above all, travel alone so far as possible; friends, relatives, wards are all hostages to fortune. A house as compared with a condominium or rental is a drag on one's existence. *Ecrasez l'infamie!*

It is evident that as the result of the two evaporations, we have the foundation prepared for a very different kind of capitalism from that of a century ago. More and more capitalism tends to "exalt the monetary unit" over the type of property that theoretically alone gives the monetary unit its value.

Central to this process of evaporation of the two kinds of property, producer and consumer, is the profoundly changed character of the family. Despite the myth of economic man, of the "individual enterpriser," the chief dynamism of capitalism was for a long time provided by the middle-class family—a family that until recently considered itself as inseparable from the future as from present and past. The typical capitalist did not work for himself; he was not a creature of atomistic self-interest. He worked for his family, meaning chiefly his children and their children, and thereby for the future—so vital to long-run investment. Schumpeter writes:

> In order to realize what all this means for the efficiency of the capitalist engine of production we need only recall that the family and the family home used to be the typically bourgeois kind of profit motive. Economists have not always given due weight to this fact. When we look more closely at their idea of the self-interest of entrepreneurs and capitalists, we cannot fail to discover that the results it was supposed to produce are really not at all what one would expect from the rational self-interest of the detached individual or the childless couple who no longer look at the world through the windows of a family home. Consciously or unconsciously they analyzed the behavior of a man whose views and motives are shaped by such a home and who means to work and to save primarily for wife *and children.* *

From devotion to family, not from ineluctable, imperishable "instinct to truck and barter," to advance oneself solely in the interest of power and status—thus came the dynamic of capitalism as the West knew it prior to the present day. Thus comes the dynamic of the capitalism of the Western Pacific Rim nations today. From consecration to, and willingness to sacrifice for, the family, then—rather than from religion—came the entrepreneur's motivation and discipline, his

---

*Joseph Schumpeter, *Capitalism, Socialism and Democracy.* New York: Harper and Brothers, 1942. p. 160

willingness to sacrifice for the future. No abstract, amorphous future was involved; it was literally the future as embodied in children, grandchildren, and great-grandchildren that seems to have mattered most to the entrepreneur of old. To work for family—the family-in-time—necessitated forbearance and sacrifice. You chose between spending annual income on self and its desires or on future generations who would carry your name proudly for all posterity. If you chose the first, you were Dr. Johnson's individual "hanging loose upon society"; if the second, you were Thomas Mann's Buddenbrooks of first and founding generation. But forbearance and prudence and an eye to future generations of family did not at all crowd out a certain type of spending: the type manifest in stately town house, perhaps in a house on the seashore for summer use, in a staff, however small, of servants, preferably those living in. As Schumpeter observes, all these and like attributes attested to the stake one had in society, the success with which a possible family dynasty in commerce was being met at an early stage. Even so, ultimate grace was the product of saving and investing, sacrificing in the present for the future. Schumpeter writes:

> The capitalist process, by substituting a mere parcel of shares for the walls of and machines in a factory, takes the life out of property. . . . And this evaporation of what we may term the material substance of property—its visible and touchable reality—affects not only the attitudes of holders but also of the workmen and of the public generally. Dematerialized, defunctionalized and absentee ownership does not impress and call forth moral allegiance as the vital form of property did. Eventually there will be *nobody* left who really cares to stand for it—nobody within and nobody without the precincts of the big concerns.*

Morals inevitably suffer, meaning particularly the morals of honesty and loyalty to others. Morals are no emanations from heaven; everywhere, from the beginning of conscience in the human race, from the time when the human mind first made the astounding leap from "is" to "ought," what we call morals are firmly set in what the Romans called the mores, customs and habits of age and sanctity. As a result of the disappearance or sharp reduction of the disciplines upon the self which went inescapably with older kinds of property, and of the rise of the present widely spread monetary unit of property—that is, of liquidity, of cash nexus—morality becomes expendable. Who needs it?

---

*Schumpeter, p. 142

* * *

The evaporation of property Schumpeter describes had its effective beginning in World War I in America. The war introduced Americans to money in a bulk and an ostensible ease of creation they had never known before. The decision by Wilson to finance the war, not by taxes on the spot but by bonds, reaching several billions in amount, in itself had a measurable effect on the American mind. For the great majority such matters as stocks, bonds, and other debentures were arcane in the highest degree. The stock and bond markets were for the few, not the many, for the classes, not the masses. One made money as one's father and grandfather had, by saving and investing in hard, tangible property. There was never a great deal of cash around in the economy, and credit was for most Americans something to be avoided like the plague. Jobs were hard to get and when one got one, he stayed with it to the end; he didn't persistently shop around for better jobs and wages. Land, of course, rural or urban, was clutched by its owners as though life itself depended upon it. It was the supreme form of capital; one lived off his capital through interest and rent; only fools ever dipped into their capital.

The vast excitement of 1917–1919 changed or began the change in this style of living. Of a sudden money, spendable money, increased immensely as the result of almost total employment and generally at high-wage jobs. Profits were generous; several thousand millionaires were created by World War I. Under Wilson's indulgent regulations, none of the appointed czars of business and commerce were likely to look too hard at undue wage increases; they kept the workers happy and productive, didn't they? The whole effect of the economic spasm that went with the war was to enlarge the average middle-class American's proclivity to spend instead of save and put by.

There were, of course, those whose immediate thought was expenditure of war-made money to buy the kind of property, industrial or consumer or both, their fathers had known, to fit into and perpetuate the older pattern of living—town house, country house, servants, and so on—to save, invest in growth industries, and in general sink comfortably into the old middle-class comfort and propriety. But there were others who, beginning in the 1920s, made it evident that the old style of business, finance, and living was not for them. The result was a substantial contribution to what became known as the "Roaring Twenties," a decade of escalating stock market values such as the world had never seen, and the birth of dreams in which the old-fashioned ways of

making money—hard work, saving, investment, production of needed and wanted goods—were scattered to the past, with the new ways of slickly managed buy-outs, mergers, inside deals, and the like taking over. The Depression and New Deal reform stopped but did not kill the new ways of making money which had been breaking records on Wall Street.

World War II, of course, did exactly what the First War had done to America, but on an immensely greater scale. And the postwar of the late 1940s and early 1950s proved to be a business and financial saturnalia without precedent. No real depression interrupted things this time. Schumpeter's principles of evaporation of property—of conversion of the hard to the soft, of tangible ownership and management of plant to parcels of highly negotiable shares, of commodity to service, and withal an ever-growing liquidity of the financial world, with oceans of cash and instant credit lying around for quick use—all these new forces moved like a single great avalanche across the financial terrain. Clearly the cash nexus was diffusing and deepening its mesmeric impact upon people to a degree that neither Marxian nor classical economists had foreseen. If cash is the real thing instead of land development, factories, manufacturing, and the creation of products and services important to society, then certain other things will automatically assume importance too: frenzied buying and selling in the multitude of markets available in this country and throughout the world, a pronounced turning from product creation to simple ordinary money creation, and, as the record makes plain, leveraged buy-outs, networks of mergers, takeovers, insider tradings legal and illegal, poison pills, golden parachutes, and much else.

In such circumstances the loose individual flourishes. For in an epoch of high liquidity, incessant turnover of shares, and fast-moving takeovers, mobility on the part of the operator is imperative. Those who are mired in tradition, in ancient concepts of trust, honor, and loyalty to house will be losers. Looseness of economic muscle is indispensable. "Conservative" was once an accolade to a bank or brokerage house. Today it is anathema. Black Monday of October 1987 may have set in motion opposite impulses here, to be sure. We shall see.

The worst part of it perhaps is the inevitable flouting of the basic conditions of economic growth over the long term. When leverage is suddenly created to pay out shareholders today, that is, right now and be damned to the future, the American economy loses not only the spurs to real development but much of the cutting edge in foreign competition. Some of the most dubious sectors of the economy receive

an inflation of ostensible value through infusions of money which shortly worsen the actual condition of the companies so infused. The role of banks, savings and loans, and all other manufacturers of credit, of money, is today vast and therefore, given the fiduciary essence of such institutions, increasingly precarious.

The pretentious and sometimes duplicitous assurances of the raiders would be the stuff of comedy if it weren't approaching tragedy. For they seem actually to believe—some of them, at least—that by raiding a decently run corporation, artificially jacking up its price on the stock market through the use of high-yield credit, including junk bonds, they are in consequence improving the management of the corporation. Those who in the old days solemnly defended horse racing and its heavy gambling profits by assurance that they were "improving the breed" have been vastly outdone by the T. Boone Pickenses of our day who assure us with equal solemnity that arbitragers and raiders of all kinds are "improving the management" of corporate America.

The cash nexus is the thing! Why build an industry when you can, if you are slick and agile enough, take one over—with junk bonds, if necessary—and then sell it off at the very second the value of the shares reaches a proper point on the market. Such slick agility doesn't help posterity but, as the congressman once asked, what has posterity done for me? What is astounding is the relative ease of the operation. If there is resolute opposition on the part of the management of the corporation being raided, it will almost certainly pay greenmail to the raider, thus ending the threat of takeover and paying off with profits even more easily accumulated than the raider had thought. At all times, of course, looseness is vital to survival.

American industry badly needs investment, which in turn requires savings, but neither is likely in an age of quick, fluid profits and instant availability of cash or immediately negotiable shares and debentures. America has very low savings and investment rates compared with other industrial nations. Not nearly enough of the enormous liquidity of our current economy is transferred into the forces which govern economic growth.

As the economic and legal consultant Benjamin J. Stein points out, management in the larger corporations—once regarded as the very backbone of the system—is frequently in a position these days that is scarcely less than subversive. The chief executive officer of a corporation "buys" that corporation at, say, forty dollars a share, a price he himself is largely responsible for setting and one that receives the endorsement

of investment analysts. Lo and behold, the corporation almost immediately proves to be worth three hundred dollars a share, with billions in profit going to the CEO who has added literally nothing to the corporation or the economy. Stein says:

> Management sees that it has operations which are overstaffed. Management sees that it has pension funds which are overfunded, management sees that it can lay off employees temporarily, generate higher quarterly cash flow, and thereby make the outside world think that once the LBO is completed, they're making more money.
>
> I think that Wall Street and the LBO industry have turned corporate America into a vast junkyard of corporate spare parts, and this is not what America needs in a competitive world economy. I think LBOs have been a tragedy, and management LBOs have been a severe violation of the law and an infringement of the rights of ordinary people.*

There is not the slightest real evidence that through such shenanigans, which in the aggregate account for many billions of dollars a year, economic growth of America is helped. The pertinent facts lead indeed to the opposite conclusion. Edward F. Denison of Brookings Institution asserts that the evidence he has studied indicates leveraged buy-outs of whatever kind—investment bank instigated, management controlled, whatever—tend to lead to a decline of productivity. This is not hard to believe. Rearrangement of the deck chairs, irrespective of whether the *Titanic* is sinking or not, has nothing to do with the strength of the ship.

The huge federal budget—a trillion a year now, with its current budgetary deficits reaching three hundred billions a year, and our trade deficits making us a debtor nation in all important respects—necessarily carries with it a staggering interest charge; that is, an utterly nonproductive, sterile, but hugely burdensome lien against growth and stability. President Reagan, all the while caterwauling at Congress and fate, has not yet, in the six years of his office, submitted a balanced budget for Congress to ponder. Strange superstitions float in the atmosphere, beliefs in fiscal magic abound, leading to the proposal of such miracle-worshiping panaceas as continuing cuts in taxes and continuing fattenings of defense and Social Security budgets. Gibbon says that Rome in the fourth century so abounded in myth and awaited miracle.

Everyone wants to be rich but, equally important, loose in his

---

*Spoken on *Adam Smith's Money World*, October 5, 1987. Copyright © 1987 by Educational Broadcasting Companies.

relationship to anything—equities, family, church, lodge, whatever. In such a scene even the rich don't feel rich. Money becomes its own end, thus leading to a kind of contempt that lies uneasily inside the narcotic-like fascination of money. It is a reasonable guess that agonized reflections of this kind were rife on Wall Street on Black Monday, October 19, 1987. For nearly a decade, as back in the 1920s, it had all been such fun; easy, relaxed fun. LBOs, insider tradings, loose margin, oceans of liquidity, consumer ecstasy, all this and much more, seemingly forever. Came the Great Crash and Never-Never Land turned into black nightmare. The loose individual has, by choice, little to hang on.

In an economy as awash in liquidity as ours is today, with Hollywood entertainers like Eddie Murphy and Wall Street specialists like Ivan Boesky netting anywhere from twenty-five to fifty millions a year, with the Haft family making perhaps twice that for takeovers *that fail*, and with the stock, bond, commodities, and options markets dealing with amounts of money that reach astronomical heights on any given day, it would be strange—it would be sociologically absurd—if unethical and, as we have learned, outrightly criminal behavior were not constantly on the rise. When the notorious bank robber Willie Sutton was asked why he persisted in robbing banks, his answer was, "That's where the money is." Not today do our Harvard-educated, elegantly attired Willie Suttons bother with banks, unless it is to merge a few; the money, the real money is not in banks but in leveraged buy-outs, in quick applications of junk bonds to buy whole corporations, and to sell immediately, and in insider trading, to cite a tiny few of the approved *modi operandi* on Wall Street.

We mustn't overlook in this richly laden scene the golden parachute, as it is cutely labeled on Wall Street. The golden parachute as an escape hatch grievously wounds the old piety that for one to be well paid, he must work hard and be a success. Not today. There is the recent story, widely publicized, of the CBS chief executive who was fired; repeat, fired. One can only assume that his work and presence were found unsatisfactory by the board of directors. If so, the act of firing him turned instantly into one of the greater success stories in the corporate world. The happy miscreant was given several million dollars outright as a bonus, a life income of several hundred thousand dollars a year, and a possible bonanza in the form of valuable stock options. Where now, we are obliged to ask, the ancient proverb of the hard-working and frugal ant and the insouciant, lazy grasshopper? In a golden parachute, that's where.

One more note on loose individuals and the cash nexus. Even treason has lately moved from ideology to cash. Recall that when the physicist Klaus Fuchs stole almost the entirety of the atom bomb secrets from Britain and America, he did so for love of Communism and the Soviet Union alone. Today, as the recent Walker case demonstrates, treason and treachery are strictly cash on the barrelhead. How loose can you get?

The loose individual prowls the halls of academe as well as Wall Street these days. What is wrong with the contemporary university will not be made right by encounter sessions on Aristotle and Rousseau under the banner of Great Books; nor will it be improved by general smatterings courses aiming to produce the well-informed mind. (The merely well-informed mind is the greatest bore on God's earth, said the late Alfred North Whitehead.)

The university was damaged well before the Student Mania broke out in the 1960s (about which I shall speak in the next section). Universities, like churches, states, and other major institutions, are to be seen in the light of their major functions; when functions change without warning, without the tacit assent of their communities, revolutionary change is almost always in the near offing. The function of the American university had been from its inception teaching; research, yes, but strictly subordinated to teaching. For the last forty years the function has been organized research; teaching on the side, as it were, but only so long as it doesn't distract the research mind from its appointed, bureaucratized duties in laboratory and computer hall.

The transformation of the university began with World War II, perhaps a shade earlier. In the First World War, although scholars and scientists were drafted for high-level war duty, the campus itself was left alone. Few were the instances in which the War and Navy Departments actually moved onto a campus, taking it over for exclusively military instruction. But in World War II there was a great deal of taking over, of militarization of the halls of ivy. Within months of Pearl Harbor campuses rang to the sound of uniformed recruits hup-hupping their marched and ordered way from class to class, building to building. Dormitories overnight became military barracks.

More significant by far was the militarization of research in the universities. This could involve structural change in the university. For centuries research was individual, self-chosen, and responsible only to the audience for which it was done. But of a sudden in early World War

ll the Project came into being, to transform university research forever. The Project was financed by the government, labeled and code-numbered by the government, and usually declared secret by the government. The Manhattan Project, which yielded up the atom bomb, is perhaps the most celebrated, but there were—and are to this day— thousands of others. Today they are typically known as institutes, bureaus, and centers. They net lots of dollars.

A new academic bourgeoisie appeared on the American campus after the war, with the new, higher academic capitalism. The short term in research replaced the old, once unique, long-term pattern of research and scholarship. The reason was manifest. Funds of institutes and for projects tended to be annual, subject to one or two renewals perhaps, but not likely to be renewed for long unless results were quickly evident. Short-term profits, short-term research, and, increasingly, short-term teaching became the rule. Faculty began to be lauded for their fundraising activities for their research; and such activity soon tended to become an expectation on the part of administrations, even a criterion of promotion.

With the infusion of ever-enlarging capital from the government and the big foundations, every infusion, of course, requiring a contract, the idea of piece-rates began to penetrate the once austere halls of learning. "Contact hours" began to be specified, especially for teaching, and the increase or decrease in these contact hours affected what was increasingly known as one's "teaching load." The power of money to influence a social organization lies in its capacity to permeate social roles. Once the big money, in the form of project and institute research, invaded the campus, two nations tended to form in every faculty: the first, institute- and project-linked, arrogant in its possession of money that required no sense of obligation to the academic community; and the second, older nation, still committed to the ideal of *teaching* as well as research and to the hoary concept of *service*. The new nation easily subjugated the old everywhere.

The first million dollars of extramural grants to individuals on campuses was far, far too much. Today a hundred billion dollars a year would not be enough to meet the swollen expectations and demands of the institutes, bureaus, and projects which crowd out traditional communities of academic life. Huge amounts of money, from war-enriched foundations as well as from government, and from constantly rising appropriations for the public universities from compliant legislatures, all

combined to change the character of the university from service to cash nexus. It is possible today—not only possible but increasingly common—for a professor to become actually rich by virtue of his aristocratic position in contemporary society. Salaries of over a hundred thousand a year (for essentially an eight-month academic year) are becoming visible, in the humanities as well as the sciences. But salary is only the beginning. There are consultantships, substantial fees for attending conferences, textbooks and trade books carrying royalty rates that with a little luck in the book market can make a professor of art or physics look like a real swinger on Wall Street. At the present time, and I do not exaggerate, it is possible for a Mr. Chips, so called, to earn at least two hundred thousand dollars a year from salary, from book royalties, consulting fees, television appearances, and rewards for attending posh conferences and directors' meetings of big corporations. We reach the figure of two hundred thousand without bringing in likely stock and bond market extras.

Nor are these bonanzas limited to physical scientists—where, it is true, they began—and business-school wizards. Economists, even political scientists and sociologists, *even* humanists, especially of the genus that comports in what is solemnly called literary theory, do very well. To be a "deconstructionist," a "structuralist," or a "minimalist" today is like being a nuclear physicist right after World War II.

For centuries in the Western world, universities were primarily institutions for teaching and scholarship, in that order. Students comprised the largest single group at any given time in a university; next was the faculty; well down in number and significance was the support staff—janitors, purchasers, accountants, and so on. I have not made a rigorous count, but I would be astounded if today in any large university in the United States the support staff does not rival, even possibly exceed, faculty in number. By entering the Higher Capitalism after World War II, the university soon found itself with a bewildering corporate infrastructure, better known as bureaucracy, made necessary by the onset of the era of high finance.

In the atmosphere of competitive finance in today's university world, of big bureaucracy and incessant fund raising, of subordination of teaching to large-scale research, it is hardly surprising that the loose individual thrives. To hang loose upon the university today, fiercely competitive as the academic world has become, makes at least as much sense as in the corporate and financial world. It is not likely that

additional courses in the humanities will reduce the number of loose individuals in today's university.

Before leaving the contemporary university in America, I must say something about the so-called student revolution of the late 1960s. As I shall shortly indicate, this revolution was much more like one of the manias of history, crowd crazes, or mental epidemics, than it was a revolution in the ordinary sense of that word.

The first point is that the student mania of the 1960s was not so much a revolt against academic authority as it was the almost inevitable issue of a prior breakdown in university authority—a breakdown almost implicit in the changes in the university after World War II which I have just described. The natural authority of the teacher, scholar, and dean had fallen between the cracks opened up by the new academic bourgeoisie and the higher capitalism. It had become apparent by the early 1960s, approximately two decades after the war, that the teacher-scholar, the academic department, the academic school or college, mattered very little in the new order. What mattered was the institute, the bureau, the center, each by nature a practitioner of grantsmanship, of the attracting of large sums of money, in which the university as a whole would share.

As the center of gravity passed ever more surely from the old authorities to the new, from department, school, faculty, college—each primarily an organization directed at teaching and at students—to the institute, center, and bureau—each anchored in subsidized, contract, large-scale research alone—something of an earthquake took place in the historic university. It was too far down in the earth's bowels, too subterranean to be felt at first by more than a small number of perhaps preternatural minds, but when it was unmistakably felt, by the end of the 1950s, it was felt with a bang—nothing less than the Great Student Mania of the 1960s. It was not a revolution. Revolutions are hard work, demand discipline and some kind of agenda. The students, from Berkeley to Columbia, couldn't abide work, they had no agenda—save what an eager television news team might quickly thrust at them to make the stories of vandalism spicier—and they couldn't keep their minds on what they had done and said from one day to the next.

The earthquake which followed the titanic struggle for authority between the old and the new powers in the university opened up crevices and then whole crevasses and chasms. Students—at most, it is well to remember, a small minority—made restless anyhow by the war

in Vietnam, the civil rights thrusts of blacks at racial barriers rarely if ever challenged on a wide front in America, and the whole heady brew of Big Government, Big Business, and Big Battalions abroad—were hardly to be expected to remain blind to what was unfolding before them; they therefore acted, beginning in late 1964. Their action, from San Francisco State to Harvard, during the next five years consisted of a large-scale dramatization of counsel said to be Nietzschean: "If you see something slipping, push it." This the Mario Savios and Mark Rudds did—precisely, shatteringly, and, in terms of impact upon the credulous and rapt American media, very successfully, between 1965 and about 1972.

As I say, it is difficult to descry anything of the nature of a revolution in the student seizure. Revolution there surely was in what the largely black civil rights movement was accomplishing—a movement that was clearly evident from the late 1950s on—and also in what the anti-Vietnam protesters were accomplishing from about 1963 on. But these two movements are clearly distinguishable, if not always physically separable, from the campus rebellions and insurrections, which were, as I have suggested, far more in the nature of manias, religious, moral, and even economic rather than revolts.

Manias seem to be connected with suddenly perceived breakdowns in the accustomed practices and guidelines of a social order. The religious manias of the late Middle Ages and early modern times in the West sprang up in the cracks of the church, which was being slowly twisted and distorted by the power of the secular state. The Reformation was quite as much a political as a religious happening, and when vacuums were created in power, there were restless and often potent groups ready to move in. Puritan manias were common and often tumultuous in England in the seventeenth century. In their diversity and division they were scarcely a revolutionary force, though the effect of organized Puritanism under Cromwell had revolutionary character. But Puritan manias like the Levelers, Shakers, Quakers, and Fifth Monarchy were just that: manias, with a common antinomianism—a nihilistic assault on the spirit and letter of all the dogmas, liturgies, rituals, even morals and ethics, which could be associated with the hated Establishment, Roman or Anglican. Hence the exhibitions in public sometimes of fornication and defecation, the use of insulting language and gestures toward the aristocracy. It was a means of achieving blessedness with the true God: that is, the calculated flouting of laws and morals which had grown up under the false god of the Establishment.

At its height the student mania of the 1960s came close to the practices of the Puritan zealots in the English seventeenth century. Obscenities flourished, chiefly of language in public places, but also obscenities of the act, the performance, as at Chicago in the summer of 1968. Puritan acts of occupation, even desecration and destruction, of churches—favored means of demonstrating blessedness being the smashing of stained-glass windows in the great cathedrals and the destruction of coffins containing the bones of early kings and prelates—were faithfully emulated by students in administration offices, classroom buildings, and even libraries, demonstrating their purity of academic faith, their liberation from the false gods of the faculty and administration.

"What Do We Want? Everything. When Do We Want It? Now." That, one of the most favored emblazonments of the so-called revolution on the campus, illustrates sufficiently, I believe, the lack of any genuinely revolutionary message. Comparing themselves to "IBM cards," "niggers," and "peons" was about as far from reality in the postwar American university as anyone could conceivably reach.

Two French phrases, both old but both used with reference to the almost equally mania-seized students in the University of Paris at the time, illustrate something important about the student mania in America. *Retour à las bas* and *nostalgie de la boue*—"return to the down under" and "longing for the gutter"—describe with equal pertinence the occasional spasms of behavior to be seen at Berkeley, Harvard, Smith, and Radcliffe. There was a conscious, almost fanatic desire on the part of many students to wallow in the most elemental, the least intellectual, practices, flaunting them at the public, including parents; to wallow in the pit of primitivism or the mud of obscenity—and in just plain physical dirt. Middle-class children, those caught up in the mania, at least, learned for the first time in their lives what it was to go unbathed, unwashed, clad in filthy garments, for days at a time.

To both liberal applauders and conservative critics, the student mania was an exercise in romanticism, in demonstrating how human beings are when stripped of the habits and customs of their civilized existence. Liberals on and off the campus thought—and think to this day—that the antinomianism of the students showed them to be, beneath all the tyrannizing patterns of middle-class behavior which they were now sloughing off, Rousseauian children of nature, happy little savages. Conservatives, presumably not liking either the Pit or the Mud, were confirmed in their belief that once the social fundament is allowed

to crack and to open up fissures, the very foundations of reason and moral decency begin to erode away, pushing human beings ever closer to the void.

Faculty members, it must be said here, participated in substantial numbers: not of course in the more egregious acts of destruction and vandalism, but in the tender, loving care bestowed upon the Filthy Speech Movement and its analogues of the mania. New depths of innocence were discovered, and with these, new depths of the sadistic cruelty done these children of God by vengeful, hate-inspired, tyranni-cal middle-class American parents. To heal these twisted victims of middle-class conformity, courses were given without assignments or even lectures, in which the entire class would be guaranteed A's; votes were taken at faculty meetings in which majorities would endorse am-nesty in advance for whatever depredations might be wreaked upon libraries and laboratories; and, never to be forgotten, newspaper colum-nists and editorialists and especially television sages, all of whom per-sisted in regarding "the kids" as innocuous and lovable young idealists. It was no less a personage than Archibald Cox who, after being hired by the Columbia University Board of Trustees to make a thorough investigation of the student turmoil at Columbia, began his report by declaring that the participant students were from the "most idealistic" generation in the history of American education. With dispassionate experts like Cox, what need had the antinomian rebels for even the best of faculty friends?

The mania ended almost as abruptly as it had begun, in that respect too like the apocalyptic, millenarian crowd seizures of old in Western history. It was almost like going to bed on a given night listening to radio news of "the kids" in their obscenity hurling and window-smash-ing and then waking up the next morning and being told that the Age of the Yuppies had just dawned. The mania lasted about seven years on the campuses, with no particular educational demands or suggestions made, and clearly no significant educational results of their activities, but, as Southey wrote in "The Battle of Blenheim," "things like that . . . must be/After a famous victory." Perhaps Bishop Butler's words, out of the English eighteenth century, are the aptest epitaph: "Things and actions are what they are, and the consequences of them will be what they will be; why, then, should we desire to be deceived?"

During World War II and after a new breed came onto the cam-puses of the major universities: individuals who were like but not quite like teachers and scholars and academic types generally. So far as teach-

ing was concerned, it was something of an irritant but tolerable when necessary and not too demanding; scholarship appeared to them as would have the bustle on women faculty members. Research was the thing, not individual scholarship; research involving dozens at its best, organized like a military platoon to hunt down its prey—facts and more facts.

These were the new bourgeoisie engaged in the new and higher capitalism that had grown out of the war. Such was the damage they managed to do to traditional academic community and traditional academic authority, both rooted in the teaching vocation, that when the mania-seized "kids" came along in the sixties, there was nothing much more to be done than to mop up with brickbats—not a few of which managed to strike even the members of the new bourgeoisie, much to their consternation, ideological anguish, and incredulity. Why *me?*, asked one beleaguered institute titan after another. They rarely waited for an answer.

The cash nexus and loose individual have many haunts beyond Wall Street and the Multiversity. It is not easy to think of a major pursuit in America in which monetary units have not yet triumphed over the motivations and discipline of old. Three, eminently diverse, areas come to mind: sports, religion, and government service.

In sports a significant evolution of power has taken place since World War I: We have seen the original amateur—once a term of honor in our society—succeeded by the professional, the respectable professional, it should be said; then by the agent, ever solicitous of his client's income and investments and, of course, his own percentage. Sports have become as conspicuous and flagrant an example of the profit motive and the bottom line as any commercial operation known. But sports are something else: a secular religion in America, one that ranks only just behind education, which is by now a civil religion.

It is good that sports are so important. They—and especially the contact or "violent" ones like football, hockey, and boxing—play a role of relieving pressures in human beings which once had no other outlets but wars, Bedlams, and public hangings. If by some major accident we ever lose the mayhem of the hockey rink, gridiron, and prize ring, if we are limited, say, to track and field, heaven help the ordinary American who wants only law and order and peace.

The question is, how long can professional sports serve this important function—or any other function beyond their own preservation for

profit? The cash nexus threatens to outstrip anything found in corporate America and on Wall Street. We honor the free agent who, having had the chains of serfdom struck off, is now at liberty to run from one team to another as fancy and financial reward determine. We are glad to see him reach the position of hanging loosely on the sport. But fans identify powerfully with *teams,* and the greatest of individual heroes from Babe Ruth and Ty Cobb down to Walter Payton and Lawrence Taylor are linked with given teams as closely as with their own names. We all know that money is important in the form of salaries, bonuses, and other forms of remuneration, but we also know that, just as it is impossible to glean genuine heroes from the ranks of stockbrokers, bankers, salesmen, and vice-presidents for production, it becomes more and more difficult to keep one's mind on the performance of a Dave Winfield on the baseball diamond when rivaling it are the lush details of his latest contract—in the millions naturally, and made a little more interesting perhaps by the division into present income, deferred income, options, a special trust, and even, so help us, a foundation in his name. What confounds some of us is that all this is printed on the once-sacrosanct sports page, not the financial.

The celebrated bottom line is the sole reason we have so many teams in baseball, football, and basketball that East-West, North-South divisions are necessary, themselves perhaps cut into sections, with play-offs today calculated to give anyone a rough notion of infinity. Further adding to the possibility of present bewilderment and future boredom, and also a product of the cash nexus and a lubricant to looseness of the individual, is the relentless specialization of play. The player who is paid for but one activity—field goal kicking, kickoff return, or whatever— obviously is hanging more loosely on the game than his predecessors who, if they played at all, played sixty minutes, on offense and defense. It is really impossible to compare current with past stars in any of the major sports. No matter how we may thrill to a Jim McMahon and a Joe Montana at quarterback today, we are getting a good deal less from them than we did from quarterbacks who once upon a time played sixty minutes, on defense as well as offense, who themselves called the plays, ran with the ball, and often punted and drop-kicked. Tocqueville, speaking of the damaging effect upon the worker's mind of the extreme specialization that went with division of labor, said that under such specialization "the art advances but the artisan recedes." Today the fan as well as the player is receding, in Tocqueville's sense.

It will be more and more difficult for most of us to keep balanced

in our minds the dual role of the player: on the one hand, the high-salaried, expert worker in a basically machine effort; and on the other, the warrior jousting as did warriors of old for victory, sweet victory, on the field of battle, and the devil take all else.

Turning to religion, more particularly to the large and extremely important part of it that exists on the airwaves, radio and television alike, we are also confronted by a passion for gold and a looseness of ethics that have little to do with religion as it was once understood, and is still understood by a large number of Americans. Churches become gaudier; their ancillary activities, ranging from elaborate hostelries for unwed mothers all the way to Disneyland types of entertainment facilities—income tax–exempt, of course—more numerous and generally profit-making; and their campaigns for gifts of money more fevered all the time. When you turn the televangelist on, you find yourself making mental bets as to just how long he will be able to restrain the plea, demand, threat, as the case may be, for money and more money the while he discourses on God and love of fellow man.

Seemingly there is nothing too crass, vulgar, and avaricious for some parts of the Christian ministry today. Anything, *anything,* is allowable if it can be counted on to yield cash and profit: whether an Oral Roberts threatening his television audience with his own death for want of eight million dollars—which, for good or ill, he got in time—or Jim and Tammy Bakker lolling in the luxury of the garden of one of their several homes, now preaching but only a little, now weeping just a little, now kissing a little, all the while beseeching their television congregation to send more money in—to add yet another thrill to their Heritage USA Theme Park in North Carolina, which is something less than Disneyland but something a great deal more than your garden-variety carnival. We switch to another televangelist and find him in the process of describing plaques that will be sent to donors if they contribute the right amounts: Blessed Shepherd will be conferred on the donor of five thousand dollars; Innkeeper, for one hundred. We switch to still another and find him reminding his congregation of not only all the regular needs for and uses of donations but the new, fresh funds required to aid him in his possible presidential pursuit.

As H. L. Mencken put it many years ago, no one has ever gone bankrupt through underestimating the intelligence of Americans. But there is still the nagging question, who in fact does support the Crystal Cathedrals and the Theme Parks? In some measure, we gather, the extremely well-dressed and prosperous-appearing folk who fill the enor-

mous churches for television. But, in a great deal larger measure, we learn, the millions of Americans who can't afford to attend and wouldn't have proper clothes if they could.

It was once thought that government service as a career, whether military or nonmilitary, was its own reward: in stability, security, and ultimate pension. One did not go into government service if his life's aim was that of making money. That too was once thought—but no longer. True, it is still impossible to earn or otherwise make sizable sums of money while actually in service, but for almost any admiral or general or civilian equivalent in the nonmilitary areas of government, there is a great deal of money to be had by cannily biding one's time. To see the government career not as a service or calling but rather as a necessary preface to the real career in business, books, lectures, articles, etc., with very high rewards almost guaranteed, *that* is the way to have one's cake and eat it too.

There seems to be no end to the public's fascination with book writing by ex–White House aides, ex-ambassadors, and ex-marines or their equivalent. Advances of up to a couple of million dollars are becoming known. For the same ex-aide, lecture fees of up to twenty-five thousand dollars are also to be had. Even so, however, books and lectures don't command the really awesome heights of the cash nexus; these are inseparable from the corporate and financial headquarters of America. The "military-industrial complex" that President Eisenhower warned of has never been more prosperous and fertile than it is today. Rare indeed the high military officer or the secretary of navy, army, or air force who has not discovered before stepping down, as it is always delicately referred to, the world of business and finance out there waiting for his rank and whatever else he may have to offer. His rank, of course, doesn't carry over functionally to the new world of high salary, stock options, pension, and the like, but it is usually not intended to. Name and influence will do quite nicely.

The revolving door between government and corporate America works overtime in the present age, in this late part of the age. Occasionally, greed becomes so imperious that a decent wait of a year or so between status of secretary or White House aide and that of entrepreneur becomes mentally and physically impossible to endure. Then, with a mighty huffing and puffing, the wheels of justice begin turning; special prosecutors may be appointed, subcommittees of Congress set up, and so forth. Rarely, though, is anyone seriously impeded as he rushes through the revolving door. The word *unethical* has become, in our

loose society, quite possibly the single most difficult word to define in the American language.

Heroes in all their familiar categories may be the greatest casualties of an age such as ours. Only with the greatest difficulty have the two entities "hero" and "businessman" been fused into one in Western history. Church; field of war; university or monastery; culture, particularly art and literature; in modern times, sports and science—these have been the nurturing grounds of heroes. But never business and finance, unless one wishes to do some stretching and bending to work in the Fuggers and Rothschilds. By dint of living a long life and giving away a great deal of money in philanthropy, it is possible that John D. Rockefeller became a hero, and also Henry Ford; if so, however, heroism sprang from charitable and educational works. The relationship between the qualities necessary to heroism and those embedded in the commercial/business/trade world is chemically poisonous.

That is why in the present age, with its surfeit of money and preoccupation with schemes to make money everywhere, in sports and government, in the university and the church, the difficulties of yielding heroes mount remorselessly. We continue to honor sports heroes of the past—Red Grange, Knute Rockne, Jack Dempsey, Babe Ruth, Ty Cobb, Christy Matthewson, Bill Tilden, Helen Wills, Gertrude Ederle, Bobby Jones, among others—and oftentimes can't even think of the names of living greats, no matter how keen and resilient their instincts and muscles. Part of the reason is that there are too many of them. Through science and technology we have learned how to develop bodies far superior on the field, in the technical sense, at any rate, to those of the Age of Heroes in the 1920s. But that's part of the problem: Are they living beings or human machines designed by Dr. Frankenstein's students? When we read about steroids and then about cocaine and the powers of each to induce sheer mindless recklessness, the potential for actual heroes went down abysmally. But above all there is the inseparability of the successful athlete today—the Dave Winfield, the Carl Lewis, the Larry Bird—and the cash nexus, the bottom line, the complex contract covering years and many millions of dollars.

Anyone for heroes today in politics? Lord Bryce was struck a hundred years ago by the paucity of great men in American politics, as compared with his own Britain. In *The American Commonwealth,* he titled a chapter with the intriguing words "Why Great Men Are Not Chosen Presidents" and another with the words "Why the Best Men

Do Not Go Into Politics." The common denominator of both chapters was the greater appeal in America of endeavors in which the cash nexus operated, in which considerable money could be made. But, as I have suggested, that need no longer be a reason, given the revolving door and, once through the door, the golden parachute. We shall see. Despite the fact that the good citizens of a Midwest state not long ago voted John F. Kennedy greatest of American presidents, it is still unlikely that any but Wilson and the two Roosevelts will rank as possible heroes at the end of the century.

The vast abundance of liquidity, of money, of cash and painless credit makes the genuinely heroic, like genuine honor, trust, and fidelity, improbable to say the least. Monetarism is a major theory in economics; it holds that when there is too little money available, growth suffers, and when there is too much, it suffers also. As a theory, monetarism might be expanded to go beyond the economy and economic growth to culture and cultural growth. Too little liquidity, and money will be hard to find for the minimum condition of any art, literature, or science at all: that is, a surplus after survival needs have been met. But too much liquidity, and there is an inundation, a flood before which cultural values begin to erode.

It is very hard to find a *sacred* in culture at this stage of the twentieth century. Everything in science, philosophy, art, literature, and drama has seemingly been reduced to the profane. The great sociologist of religion Emile Durkheim called the contrast between the sacred and the profane the widest and deepest of all contrasts the human mind is capable of making. Everything above the level of the instinctual, Durkheim concluded, began in human veneration, awe, reverence of the sacred—be it a god, spirit, grove of trees, or lake or stream. Religion in the sense of gods, churches, liturgies, and bibles emerged in due time from the primitive sacred essence. So did the rest of human culture, its signs, symbols, words, drawings, and acts.

There was one reason alone that books and songs and dramas and then philosophy and science became as important as they did at the dawn of civilization: the sacred. Because all early art and literature and philosophy were limited to explication and interpretation of the sacred, these pursuits imbibed some of the essence of the very sacred force that they were contemplating. As Durkheim pointed out, the most basic categories of human thinking—cause, force, time, space, and so forth—all had their origins in religious reflections and ruminations. So did morals and ethics, more particularly in the care given to the sacred

essence, be it the perpetual flame at the Greek and Roman hearth or a protecting god. Honor, trust, loyalty, and fidelity were important not because they advanced one in life—though they generally did—but because these were qualities vital to the sacred core of all human life.

In the contrast between the sacred and the profane, nothing more perfectly epitomized the profane than commerce and the money by which commerce began to be conducted at an early point in civilization. No greater impiety, act of desecration and dishonor, could be imagined than commercializing the sacred, putting it up for sale, making money from it. Throughout most of history, in every civilization known to us, the individual of mere wealth, that is, monetary wealth, was on the defensive so far as honor and dignity were concerned. Hence the eagerness of the newly rich manufacturing circles in the last century to buy old wealth—landed estates, paintings and sculptures, titles when possible for daughters, and the social privilege of giving philanthropic money under high auspices. Art came close to superseding Christianity as the religion of the established and wealthy at the coincidental time when a great deal of new money was available to buy and thus be able to worship art.

Always the ultimate distinguishing mark of the gentleman, the individual of honor, was his relative separation from moneymaking as the primary vocation in life. In the beginning only the aristocracy, royalty, and the clergy could be men of honor, then one by one, slowly, almost grudgingly, lawyers, judges, doctors, bankers, professors, novelists, poets, dramatists, and others. Some of these acquired honor, or the capacity for honor, early in the modern age, as lawyers and scholars did; others like writers, publishers, engineers, and dentists relatively late. But always where honor and dignity existed there had to exist also the presumption of the *non* monetary as the raison d'être of one's life. Money and the spiritual or esthetic were and still are in some degree deemed incommensurable, alien. To tip a menial with money was fully accepted as a custom; there was no possibility of honor between the gentleman and the menial. But to tip someone of one's own general rank in society—a professor tipping a professor, for example—was unthinkable. One did not *buy* the trust and honor and service which were expected to exist in the world of teachers, bankers, lawyers, doctors, and scientists. One *assumed* honesty in a colleague; it wasn't something that could be bought, or quantified. That, at least, was the omnipotent myth society lived by.

There is still honor, still trust, obligation, loyalty, and the like in

American society. We should be hard put if there weren't. Perhaps we shall never know what life would be like in which literally every social act was subject to cash payment, never the bond of love, mutual aid, friendship, trust, and honor. There may well be a point beyond which chaos must reign in an evolution toward a total monetary regime.

But our society and culture today are manifestly closer to the complete cash nexus, the total monetary regime, than they were at the beginning of the century. Sharp, unethical, self-serving practices are, or so the vast bulk of ongoing journalism and social criticism tells us, no longer limited to the ranks of those living on the margins of society. Such once-common and respected exclamations as "You have my word on it," "It's a matter of honor for me," "No contract is needed between friends" would today invite derision for the most part. Honor was once the essence of the officer corps in the military. Officers, by dint of commissioning by king or president, had honor; enlisted men did not. That is why for the same offense an enlisted man could be jailed for years, an officer merely demoted or possibly forced out of the corps. The unspoken premise was that nothing could be more punitive to the individual with honor than to be stripped of it.

It all comes from the primeval sacred. The sacred can suffuse parts of nature, books and documents, social classes, some men and not others, some relationships with women and not others, occupations and professions, given acts, and so on. It is the historical and continuing core of culture, including high culture. Without the sacred, all is cash value. As a final note, the beggar had a modicum of honor in the Middle Ages. The tradesman did not.

We hang loosely upon the once-honored, once-cherished, once-explored past. What T. S. Eliot, in *Four Quartets,* refers to as "disowning the past" is not uncommon practice. Concern with the past seemed to the Greeks of the Age of Pericles concern with the very reservoirs of creativity. We cannot read the future. Where else but the past can we repair to when the present seems barren of inspiration? The past, correctly approached, is a dynamic composition of myriad human experiences in all kinds of settings. We came out of it, but such is the time-binding capacity of the human species that we never completely get away from it. Nor should we. Present and past are, or should be, fused, not separate worlds.

Antiquarianism is not the same as genuine study and understanding of the past; it places a value on old things simply because they are old.

But there is dross as well as gold in the past, and mere age won't make up the difference. We don't turn to the past as a narcotic but as a unique treasury of other human experiences, in different time frames, and also as the setting of the roots of our own civilization. The modern idea of progress directs our minds just as much to the past from which we derive as to the unchartable future. With loss of the real past, in our search for meaning, we unfortunately turn to idle nostalgia. Nostalgia has become epidemic in contemporary American culture. Even decades as recent as the 1950s are made the subject of nostalgia by Hollywood and Madison Avenue. Nostalgia is very different from respect for or genuine intellectual interest in the past; it is really the rust of memory. One form that has become particularly rampant, not least on Broadway, is nostalgia for one's roots in poverty, primitivism, whatever, the essential point being one's rise out of all that. One recreates an early Brownsville, Hell's Kitchen, Salt Flats, or Brighton Beach, inundating readers or theater audiences with the idiosyncrasies of Dad, Mom, Uncle Oscar, and assorted family types. This is *nostalgie de la boue* and also a good opportunity to sentimentalize and to dramatize an author's Shakespearean rise in the world.

Nostalgia, we must make no mistake, is good politics as well as good retail sales. For want of a real and used past, politicians blandish us with sentimentalizations of past presidents and events. The Depression and World War II have become staples of nostalgia in our time. But there is little that is safe from nostalgic use. We are barely out of the 1970s, but they are already nostalgia food.

The great danger of nostalgia is that it narcotizes us and helps prevent a proper sense of the past—which is closely woven into the present and helps us guard against destabilizing fads, fashions, and foibles in important areas of thought and allegiance. Quite rightly did Orwell make the calculated destruction, and remaking, of the historical past the foundation of the totalitarianism of *Nineteen Eighty-Four*.

Utopianism is one of the major passions of the Western, especially American, mind in our age, and also a favored refuge of those hanging loose upon the present. B. F. Skinner's *Walden Two* demonstrated the mesmeric appeal utopia has for the college generation, just as the numberless variations of *Star Wars* and *Star Trek* demonstrate the utopianism that lies in the minds of children.

But the really important utopianism of our age, the type that gives a cast to much philosophical and historical thought, is the eudaemonizing, the making into a happiness frolic, of the great philosophies of man

and nature of the past century: Darwinian evolution, Marxism, and Freudianism. Even Einstein's austere theory of relativity has been invoked in the name of man's liberation from ancient dogmas. Examples are legion. The twists given by the otherwise eminent scientists J. B. S. Haldane and J. D. Bernal to Darwinian natural selection reflect the triumph of political ideology over science. Man, it is declared, will become ever more rational, liberal, kind, and tolerant through indefinite perpetuation of current processes. Teilhard de Chardin, eminent Jesuit and paleontologist, sees evolution as a process inevitably reaching a spiritual stage, with the sacred being of Jesus Christ central to the saga.

Marxism and Freudianism have both, under the spell of contemporary utopianism and progressivism, been transformed. The grim Marx of the 1930s in America, the Marx of the Marx-Lenin Institute in the Soviet Union, is no more; at least not in America, not since World War II. He has been replaced by the humanistic Marx, the Marx of the Paris essays, of alienation, and of all-round jolly fellowship, the toast of the New Left and its Greening of America in the 1960s. I shall come back to this Marx later in the chapter, for he far outstrips the mere uses of utopianism. Let me turn to the comic-opera surgery performed on one of the greatest, most dour, and most profoundly pessimistic of prophets in the twentieth century: Freud.

Freud saw man as the eternal embodiment of two sharply contrasting drives: sex and aggressiveness; the first capable of generating relationships of love, friendship, and trust, the second of conflict, hate, and perennial war. Apart from occasional, brief, and minor liberations from this biological determinism, liberations effected by mental therapy, human beings were effectively condemned by Freud to an eternity of war within themselves, war between sex and aggression, between the id and the superego, between a primal barbarism and the sporadic vision of a heaven. In his *Civilization and Its Discontents* Freud paid melancholy tribute to the future of man: a future of unhappiness, of incarceration within biological bars which would never be broken down, and of permanent pain stemming from the absolute incapacity of man to come to terms with himself or with his fellow creatures.

This Freud, the authentic Freud, exists in America, but only in tiny, therapeutic manifestations. The authentic Freud is far outweighed by the bogus Freuds created by those such as Erich Fromm, Herbert Marcuse, Norman O. Brown, and their like who have, with wanton strokes of the scalpel and needle, liberated Freudianism from its natural body and fused it with a similar liberation of Marxism from its natural

body. The deadly serious Marxism of *Capital* and *The Gotha Program* joins in extermination the deadly serious Freudianism of *The Interpretation of Dreams* and *Of Civilization and Its Discontents.*

What emerges from cosmetic surgery is something that might be called a Freudomarx or a Marxofreud. It was probably the incredible Wilhelm Reich who started it all, with his tortured twisting of Freud into a prophet of sexual liberation and thence happiness. For Reich there was a magic alternative to the future of struggle and pain foreseen by Darwin, Marx, and Freud; this alternative was, or could be with slightest effort, the free, spontaneous, and persistent orgasm.

From Reich and his Promised Orgasm it is but a few steps to the Freudomarx of Brown, Fromm, Marcuse, and other "scientific" purveyors of the millennium. What Frank and Fritzie Manuel write in their magisterial study of utopianism in history is sufficient here: The successors of Reich

> represent a characteristic resurgence of the Adamite utopia in a mechanized society where relationships are endangered by an atrophy of love. They negate the Freudian negation of the eudaemonist utopia. They reject the underlying dualism of his system and admit no intrinsic reason that the libido cannot enjoy free expression, once mankind has been emancipated from the economic and sexual repressions that may have been necessary for culture-building in lower states of civilization.*

Utopianism takes many forms in the American twentieth century: those I have just touched upon; that of Woodrow Wilson and his dream of a world safe for democracy; that of Franklin Roosevelt in which he, in happy fellowship with Stalin, would banish war forever; those of the New Left and Consciousness I, II, and III; and, current now, the utopianism of Ronald Reagan and a Strategic Defense Initiative that will negate all future danger of nuclear weapons just as the dome of a stadium negates all raindrops. If one can believe Reagan, I can't resist thinking, one can believe anything—even Wilhelm Reich.

For the largest of all manifestations of utopianism in the present age, we are obliged to return once more to evangelical religion—with or without television cathedrals. It is a mistake—it always has been— to suppose that the Christian fundamentalist or charismatic or Pentecostalist is interested solely in future, eternal heaven. He is so inter-

---

*Utopian Thought in the Western World. The Belknap Press of Harvard University Press, 1979. p. 793

ested, to be sure, but under the doctrine of Christian millenarianism there is a preheavenly, earthly, period of paradise—that is, for the saved, the holy ones, those who kept up their commitments. This period is the millennium, to last roughly a thousand years, though it could be longer. Jesus Christ will return to the earth to rule personally over mankind from a golden throne sited at or near the center of mankind. The millennium will be a sacred age, steeped in spiritual being, but it will have its due share of the more earthly pleasures; there will be gold for those who knew only poverty, rich foods for the hungry, and earthly delights of other kinds, too, including perhaps perpetual recreation and relaxation—and without danger of becoming bored by such affluence.

However, the precondition of this golden millennium is a time of troubles, an Armageddon in which the good and the evil forces in the present world become engaged in a fearful war, one that will not end until the evil have been vanquished from life on earth. Then and only then will Jesus descend to his golden throne and announce the beginning of the millennium. Armageddon is a fascinating, almost obsessing concept. We have to imagine a war on a scale vast enough to engage all humanity and to rid the world of all the evil people. Whatever may have been the picturizations of Armageddon before 1945, they have inevitably taken on some of the flavor of the atom bomb and, today, the enormous numbers of nuclear missiles in the world, nearly all—but not quite all!—in the hands of the Russians and Americans. Could Armageddon and then the blessed millennium possibly hinge upon nuclear wars, with a denouement in so mighty a holocaust? Who knows? But we do know that among those who have expressed great interest in Armageddon is the current president of the United States. Good citizens will hope, pray, and assume that Ronald Reagan's interest is solely academic; that is, in Armageddon and the consequent millennium.

A conservatively estimated sixty million Americans, born again, individually convinced of a state of blessedness connected directly to Christ, and confident of reaching the millennium with its endless fountains of delights, fall in the aggregate of utopians I have just described. It is the utopian imperative that allows so many millions to be seemingly indifferent to the scandals of monetary enrichment and the occasional indulgences in embezzlement, fornication, and other peccancies which now and then come over the great world of televangelism, with its

Bakkers, Robertses, Copelands, Swaggarts, Falwells, et al. presiding. After all, it could be thought, and correctly too in terms of revelation, that such sins are simply the faint beginning of what will shortly be the welcome Armageddon and its promised issue, the millennium.

The death of socialism in the West opened the field of ideology, of "isms," to a number of entries which had not been especially noticeable before the Second World War. Egalitarianism is by all odds the most powerful of ideologies in postwar America—and in Great Britain and many parts of Europe as well. The struggles for equality between the genders, between age groups, and between races and ethnic minorities tell the story of a great deal of postwar American history.

As long as socialism was the serious dream of American intellectuals, and of large numbers of blue-collar workers at one time, its own relative cohesiveness as doctrine kept any possible *disjecta membra* from flying about social space. Today these *disjecta membra* are everywhere, most commonly perhaps in the form of "issues" courses in the grade and the high schools. Behind the whole miscellany of women's studies, black studies, Hispanic studies, Jewish studies, consciousness studies, et al. lies the ideal of an equality in the social order that cannot now be easily found, for all the staggering number of laws passed, actions made affirmative, and entitlements given.

Socialism held these vagaries—to the extent that they even existed as ideals in the minds of most intellectuals—together or kept them down as mere latencies—for exfoliation perhaps in the very distant future. But when socialism ceased to be the energizing faith of the Left in the West—primarily because of the repulsiveness of the Soviet Union, Fascist Italy, and Nazi Germany, one and all founded by lifelong socialists, but also because of the indisputable fact that the Third World nations that took up capitalism—as in the Pacific Rim countries to the west—were faring immeasurably better than were those that took up socialism—when the socialist dream passed, the result was a mess of new idols in the marketplace.

One has stood out: Jean-Jacques Rousseau. We considered this extraordinary thinker above under the rubric of political power, more pointedly his theory of the General Will and its absolute authority over the individual. But along with Rousseau's theory of authority is to be seen the veritable elegy in his political writings to equality and to the revolutionary potential that lies in his combination of the General Will and absolute equality. Conservatives who have somehow become en-

chanted by Rousseau simply have failed to see the overpowering mien
of the revolutionist in Rousseau, the egalitarian revolutionist. His is the
theory of permanent revolution, which is not the case with Marx; at
least the orthodox Marx. Rousseau ceaselessly talks about freedom,
which is lulling, even beguiling to present-day readers; but what he
means by freedom is not freedom from power but the "freedom" that
allegedly emerges from participation in power. He is quite blunt about
this. Very early in *The Social Contract* we are told that the "social
compact" that brings about the good state

> "will defend and protect with the whole common force the person and
> goods of each associate . . . in which each while uniting himself with all,
> may still obey himself alone and remain as free as before." (Bk. 1, Ch. 6)

A little later on in the same work, Rousseau adduces what he calls
The Legislator, a kind of composite of all the legendary lawgivers of the
ancient world. It will be the task of the Legislator to transform human
nature.

> He who dares to undertake the making of a people's institutions ought to
> feel himself capable, so to speak, of changing human nature, of transform
> ing each individual, who is by himself a complete and solitary whole, into
> part of a greater whole from which he in a manner receives his life and
> being. . . . He must, in a word, take away from man his own resources and
> give him instead new ones alien to him, and incapable of being made use
> of without the help of other men. (Bk. 2, Ch. 7)

This is revolution carried to the very marrow of human nature. The
new political man! In Lenin's imagination at the beginning of the
Bolshevik regime the new political man of Rousseau became the New
Soviet Man, courtesy of Marx and Lenin himself. It is the kind of
revolution that has special appeal to the present age in America; one
carried to the laws and customs that are barriers to equality but that
then goes on to the recesses of the human psychology. Equality, Rousseau tirelessly enjoined, requires revolutionary destruction of the infinity
of inequalities contained in human history. It also requires a corporate
community based on absolute power. The social compact that marks
our progress to the new and just state demands

> "that instead of destroying natural inequality, the fundamental com-
> pact substitutes . . . an equality that is moral and legitimate and that
> men . . . become every one equal by convention and legal right." (Bk. Bk.
> I, Ch. 9)

The great merit of Rousseau today is that unlike Marx his ideal is very far from the "withering away" of the state. The goal is nothing less for Rousseau than the creation through a social compact of the absolute, permanent state—a state, however, grounded in the general will of the people. That grounding in Rousseauian, and much contemporary political thought, makes it totally impossible for any tyranny to arise since no one already sharing power could have any interest in usurping someone else's. That at least is the theory of equality-as-freedom. To a generation of intellectuals in our time wedded to the ethical theory of John Rawls, the fresh study of Rousseau can be highly recommended. For unlike Rawls and Christopher Jencks and others who seek to make equality simply and effortlessly accomplished, Rousseau deals frankly and fully with the role of political power in the achieving of greater equality in society. His chapter on the Legislator in *The Social Contract* is about nothing else but the absolute and relentless power necessary to remake human nature in order to achieve equality.

In Rousseau there are three themes which have a great deal of relevance to contemporary egalitarianism. The first is the virtually nihilistic attitude toward the whole network of social relationships that lie intermediate to the individual and the state. Such relationships, Rousseau tells us in *Discourse on Inequality*, are the very sources of the inequality we suffer under. The second theme is the perfectibility of the individual once he has broken loose from the corrupting influences of the social relationships just referred to. Third is the theme of power: of the necessity of power in the process of extermination of evil traditions and of the moral development of the individual. "If it is good to know how to deal with men as they are, it is much better to make them what there is need that they should be." To which Rousseau adds the words, in his *Discourse on Political Economy*, "It is certain that all peoples become in the long run what government makes them."

The appositeness of Rousseau's philosophy to public policy in the United States during the past forty years is immediately evident. Equality has been the most admired moral end of our philosophers, legislators, and jurists alike. Rawls's *A Theory of Justice* and Jencks's *Inequality* have had immense influence on the intellectual mind and, in a filtered way, the politician's. The major contributions of the Supreme Court and the Congress have been in the direction of equality—for women, for ethnic minorities, for workers, and other groups. There is not the slightest question that even as late as the end of World War II there was much work in this direction that badly needed doing. Women, for

one, had won the vote at the end of the First World War, but little of an economic character followed from that needed reform. In many states, married women were still virtually barred from control, or even voice in, the finances they may have brought to their marriage. Discrimination in the marketplace, in the office and the factory, was notorious. There was much to do, and in the egalitarian climate of opinion that has prevailed, a fair amount has been done. To compare the status of gender, race, religion, and social class today with what was commonplace at the beginning of the present age is to envisage some very large social changes. It is not too much to say that in the respects just cited, most of the grosser forms of political and economic inequality have been met if not actually remedied in detail. And I know of no polling evidence to suggest that the vast majority of Americans do not accept and approve.

We are entering now, though, a potentially critical time in the development of egalitarianism in America. Two forces of uncommon power in human relationships have entered the scene. The first is the inevitable dynamic of rising expectations in nearly all matters of reform. The second is the passage of the egalitarian ethic from the large political and economic areas, the areas of institutions it has occupied for over a hundred years in this country, to the smaller, more intimate and subjective areas of family, marriage, and other close personal relationships.

On the first, rising expectations, Tocqueville wrote some prophetic words in *Democracy in America:*

> It is easy to conceive of men arrived at a degree of freedom that should sufficiently content them. . . . But men will never establish any equality with which they can be contented. . . . When inequality of conditions is the common law of society, the most marked inequalities do not strike the eye; when everything is nearly on the same level, the slightest are marked enough to hurt it. Hence the desire for equality always becomes more insatiable in proportion as equality is more complete. (Vol. II, Bk. 2, Ch. 13)

Without the slightest question the grosser inequalities that bound women and minorities in 1914 have been eradicated. But in the very process of eradication, the spirit of egalitarianism has grown and spread, become almost obsessive, in the American political mind. During the past two decades we have seen feminism and ethnicism both pass well beyond the marks of simple reform, of correction of old legal and

customary injustices, to reach existential status in many spheres: sufficiently illustrated by "the feminine mystique" and "the black soul" in
cultural areas. And why not? For countless centuries masculine gender
and Anglo-Saxon mystique played a heavily dominant role in the West.
In literature, the arts, philosophy, and religion there is ample room for
mystiques and existential essences.

Our age may be reaching a crisis, however, with respect to feminism
as philosophy and thrust of mind, in its demonstrable impact upon the
family. The family remains in our age of high-tech and middle-class
affluence just what it has been for hundreds of thousands of years:
utterly vital in socialization of the young and in meeting the social and
psychological tensions that go with difference of gender and generation.
All of the easy, rationalist, and clever dialogue of a half-century ago—
most of it based on Americanized Freudianism and Marxism—about
the "bankruptcy" of the family and its imminent, unlamented disappearance rings hollow today.

We are learning just how vital has been the middle-class family, the
kind of family that began to be evident in Western society in the
seventeenth century and that has had extraordinary effect upon
the motivations—economic, political, social, architectural, educational,
and recreational—which have transformed the West since the Middle
Ages. Almost all of what we are prone to call middle-class ways of
behavior are in fact middle-class *family* ways of behavior. The difference
is very large. We are witnessing today the maintenance of middle-class
levels in income distribution and in housing construction; but we are
also witnessing the near collapse of the kind of household that for
several centuries was inseparable from economic level.

We see the collapse chiefly perhaps in the loose relationship between children and parents. What optimists call the new freedom of
children under the contemporary ethos of "permissiveness" takes a
variety of forms. Some we applaud: earlier onset of mental and physical
strengths, as the result of improved diet. But some we don't like: the
constantly increasing rate of teenage suicides, teenage thrill crimes,
ranging from robbery to murder, teenage pregnancies, narcotics and
alcohol use, prostitution, runaways, and the like.

One of the more interesting ideological changes of the postwar
period has been the status of the middle-class family in liberal and
radical thought. During the earlier part of the century, under both
Marxian and Freudian influences, the trend among intellectuals was
denigratory toward the family; there was much vague talk about the

greater liberty and opportunity for full-scale development under non-family circumstances—such as the compound in traditional China or the kibbutz in Israel. The family, it was said solemnly by the Marxist Frankfurt group, Horkheimer, Adorno, Marcuse, et al., tended to create an "authoritarian" personality—given to ugly racism, even fascism. Family discipline was the preparatory process for the kind of discipline one saw in the Nazi corps.

For the last quarter-century, though, a profamily sentiment has grown up on the Left, one primarily concerned with the affectional and other psychological traits rather than the structural relationships of family to society and the host of functions they perform for other institutions and groups—for education, public and private; law and order, cleanliness—beginning at home and reaching the city streets—ambition in career, respect for the woman in her role of mother and domestic manager, and for a few other related ends and purposes.

There are certainly wraiths present today to suggest the middle class I have just epitomized, but it would be very difficult to describe without extensive qualification and disclaimer the middle class of present-day, post–World War II America. Single-parent families abound and grow in number by the day, a condition which virtually all studies unite in deploring—for psychological as well as social and economic reasons. As for the value set on chastity and on cohabitation before or outside marriage, on morality, dress, ambition, respect for the social bond, and so on, the less said the better. Statistically, divorce is almost predestined.

So too has a genuine upper class just about disappeared, with only patches left to suggest its nature and reality prior to this century: family obligation and loyalty; wealth; high status; virtually its own system of education from nursery to Harvard, Yale, and Princeton; great houses in town and country; a highly distinct, if secluded, style of living that brooked few outsiders; a noblesse oblige of sorts (think of the Roosevelts, Hyde Park and Oyster Bay); and, for the most part, a bearing and an authority that really became noticeable in a few novels and essays of manners only when they were skidding down the slopes of popular egalitarianism. Never having had proximity to, much less membership in, the upper class I have briefly noted, I cannot speak of its intrinsic worth to American culture and morality. But I suspect that such a class was, in subtle but puissant ways, necessary to a real middle class. We lost the upper class and are now in the painful process of losing the middle class, leaving—what? Primarily, I would suppose, a great sense of vacuum even among the most ardent of the new individualists, the

most consecrated of yuppies, rebels, and escapists. Otherwise why the craving for "community" wherever it might be found?

Even the nomenclature of social hierarchy seems to be absent from our society today. For a long time, beginning perhaps in the last century, the consciousness of being upper class—when in all necessary attributes one actually was—has been seemingly unbearable to Americans. It is interesting to read in the biographies of the early great millionaires, Rockefeller, Ford, Carnegie, et al., that the wealthier and more powerful they became, the more closely they adhered to working middle-class rhetoric and plumage. It is hard to believe any ideological radical ever outdid the first Henry Ford in the ardency of his egalitarianism. It is hardly to be wondered at that during the first half of this century, when socialist parties were accumulating in Europe, there was little serious interest in socialism by American workers. With such revered financial titans as Ford, Rockefeller, and Carnegie preaching at least the psychological and social aspects of socialism and with all three plainly oriented toward immense largesse to their fellow citizens, not much was left to be said by socialist voices. "Classless" is too strong a description; but it comes closer than the Marxian image of class to describing America.

Class ties, such as they were in this country, are plainly eroding away at heightened rates in our century. This does not mean, however, that there is an eroding desire for status, visible status, in elites, cliques, and fashionable minorities. The often frenzied efforts of parents today to get their children into the most prestigious of schools and colleges are, when compared with the behavior of identically situated parents at the turn of the century, clear signs of a loss of the assured, institutionalized status enjoyed by grandparents and of a desperate desire to compensate with school ties. The Groton-Harvard connection is even more valuable today in our supposed egalitarian culture than it was when FDR attended.

Individuals are looser upon society now, measured solely in status terms, than they were when there was a recognized class system—one that was built around the families of Hyde Park and Oyster Bay. Descent, heredity, kind of property, and the like were securer foundations for anyone's status than are the often treacherous and self-defeating criteria of membership in the elites and jet sets which stretch from San Francisco to New York. Scientists, academics, and intellectuals also know the precariousness and ephemerality of elites. There are real elites in the worlds of letters and art, of scholarship and publishing, journalism

and think tanks. Conflict within elites and between elites can be as sharp and lethal as the kind of class conflict the Marxists once postulated. Social class, in any genuinely cognizable sense, is of all affiliations the weakest in capitalist-democratic society. But elites, self-serving minorities, and other status groups would appear to become stronger all the time. Hence the paradox of the bitter struggles and animosities on the political left and, more recently, on the political right, having to do with pecking order. Darwin noted that the struggle for survival is greater within the species than between species. The passionately religious in our age do not waste time hating nonbelievers, atheists, but rather others who also believe in God and religious grace. The Iranian *Shiite* Moslem under fanatic mullahs does not hate the great atheist bear to the north nearly as much as he does the other Moslems who do not choose to see exactly the right light. It's that way in somewhat moderated intensity among radicals, conservatives, and liberals in present-day society. Each category is the setting of ferocious fighting for fame and glory.

It is in the smaller, more intimate areas of life that equality as doctrine seems to create the most tension and unhappiness. And it is necessarily within the family or other comparable male-female relationships that the pains of equality are most often felt. It is one thing for continuing inequality of gender statuses to be confronted in the office or factory. It is something else for it to be confronted in the intimacy of love. The tensions of ordinary appraisal and self-appraisal between the male and the female worker are transmitted to the bedroom and, hardly less important, to the kitchen and its responsibilities. The wisdom of our ancestors argued that the woman in career or preparing for career becomes desexed, in subtle but powerful ways less capable of attracting a mate and then of holding him. How much evidence there is for this hoary belief, real evidence, is highly questionable. Suffice it to say that today, indeed for just about all of the present age, that particular bromide does not have much conviction.

And yet, as more and more women are discovering—and writing about in novel and essay—the new equality, such as it is, creates perturbations in marriage and in relationships which are very difficult to handle. No doubt mediating processes will evolve, but millions of young women and young men are discovering that the old, now obsolete, worker-homemaker partnership between husband and wife was the sturdy foundation of many interpersonal relationships which today are difficult to create.

The biology of sex being what it ineradicably is, the surrounding culture was for centuries and millennia one in which initiative and dominance were also masculine. That superstructure of culture is today being ravaged by more sophisticated views of equality. Physicians, mental therapists, and the confessionally-minded writers of fiction, documentary, essay, and drama, tell us in a veritable chorus of disclosure that a mutually enjoyable sexual relationship is not nearly as common as one might have predicted when the bars of prudery and male chauvinism were first being broken down. Sexual freedom—that is, the kind of spontaneous, zestful freedom that accompanies a successful romance—seems to elude a considerable number of males and females who are most earnest about equality of the sexes and most solicitous about pleasure for the female at least equal to that of the male.

It is a worthy ideal, and when it fails it is by no means the sole fault of the ethic of equality. The great difficulty with equality as a driving force is that it too easily moves from the worthy objective of smiting Philistine inequality, which is tyrannous and discriminatory, to the different objective of smiting mere *differentiation* of role and function. There is, abstractly viewed, no good reason why the commendable objective of economic equality, at home and in the market, wherever, must become a fevered desire to reduce all that differentiates male and female. But it too often does. And sexual differentiation sacrificed to the gods of equality in the marketplace is not exactly what the great pioneering feminists sought.

For countless millions of years the dominance of the male was upheld by both natural selection and social selection. Among human beings, once the species was emergent, social selection doubtless took precedence in importance over natural selection. But it was not the less potent in effect. In the extraordinarily complex union of heredity and culture that is the essence of every human personality, it would be astonishing if the fingers of the past didn't constantly intrude upon ideas of the present and for the future. It is "all our yesterdays" more than "tomorrow and tomorrow and tomorrow" that rise the oftenest to challenge our dreams.

If, as seems to be the case, there are many more homosexuals, male and female, among us today, some of the reason surely lies in retreat to masculine and feminine company respectively by a rising number for whom the boy-girl relationship has become just as difficult and sensitive as the man-woman relationship under the new equality and with it the prescription inherent for the new man and the new woman. Inequality,

Rousseau to the contrary, comes more easily and more naturally, alas, than does equality—which, the evidence suggests, is hard work at diminishing wages.

The loose individual is as prominent in high culture, in literature and art, as he is on Wall Street and in the university. Minimalism, deconstruction, literary theory, narcissism, all reflect a hanging loose on culture. Each is an analogue of what arbitragers and golden parachutists get away with in high finance, not to forget grantsmen in the universities and free agents in professional sports.

In culture a blanket of subjectivism dropped on American writers and artists shortly after World War II. It is largely under this blanket that such egocentric activities as minimalism and deconstruction operate today. Once free fall, stream of consciousness, and narcissism were declared the Right Stuff for novelists, poets, and painters, with the author's or artist's God-given self the true hero or protagonist, replete with endless cataloging of feelings about feelings, the way was open for a new chapter in modernism.

World War II yielded no cultural efflorescence to match that of the twenties. We might have foreseen that from the difference in the two wars, from the viewpoint of Americans. There was little of the ecstasy, the sacred crusade, and the ardent "it is good to die for country" that had developed in the First War. Perhaps it was the lack of a George Creel. On the record Hitler was much more a Beast of Berlin than the well-meaning, simple kaiser, but alongside that fact was another, starting June 1941, and that was alliance perforce with the Beast of Moscow, as many Americans saw Stalin and the Soviets. There was strong opposition toward Lend-Lease for the Russians during the early months, and any thought of working toward an alliance with the Soviets comparable to what we had with the British and French was a trigger to discord in Congress and in the public. It is interesting to speculate on whether, after Pearl Harbor, Congress would have reached agreement on a declaration of war on Germany. Fortunately, Hitler, in an act of strategic bravado, saved Americans the further furor by declaring war on the United States a few days after Pearl Harbor.

Even so, and not forgetting the major contribution America made to the winning of the war in Europe as well as the Pacific, we tended, both as civilian public and as fighting force overseas to hang rather loose upon war and cause. The most pathetic individuals in the army were the Information and Education (I & E) officers, charged with responsi-

bility for whetting Our Boys' appetite for crusade. It was hopeless. If you volunteered, as a few did, you were well advised, once in the service, to keep it to yourself or else you would be jeered. Best to beat the draft; second best to wangle stateside service throughout; third, rear echelon strictly if you were sent overseas; after that, earliest possible discharge so long as it wasn't a dishonorable one. In many a Pacific unit I discovered more resentment, more actual hate by enlisted men for their own officers than for the Japanese, though I make haste to explain that that particular feeling was very much less evident in the combat sphere than in the rear echelons.

As we hung loose on the war and its crusade from 1941 to 1945, so did the millions of returning veterans seem to hang loose on the home front that had been so impatiently awaited all through the war. It is unlikely, I have always thought, that America would not have escaped something like the bitterness and internecine civilian-political strife of Germany and France and Great Britain after the First World War, had not the vast cornucopia of the Veterans benefits been opened immediately after VJ Day. The intelligent, ambitious young who otherwise might have exploded, were of course welcomed to the universities, colleges, and vocational institutes, many expenses paid by the government, thus ensuring a significant and honorable chapter in the history of American higher education. There were many other benefits, including low-interest mortgage loans for homes and new businesses. Finally there was the great gift of economic prosperity that, despite the dour forecasts of nearly all economists, lifted almost all boats in its ever-rising tides.

It is not too much to say that Our Boys were bought off, wisely, shrewdly, and humanely from what could well have happened in different circumstances. It is interesting to note that whereas out of the First World War came quasi-military organizations like the American Legion—a distinct force in American politics until after World War II—none such appeared, though a few were attempted, after 1945. The spirit of war was dead, to the extent that it had ever been alive, after that date.

There is a good deal of cultural character to reinforce that judgment. Earlier I stressed the almost instantaneous effect of the Great War on American culture—the Roaring Twenties. Except in eminently welcome economic and political respects, the forties did not roar, nor did the fifties. There is simply nothing in the literature, art, music, and film of these latter decades to compare with the already described cultural

efflorescence that filled the twenties—well into the thirties. Instead of Hemingway, Faulkner, Fitzgerald, and Dos Passos in the postwar novel, this time we got not much more than Norman Mailer's *The Naked and the Dead*, after which it was pretty much downhill with James Mitchener and Herman Wouk. World War II itself had been singularly sterile of song, verse, and film, and so was its immediate aftermath. Compare the movies, starting with the appalling *The Best Years of Our Lives* in 1946, of the second war with the first. There was no *Big Parade*, no *All Quiet on the Western Front*. In music there were Rodgers and Hammerstein waiting with *Oklahoma!* and shortly after some highly affected classical jazz, but nothing after World War II to compete seriously with the Gershwins, Irving Berlin, Lorenz Hart, Cole Porter, Duke Ellington, and Fletcher Henderson earlier.

It is no wonder that subjectivism has been the overwhelming mood and mode of literature since World War II. There was a manifest incapacity among American writers to deal with the objective phenomenon of the war—as the Hemingway generation had dealt with the First War—and to do the Second War justice in novel, poem, drama, or song. Add to that the early beginning in America of the spirit of egalitarianism (substitute, as I have said, for dying socialism); and with that the inevitable juices of envy and resentment which begin to be felt when the dogma of equality penetrates the intimate and personal recesses of life, beginning with the family; and add still further and finally the enormous wave of affluence that rolled over America starting in the fifties and that seemingly still rolls in the consumers' paradise that is America (unless there are more Black Mondays ahead); add all of this, and we have the most fertile possible soil for the excretion of subjectivism. When the personalities of other human beings and their events, accomplishments, joys, tragedies, and accidents become impenetrable to whatever literary and artistic talents lie around, then, by all means, turn to the subjective; to one's own little ego and assembled feelings. Explore it and them unceasingly, laying before readers every little detail of what one did, thought, felt, loved, hated, throughout one's life; that is, from hateful toilet training to all the *sturm und drang* of middle-class life in the United States.

Goethe said to Eckermann:

Epochs which are regressive, and in the process of dissolution are always subjective, whereas the trend in all progressive epochs is objective. . . .

Every truly excellent endeavor . . . turns from within toward the world, as you see in all the great epochs which were truly in progression and aspiration, and which were all objective in nature.

What one may add to Goethe's words, in large measure drawn from Tocqueville, is the reciprocal relation that obtains between subjectivism and egalitarianism. In ages of accepted differences in rank, one does not feel beaten or humiliated by life when stark reality forces one to awareness of one's individual limitations and weaknesses. These of course are cultural as well as biological, but perceived inequalities are just that, and in no way moderated by either the cultural or the biological factor. All that matters is the sense of isolation, of vulnerability, of alienation, that attacks the individual as the waters of egalitarianism commence to flow. And from this sense it is an easy, an almost inevitable step to subjectivism, to retreat to the warm and welcome recesses of one's own little inner reality.

The postwar has mostly been a vast pumping plant for subjectivism. It became evident in the fifties, symbolized by *The Catcher in the Rye*, whose protagonist, Holden Caulfield, seems to have caught the mind of every high school and college undergraduate in the country. Under the guise of motivational studies, subjectivism entered the social sciences and the humanities, to come to volcanic intensity in the sixties. *Feeling* was the lingua franca of seminar as well as novel or poem. In high school during these years, how a pupil personally felt upon first learning about, say, the First World War and World War II was deemed more important than either of the events.

The *New York Times* book critic Michiko Kakutani, in a recent review of a not untypical novel, mused briefly on the significance of the ever-widening preoccupation with the self and its inner recesses, so often at the expense of the great outside, the real world of diverse, behaving, acting, doing people. "What it does mean," wrote Kakutani of the characters in the novel she was reviewing, "is that they're constantly assessing their happiness, monitoring their emotional damage, and charting their ability to take spiritual and sexual risks. And perhaps as a consequence they spend most of their time being miserable— lonely, isolated, and pretty much paralyzed when it comes to making decisions." In *Swann's Way* Proust describes the neurasthenics of a certain genteel asylum in Paris; they were able to discourse endlessly and happily about the recesses and convolutions of their respective selves; but any task as complicated as deciding which shoes to wear for the day,

or actually tying their laces, plunged them into fear and uncertainty.

Feeling often seems the sovereign state of the human nervous system when we examine the pufferies of liberal arts education and, not least, of Great Books programs. The vocabulary of hype for these, written by college deans and publishers' assistants, is meticulous, of course, about the improvement, the stimulation, the arousal of the mind. But not much is required in the way of research to see that what the average college of liberal arts, and the Great Books program, are appealing to are students' and readers' feelings. Thus the celebration of discussion groups, of college classes in which all pretense of the dispensation of scholarly knowledge about the liberal arts is dropped in order to make students comfortable in, one by one, retailing how they *felt* about the *Crito, The Social Contract, Origin of the Species.*

The reading of Great Books as such—that is, simply because they have been thought of and catalogued as such for centuries—is as sterile as anything I can think of where serious education is involved. Religious meditation may be advanced by the devout's reading of the Bible. But it is hard to see what is accomplished in the stimulation and nurturing of ordinary, eager, ambitious minds by spending weeks, months, on the reading, followed by group discussion, of a book certified as Great by discussion leader and publisher.

Can we suppose that any of the minds of the authors of the Great Books, from Aristotle to Schweitzer, were ever prepared, and then shaped, by the reading of the Great Books of their own respective ages? Hardly. Aristotle read Plato as Plato had listened to Socrates, not to masticate and digest a great book or discourse but to pursue truth or knowledge through the best available means—all the available means, not just a preselected list of classics. No doubt there is a pleasure in reading Darwin, but would any sane person use *Origin of the Species* as the required foundation stone for becoming a biologist today? Adam Smith's *Wealth of Nations* is also a great book, but it is unlikely that it by itself has stimulated and energized any mind destined to become a serious economist in the present age.

Great Books programs confuse the education of the mind with the catechization of the mind in seminary. The most important thing in the world, whether in comparative literature, philosophy, and social studies or in biology, chemistry, and physics, is the induction of the tyro into the living world of problems, not the world of books which have the imprimatur of Great on them.

Given the intoxication produced by the idols of consciousness and

subjectivism it is only natural that psychobabble threatens to inundate us at the present time. Psychobabble is the pidgin version of crossings of psychoanalysis, sociology, and liberation theology. R. D. Laing won renown for his work with schizophrenics; not his therapy as such so much as his riveting demonstrations of how much wiser and far-seeing schizophrenics can be than are those of us who waste time with reason, logic, and science. He praised the kinds of consciousness which come from "our looking at ourselves, but also by our looking at others looking at us and our reconstitution and alteration of these views of others looking at us." The social sciences have been markedly touched by the rage to the subjective. The ultimate goal of sociology, declared the late Alvin Gouldner in a book proclaimed by its eager reviewers to be a "soaring achievement," is "the deepening of the sociologist's own awareness of who and what he is in a specific society at a given time." Such a goal would not have electrified the Mermaid Tavern or later the haunts of Marx, Darwin, and Freud, but it is a true reflection of the subjectivist state of mind that dominates culture at the present time.

Ages of subjectivism such as our own and that of the ancient world in which Christianity and a myriad of other religions grew up are invariably ages too of the occult, the irrational or transrational, the magical, and the mystic. The pictures historians have given us of the Mediterranean world, especially the Greek world, as it was during the two centuries leading up to the dawn of Christianity, or of the Renaissance world in Europe of the fifteenth and sixteenth centuries are necessarily pictures of the occult and irrational as well as of mystic intuition and self-exploration.

It comes as a surprise, though, no matter how accustomed we believe we are to the subjectivism of our day, when we read, as we did in *The New York Times,* September 29, 1986, of the uses which are being made today of subjectivism and the alchemy of altered states of consciousness by corporations of the stature of IBM, AT&T, and General Motors. The thought of individuals hanging loose in the offices of the legendary fourteenth floor of the General Motors headquarters does have its touches of humor.

The great fallacy, ultimately the evil, of subjectivism is that from it one comes to be convinced that what lies within consciousness, within one person's consciousness, has more reality, more value, perhaps even more truth, than what lies outside the person in the world of external event and change. The objective, the dispassionate, even as ideals, are derided by the subjectivist, who even bends the school to belief that

what pupils know, or think they know, about their feelings, natural impulses, likes and dislikes, is more important than what might be taught them about the external world.

Descartes, master of intellectual terror, really started it. Rousseau would be his greatest, most powerful pupil. "I think; therefore I am," announced Descartes in 1637. With this as his axiom, Descartes quickly proved, too, the existence of universe and God. Above all, he said, were the beauties and satisfactions of the new subjective, deductive, and absolute method of inquiry he was proposing. The senses will henceforth lie in oblivion. The profoundly self-conscious mind will go far beyond the chameleonic data of the senses. There is instant terror in Descartes' injunction to burn libraries—because their contents are ultimately duplicitous. Not from books and their ridiculously sensory, experiential, and transitory methods of accumulation, but from pure introspective reason comes the only knowledge that is worthwhile. Scholars, Descartes added, are learned cretins who spend a lifetime trying to recover about Greece or Rome what every "serving girl" of that time knew. Cartesianism is even more deadly a force of destruction of the traditional and revealed than is the general will philosophy of Rousseau, whose method is strictly Cartesian.

There is a distinct and clearly influential climate of Cartesianism in the humanities at the present time. It has been growing ever since World War II and its manufacture of the Loose Horde in America after the war. Neither scholarship nor its indispensable ways of working and thinking have the appeal and strength today in the humanities that they had up until the war. More and more the Cartesian adjuration to banish everything from the mind ever learned, and then think intuitively and geometrically by oneself, is the sacred writ of our time. With his usual genius, Tocqueville pronounced Cartesianism the basic religion of democracy, for no democrat has ever been known—and this Descartes himself pointed out—to wish for more common sense, more natural insight, wisdom, and judgment than he already has. Everyman need look up to No Man!

Looseness of individuals, factions, and ideas is conspicuous in the whole area commonly lumped in the label "humanities." Whether inside or outside the walls of academe doesn't seem to make much difference. In want of any organic in the way of ties, anything even as real and constitutive as existed in the Marxist thirties in America, humanists find themselves forsaking books and authentic scholarship and turning to what are clinically called texts and to a kind of scholastic dogma for guidance. The names of Georg Lukacs of Hungary and Antonio Gramsci of Italy, both ardent Marxists in their day who counseled a storming of culture instead of the economy when the Revolution broke, are heard almost everywhere in the humanities. But at the present time the French philosopher Jacques Derrida leads all others in humanistic authority. What Cynthia Ozick has written is very much to the point:

> In the literary academy, Jacques Derrida has the authority that Duns Scotus had for medieval scholastics—and it is authority, not literature, that mainly engages faculties. In the guise of maverick or rebel, professors kowtow to dogma. English departments have set off after theory, and use culture as an instrument to illustrate doctrinal principles, whether Marxist or "French Freud." The play of the mind gives way to signing up and lining up.

The prominence and surpassing attractiveness in humanities faculties with of what are called literary theorists is a sign of the times, of the widespread efforts of the loose in the humanities to find some kind of dogmatic underpinnings. What precisely "literary theory" is, what could possibly make it cognizable by the great poets, dramatists, essayists, and novelists of the Western tradition, we do not know—any of us, I would judge from examining some of the literature of theory in the humanities.

Doubtless "deconstruction" and "minimalism," currently two humanist idols, derive in some way from literary theory—surely not from impulses born of genuine literature and art. Each is a textbook, clinical example of individuals hanging loose on culture. Deconstruction, so called, is, as the supreme pontiff Derrida conceives it from Paris, the technique of reducing the great to the merely subjective, the solipsistic. Every *War and Peace* is in reality a text resembling a Rorschach inkblot test. There is no "there" there in the purported book or event in history, institution, culture; only an almost infinitely diverse possibility of images formed by the reader or student of the "text." Objectively viewed, deconstruction, which is currently the most fashionable school of literary theory in the humanities, is a sustained assault upon the great tradition in literature, philosophy, and history. If it hangs loose on this tradition, it is a veritable scholastic *Summa Theologiae* for those today enjoying the fruits of literary theory, post-structuralism, post-Marxism, post-Freudianism, and other lucubrations of the Loose Horde.

The mien of minimalism is one of innocence, and surprise when questioned. Am I not, asks the injured minimalist, but following humbly in the footsteps of Flaubert and of Hemingway, still seeking the right word, the right economy of style, and liberation from the maximalism of the Thomas Wolfes of the world? The answer is an emphatic no. It is not the maximalism of the Wolfe that the minimalist is opposed to, but the maximalism of the great tradition in Western thought and art. These lean, spare, constipated little novels of the minimalist creative-writing-school graduates are as self-conscious as any manifesto of the subjectivist in philosophy and criticism. Their mannered, often prissy style suggests bloodlessness, sweatlessness. We see all too clearly the restraints, blocks, stoppages, but little else; very little indeed in the way of plot, character, and event. "They use the snaffle and the bit all right," wrote Roy Fuller many years ago, "but where's the bloody horse?" We need Fuller today, or the child in the Hans Christian Andersen tale who blurted out, "The emperor has no clothes on."

There is minimalism in art and music as well as in letters. The triumph of minimalist art seems to be a canvas on which either nothing or as absolutely little as possible is emblazoned. A great event was recorded when a collection of blank sheets of white paper was exhibited in New York. There is a musical composition called "Silence" in which the pianist sits playing nothing for some three and a half minutes. Presumably applause consists of silence and motionlessness.

The eminent zoologist V. G. Dethier, in a recent article on minimalism in the arts, points to some of the neurological-psychological effects possible when in the presence of extreme and prolonged minimalism: "The ultimate in unchanging stimulation is a reduction to zero. . . . The subjective result is a sense of extreme discomfort . . . images originating higher in the central nervous system; that is, hallucinations." Rock gardens consisting of a few rocks positioned on a bed of white, even sand can, if looked at intently long enough, yield either a hypnotic state of mind or, if the viewer is lucky, a passionate desire for maximalism, to restore sensory stimulation.

Charles Newman, in a cool-eyed study of minimalists, suggests: "If we are to take our recent 'minimal' fiction seriously, we are in the presence of a new class, one Max Weber anticipated. . . . 'Specialists without spirit, libertines without heart,' this nothingness imagines itself to be elevated to a level of humanity never before attained." Precisely; as I said, without blood, toil, sweat, and tears; only technique twisting in the wind. Newman adds to the above: "But this fiction does not clear the air so much as it sucks it out, so that the prose is stripped not only of rational content but also of formal awareness of itself." In the end, minimalism is as nihilistic, as dedicated to the destruction of the sacred, traditional, human heart of civilization as is the deconstruction of Derrida and his predecessors back through Gramsci in Italy and Lukacs in Hungary, Marxians both, but gifted with the post-Marxian cunning that makes culture rather than economy the prime object of revolution- ary assault.

EPILOGUE

FRAMERS of the Constitution who may steal back to look at the bicentennial of their labors in Philadelphia, will find a colossus, a giant. But it is a deeply flawed giant; not yet moribund but ill-gaited, shambling, and spastic of limb, often aberrant of mind. People shout at it incessantly, each shouter confident that he has the right diagnosis and cure for the giant.

It is a giant in military resources but not in the exercise of military power and responsibility. Befuddled by belief that God intended it to be morals teacher to the world, our giant stumbles from people to people, ever demonstrating that what America touches, it makes holy. Convinced of effortless superiority, devoted to the religion of Know How, Can Do, and No Fault, the giant commits one Desert One after another, on land, sea, and in the air.

America is a giant too in its domestic bureaucracy, the largest in the world, the most benignly oriented, and surely the most solicitous of all bureaucracies in history. The citizens, all the while enjoying the usufruct of bureaucracy, its gifts to life, health, education, and old age, don't like it; or at least they repeatedly say they don't like it. They curse it. That is why each incoming president dutifully vows to reduce immediately the size of the bureaucracy and the awful total of indebtedness caused by it. But, also dutifully, each president departs office having increased the size of the bureaucracy, the national debt, and budget deficits.

In structure, our giant is a horde of loose individuals, of homunculi serving as atoms of the giant's body, as in the famous illustration of Leviathan in Hobbes's classic. There is little sign of organic connection among the tissues and organs. Economically, our giant is bemused by cash in hand rather than property and wealth. Growth is for weeds and idiots, not for the illuminati and literati. Culturally, reigning symbols are two in number: deconstruction and minimalism, each resting securely on the conviction that self-exploration is the mightiest truth of them all.

What does it all portend? Spengler, not aiming simply at America, but instead the whole West, said that our civilization has entered its final stage. Just as all other civilizations have gone through, at least by Spengler's assessment, the stages of birth, growth, maturity, old age, and death, so, *ex hypothesi* and also *ipso facto*, will the West, America included, its exceptionalism notwithstanding. Spengler even described the symptoms of decline, the stigmata of decadence and fall: a surfeit of wars and of military commandos, political despotism everywhere, and torrents of money pouring through weakening moral foundations.

But that, our optimists say, is simply Spengler, dour, dyspeptic, Prussian philosopher, resuscitator of the oldest fallacy in human civilization: the fallacy that a people, a society, a culture, a state is in truth an organism. Plainly human societies are not organisms, and if the Spenglerian fallacy is the only basis of prediction of decline and fall, then the prediction is otiose.

Optimists and indifferentists are free to make what they want of the analyses and predictions of Spengler—or of Tocqueville who, in his *Recollections,* saw and foresaw a Europe not very different from Spengler's. And in our own day, besides Spengler, there have been other deeply learned scholars like Toynbee and Sorokin to distill from the comparative study of history the attributes of growth on the one hand and decline on the other, and to affix the latter to the West, including America, in our time.

We may take comfort from the fact that in civilizations, unlike physical universes, there are no inexorable, unalterable laws against which the human will is impotent. Intimations of long term, irreversible decline in our civilization may indeed be based as much if not more on the temper of the observer than the facts and propositions he adduces. Short of loss of the life-sustaining ozone or other indispensable physical force, there is nothing that can afflict civilization and its component structures that is not theoretically subject to correction when necessary. For, everything cultural, from family to state, from nursery rhyme to epic, rests upon ideas. So do the diseases of civilization which occasionally assert themselves. They too are at bottom dynamical patterns of ideas, bad ideas but ideas nonetheless.

The problems or conditions which have persisted throughout the present age—militarism, bureaucracy, the monetarization of the human

spirit, and the trivialization of culture—are all subject to arrest and reversal. It is not as though we were dealing with the relentless advance of senescence in the human being or the course of a cancer. Ideas and their consequences could make an enormous difference in our present spirit. For whatever it is that gives us torment—the cash-nexus as the new social bond or the spirit of deconstruction and minimalism in the arts and perhaps areas too of the sciences—it rests upon ideas which are as much captive to history today as they ever have been.

The genius, the maniac, and the prophet have been responsible for more history than the multitudes have or ever will. And the power of these beings rests upon revolutions in ideas and idea systems. The whole course of humanity was reshaped by a major revolution in Eurasia in the sixth century B.C. That was when a small number of geniuses and prophets—Confucius, Lao-Tze, Budda, Zoroaster, Mahavira, Thales, Ezekiel, and Pythagoras—spread out over a vast continent nevertheless simultaneously introduced a revolution in ideas, one in which the individual was for the first time liberated from the role of automaton in a heavily oppressive culture and brought face to face with the entire cosmos, or its ruler at any rate. There have been other, analogous revolutions of ideas—those associated with the names of St. Augustine, Newton, Darwin, Marx, Frued, and Einstein among others.

We are obviously in dire need of a revolution of ideas right now in America. But it seems not to be the privilege of man to will his own revolution when he wants it. Time and circumstances are sovereign. Fashions, fads, and fancies in ideas come and go like cicadas. Intellectual revolutions tend to stay on for long periods. It was an intellectual revolution in the Colonies that led to the United States.

Perhaps the time is ripe now for a comparable revolution in ideas. Tocqueville, in a little known, fascinating footnote in *Democracy in America*, writes:

> If I inquire what state of society is most favorable to the great revolutions of the mind, I find it occurs somewhere between the complete equality of the whole community and the absolute separation of ranks. Under a system of castes generations succeed one another without altering men's positions; some have nothing more, others nothing better, to hope for. The imagination slumbers amid this universal silence and stillness, and the very idea of change fades from the human mind.
>
> When ranks have been abolished and social conditions are almost equalized, all men are in ceaseless excitement, but each of them stands

alone, independent and weak. This latter state of things is excessively different from the former one, yet it has one point of analogy; great revolutions of the mind seldom occur in it.

But between these two extremes of the history of nations is an intermediate period, a period of glory as well as ferment, when the conditions of men are not sufficiently settled for the mind to be lulled in torpor, when they are sufficiently unequal for men to exercise a vast power on the minds of one another, and when some few may modify the convictions of all. It is at such times that great reformers arise and new ideas suddenly change the face of the world. (Part II, Bk. 3, Ch. XXI)

Perhaps we in America are in such an intermediate period as Tocqueville describes. There is much reason, it seems to me, to think we just may be. The present age I have described in this book answers reasonably well to Tocqueville's specifications. We have moved since 1914 from a highly traditionalist, hierarchical, decentralized and inegalitarian society to one that in our time approaches the diametrical opposite of these qualities. We are approaching rapidly the kind of egalitarianism that Tocqueville describes as being no less sterile of thought than the highly stratified social order. But we still haven't reached it; there is hope. There is a manifest revulsion in America toward moralizing militarism, toward superbureaucracy, toward a social order seemingly built out of the cash nexus, and toward the subjectivist, deconstructionist and minimalist posturings which pass for culture. The time would appear to be as congenial to a revolution in ideas as was the eighteenth century in America.

One thing is clear at this late point in the age that began for America in 1914 with the Great War: The popular, the folk optimism—what an admiring and affectionate, but troubled, Lord Bryce called the fatalism of the multitude in America is fast waning. Americans are much less likely than they were a century ago to believe there is a special Providence that looks out for America and guides her purity of conscience to ever greater heights. And they are immensely less likely than were their Puritan forebears three hundred fifty years ago to see America as the "city upon a hill," with the world's eyes upon it. On the basis of recent White House occupants, it is unlikely that Americans will be coaxed and preached back into the American Idyll.

INDEX